In Their Own Words

Stefan Sokulsky

In Their Own Words

This book is dedicated to Leon and Maria Sokulsky
and Maria (Maryl) Winder.

In Their Own Words
ISBN 978 1 76109 451 4
Copyright © text Stefan Sokulsky 2022

First published 2022 by
Ginninderra Press
PO Box 3461 Port Adelaide 5015
www.ginninderrapress.com.au

Contents

Introduction		7
The Pilgrimage		9
1	Growing up in Germany – Maria, 1920s	11
2	Growing up in Ukraine – Leon, 1927–33	19
3	Hard Times in Germany – Maria c. 1929–33	28
4	Storytime – Leon, c. 1934	32
5	First Memories of Hitler – Maria, 1933	35
6	Calm Before the Storm – Leon, c. 1935	43
7	Did You Join the Hitler Youth? – Maria, c. 1935	47
8	School and the Doctor's Car – Leon, c. 1935	53
9	Die Jude Eisfeld – Maria, 1936	57
10	Milestones – Leon, 1937	65
11	Brückls, Stepfather, Referendum – Maria, 1937–38	68
12	Julik – Leon, 1938–39	75
13	What Happened With the Czechs? – Maria, 1938	78
14	First, Came the Russians – Leon, September 1939	84
15	War Begins – Maria, 1 September 1939	89
16	Germany Invades Russia – Leon, June 1941	94
17	Why Did We Attack Russia? – Maria, 1941	105
18	The Schutzstaffel (SS) Arrive – Leon, 1941	107
19	Two Heinrichs – Maria, 1941	111
20	Holocaust – Leon, June/July 1942	116
21	Fatalities, Women in War – Maria, 1942	126
22	The Pilot – Leon, 20 April 1942	128
23	Xaver – Maria, 1942	132
24	The Bomb – Leon, April 1942	134
25	Arrests – Maria, 1942	141
26	One From Each Family Must Go… – Leon, Mid-1942	142
27	The Tide is Turning – Maria, 1943	156

28 Verflucter Ausländer, Arbeit – Leon, 1942/43	159
29 Meeting Leon/The Doctor – Maria, 1942/43	163
30 Georg Brückl – Leon, Mid-1943	167
31 For Whom the Bell Tolls – Maria, Winter 1944	171
32 Soviets Regain Ukraine – Leon, 1944	175
33 To Help a Friend – Maria, 1944	177
34 Work and Leisure – Leon, Late 1944	187
35 To Altötting – Maria, Late 1944	189
36 Where Is She? – Leon, Late 1944	197
37 In Hiding – Maria, Winter 1944	199
38 The War Is Nearly Over – 1944–45	202
39 Stephan Mykulyshyn – Leon, c. Late 1944–Early 1945	204
40 Death March – Maria, April 1945	208
41 The Last Battle – Leon, 1945	224
42 Trapped in Battle – Maria, April 1945	228
43 The Volkssturm – Leon, April 1945	237
44 The Ceasefire – Maria, 1945	240
45 Freedom and Work – Leon, May 1945	244
46 Aftermath – Maria, Autumn 1945	246
47 Revenge – Leon, Autumn 1945	252
48 Engaged and Married – Maria, 1946	259
49 Stolen – Leon, 1946	261
50 I Am Nothing – Maria, 1946	267
51 To England – Leon, 1948	270
52 Poverty, Faith – Maria, 1948–53	275
53 Post-war – Leon, 1948–58	279
54 Leaving Germany – Maria, 1954–69	283
55 To Australia – Leon, 1968	288
56 Why Did We Go To Australia? – Maria, 1968–69	290
Epilogue	291
Appendices	301
Notes	305
Acknowledgements	313

Introduction

This book comprises the wartime recollections of my parents, Maria (née Keil) and Leon Sokulsky, who lived under Nazi rule during the Second World War. Their accounts as I was growing up always fascinated me and fostered my love for history. For that reason, I decided to interview my parents so that we could keep a record of their experiences for posterity.

The interviews occurred sometime in 1998, at our family home in Elermore Vale, a suburb of Newcastle in New South Wales, Australia. I recorded them separately on two C90 cassette tapes. Mum and Dad passed away in 2011 and 2014, respectively, but it was not until late 2018 when rummaging through my old cassette collection that I came across the recordings that had lain there in a box for nearly twenty years. It was then that I decided, for the first time since the interviews, to listen to them. As I sat with there with headphones on at my home in Muswellbrook, in northern New South Wales, I found myself transported into the past; not just to 1998 but back to the 1920s. It was an eerie and emotional experience to hear my parents speak again. I knew then that I needed to write down what they had said.

For the days, weeks and even years to come, I sat with headphones on, sometimes for hours, trying to translate their English, still accented after all these years, while appreciating their context and significance in history. I have reflected often, berating myself for not, at that time, asking for more detail; a simple question asked then could have saved me many hours of deliberation and extrapolation as I tried to figure out precisely what had happened. Regardless, I had to acknowledge that there were, and always will be, stones proverbially unturned.

I have turned to many sources in my quest for answers, none more valuable than my family. My siblings and I grew up hearing our parents' recollections, and they were keen to help by sharing their memories of events that they had heard about from our parents. Some of their anecdotes were gruesome, the stuff of nightmares, but the main points were always the same. Sometimes, my parents would recall details that they had omitted on other occasions. However, there was an overwhelming sense that the greater good allowed them to survive in the face of extreme adversity, so they did not mind sharing their story with us. Dad sometimes joked that without Hitler, we would never have been born. While nothing would condone the evils of Nazism, he was, in effect, right.

The philosopher and poet George Santayana famously said, 'Those who cannot remember the past are condemned to repeat it.' I hope that these reflections add testimony to this ideal and that social justice and humanity ultimately prevail over evil.

The Pilgrimage

The idea of the family pilgrimage began sometime early in 2018 when I told my sister, Milla, that I was starting to write a book about our parents' experiences during the war. To better understand their circumstances, she suggested that we journey back to where Mum and Dad grew up, to Germany and Ukraine, respectively. Milla stressed that we needed to leave as soon as possible because the longer we waited, the harder it would be to gather evidence from any living witnesses.

On a Saturday morning in late 2018, I met at a coffee shop with Milla and her daughter, Steffany, to plan our route. Steffany, a lawyer, proved to be a brilliant organiser, and soon our itinerary began to take shape. We knew that Dad travelled from Ukraine to Germany on a cattle cart to work as a slave labourer during the war, so we decided to follow his journey from Zolochiv, the nearest large town to where he lived in Ukraine, to Cham, near where Mum grew up in Germany.

Before Christmas in 2018, we three met again, this time with our travel agent, Madelaine, at Flight Centre, to organise our flights. Serendipitously, our sister, Josephine, happened to pass by the shop.

'Oh, you've come to join us, have you?' asked Milla.

'Well, I guess so,' she replied, and three became four.

Before long, Milla's sons Michael and James, Josephine's son Chris, my sister Elizabeth, and brother Leon, had joined us on the Pilgrimage.

Finally, after several months of further planning and armed with our travel visas, passports, and extensive itinerary, we were ready to go. On Monday 8 June 2019, we pilgrims were on our way to Sydney International Airport.

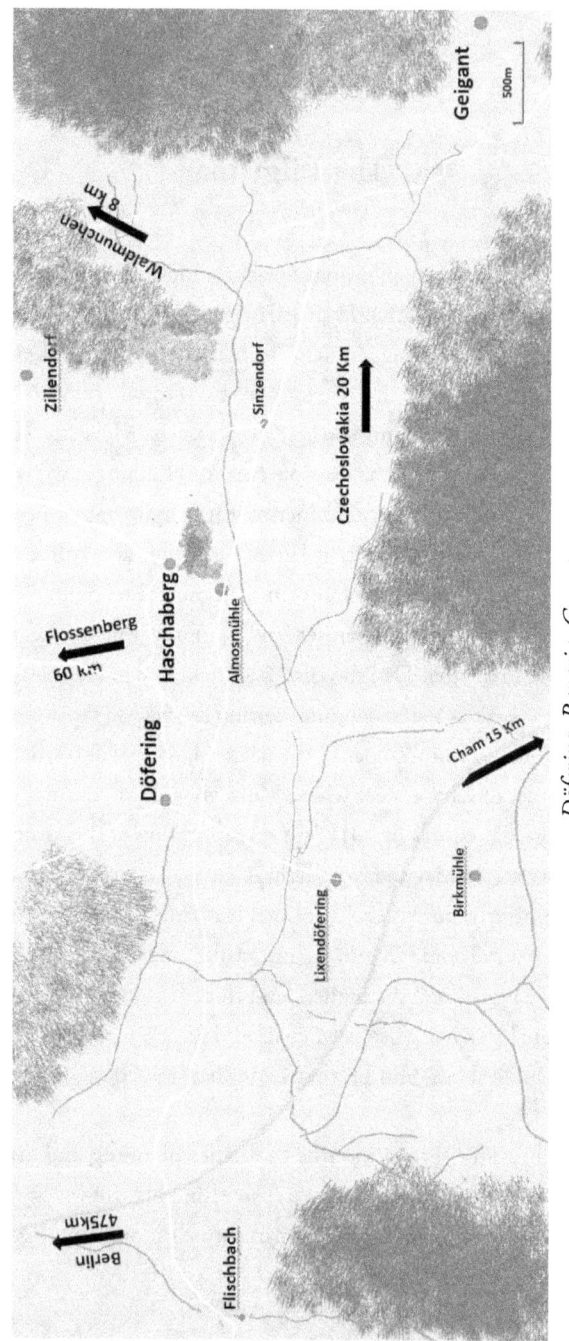

Döfering, Bavaria, Germany.

1
Growing up in Germany – Maria, 1920s

A blanket of snow covered the fields around a little village called Döfering when, on 12 February 1920, Barbara Keil gave birth to her first child. In the early twentieth century, this was the single, most dangerous undertaking a woman and her child could endure – it was more common to lose five babies than to have five.[1]

Twelve days later, Adolf Hitler delivered his Nazi Party platform speech to a small but fanatical group of fledgling Nazis in Munich. Apart from a few radical dissidents, Germans did not initially embrace the enigmatic First World War soldier's revolutionary ideals. It would be well over a decade before they were ready to come on board. In the front room of a small cottage farmhouse, *der Keil Haus* (the Keil House), Barbara, her parents and siblings had never heard of Nazism.

Hitler's speeches were conspicuous by his hatred of the Jews. He likened them to a disease that must be eradicated, like tuberculosis. The Keils, however, were more concerned with the actual diseases that killed many thousands of Germans each year. Were little Maria to fall ill in the depth of winter, with no telephone and several hours from the nearest doctor, her chance of survival would be virtually zero. Fortunately, Barbara delivered her first child in perfect health. There was, however, no father nearby to congratulate.

When Maria entered the world, Döfering, a small village with no more than fifty or so scattered houses in south-east Germany, was, like the rest of the world at the time, recovering from the physical, social and economic fallout following the Great War of 1914–18. Tragedy gave way to optimism; employment rose, the war was over, and people could get back to normal.

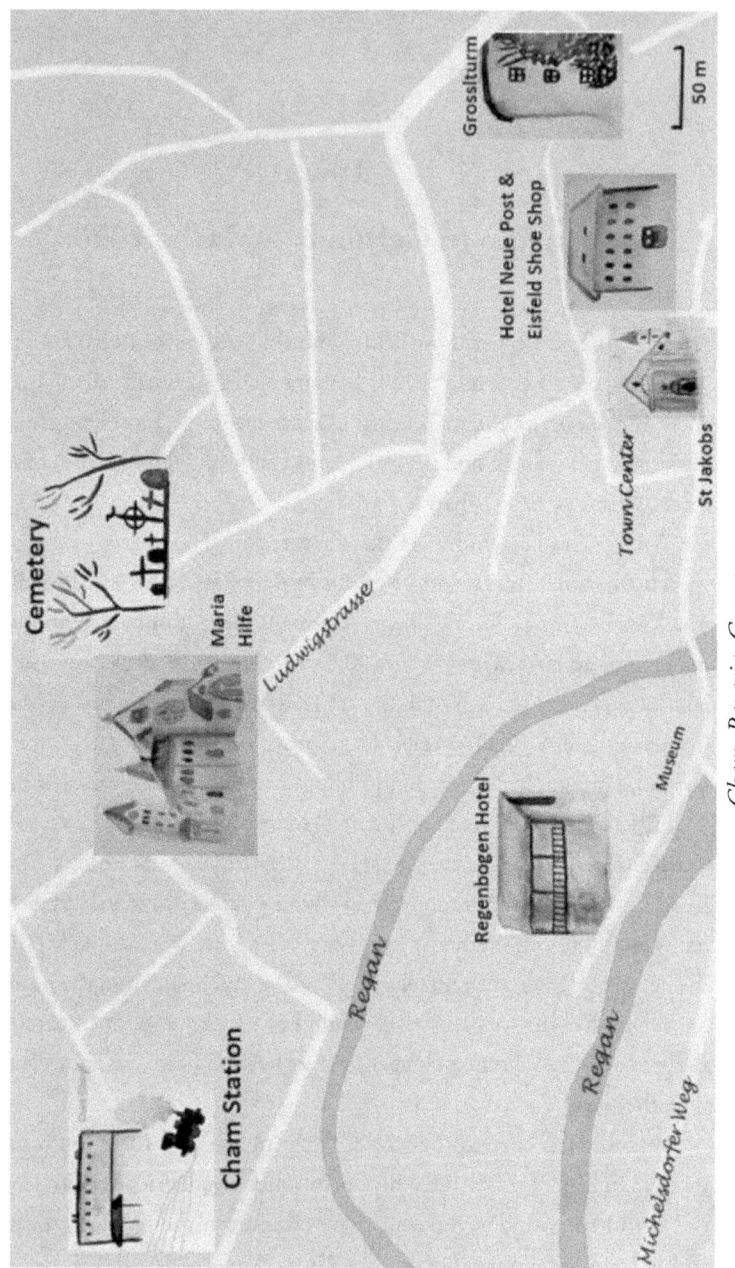

Cham, Bavaria, Germany.

Given the catastrophic loss of life in the First World War, fatherless children were typical in the 1920s. However, Maria's father was a mystery. Barbara was still in her teens when, despite protestations from their families, she began seeing a local boy named Johann Wutz, who, in his early twenties, had served and survived the Great War. However, in autumn 1919, when Barbara Keil announced news of her pregnancy, Johann's family strenuously denied his parentage, causing marriage plans to stall. According to Maria, it was 'because she was poor and they were rich'. Despite his affection for Barbara and his better judgement, Johann felt that he had no option but to side with his family. With no way to prove parentage at that time, Barbara had to bring up her child as a single mother.

The accepted belief amongst Catholics was that without baptism, you could not enter the Kingdom of Heaven. With infant mortality rates so high and not wanting to tempt fate, Maria had her baptism the day after her birth. On the day of the christening, and much to the surprise of those in witness, another veteran named August Mauerer arrived and announced that he was Maria's father. Why he acknowledged paternity if he was not her father remains a mystery. At the time of her birth, both parents were unemployed and living with their parents. Maria's baptismal certificate shows her father and mother's occupation as a cottager's son and daughter (Appendix 3).

Barbara, barely twenty-one, remained an attractive, eligible and outgoing young woman for whom Döfering offered little in the way of interest or employment. After a short period of recovery, she moved, alone, to the far bigger town of Cham, which lies about seventeen kilometres south of Döfering. She soon secured employment as a cleaner at the Neue Post Gasthof (New Post Hotel) in Cham's town centre. Working long hours meant that Maria had to stay with Grandma Keil in Döfering.

There, at the Keil House, located in an idyllic country landscape, Maria enjoyed her childhood surrounded by a community of friends and relatives. However, the arrangement prevented the two from developing a typical mother-daughter relationship. 'I didn't see her very much. She was working all the time.'

Barbara loved her daughter, but the relationship was never as strong as young Maria would have liked. Barbara was an idiosyncratic woman who, for some reason, zealously rejected dirt and filth. While this made her perfect for her work, it served to increase the divide that was to grow between mother and daughter. Maria recalled a time when she ran to her mother full of excitement to give her some special news, only to have her love unrequited on the basis that she failed to present herself as clean enough for her mother's liking. On another occasion, when her mother uncharacteristically wore out her long, wispy, black hair, Maria received a scolding for trying to caress her locks.

The difficulty and time needed to go between Cham and Döfering meant that mother and daughter saw each other infrequently during Maria's formative years. Cars were rare at the time, and the journey by train was problematic, given that the nearest station, Geigant, was about an hour's walk away. However, as she grew older and more independent, Maria made a point of travelling regularly to Cham on Sundays, her day off. There, she would soak in the sights of the big city, shop, go to mass, and spend time with her mother.

Maria nevertheless grew to be a bright and energetic girl. Her earliest memories are happy times, spending her days playing in the woods or down by the river. It was beautiful to grow up living there. Maria connected deeply with her grandma, who was the kindest person she ever knew. The two shared a strong affinity with the natural world that extended into the spiritual. They fed the birds and the wildlife and cared for any that were sick or injured. Maria's gift for relating to animals with care and compassion lasted throughout her life.[2] Her favourites growing up were reindeer, hares and cuckoos. Living on the land, however, meant that to survive, you killed your food. That job they usually left to the men. Uncle Michel and Grandfather Josef customarily killed the farm animals for food, while the women cleaned, gutted, prepared and cooked them.

Döfering was part of a parish that included the nearby villages of Rhan, Haschaberg, Lixendöfering and Almoosmühle. It was a lovely place to grow up. Nestled in a beautiful valley, surrounded by picturesque mountains, streams and fields, every day was an adventure. Every Sunday, almost all of the majority Catholic population packed St Ägidius Church in Döfering for one of the Sunday masses. Afterwards, there was always something to do. The community gathered frequently to celebrate the many religious festivals that occurred throughout the year. However, it was the time she spent with her cousins and close friends that Maria loved the most. From climbing mountains to swimming in the rivers, Maria's life was blissful.

The Keil property had a relatively small yard compared with the neighbouring farms. Still, like everybody at the time, the family could trade or barter their surplus vegetables, fruit and livestock at the local markets. Maria loved helping her grandma with her work.

> Grandma had a little business in Cham, and she transported eggs and all these things into town [which we swapped] for bread from the shops, you know the bread…and the sugar cake and things like that… I know just the train in Zillendorf that was so good for me, the train. We came to the train with our little hand wagon, with Grandma in the summertime, and the wintertime, we took with the sleigh.

Maria recalled her excitement when she, Grandma and her cousins Willie, Johann and Albert waited for the conductor to herald the next train's arrival.

> We were waiting for the train, and then came the conductor outside. 'Zillendorf. Geigant.' We took the basket of bread and things like that, and we drove it home, I, and my cousins – they are all dead now. They were little boys, or a bit older [than I was]. Grandma opened the basket and gave everybody a bun or something, you know, for helping, so we took this home, every day, every week. That was my first childhood experience that I had. I was just a few years old.

About this time, Maria witnessed some of the first airplanes and automobiles that arrived in Europe. Just as today's generation may fail to comprehend how sophisticated technologies work, Maria, curious and creative by nature, was in awe at how these machines operated.

So far as I remember when I was very young, I was outside in the field on the border, we were right on the border, there was the Czechish planes, all double-decker, little ones, you know. They came from the mountain, from the base up there, down and along the border. I looked up, and I thought to myself, 'I wonder, would I ever see how the plane looked on the ground.' I wondered how that is. I had never seen a plane. I never thought that one day I would fly in one.[3]

To those in her village, Maria was the 'Pachel Marie'. Her name derives from the Bavarian tradition in the district whereby a child adopts the original house name rather than their family name. The family house once belonged to the Pachel family. Even if the house swaps ownership, it retains the original family name. Thus, you would know a person not by their surname but by the house in which they lived.

Maria's love of reading sometimes led to another name. From a very young age, she quickly fell in love with books and the world of fairy tales, adventure and history, all of which fostered what came to be a lifelong adventure of discovery. Maria would spend hour after hour with her head in a book. Thus, in the Bavarian dialect, she became the Buachel Marie, or Book Marie.

Maria's grandma was born a Preiße (Price). The family held much of the land in the district. However, in a similar scenario to the Wutzes, they were displeased when Grandma fell for the goose-herder Josef Keil. Some said the reason was that the Keils were of a different class, while others pointed to a generational feud between the families. Regardless, Grandma's love was strong and she married Josef all the same. Together they went on to have five children, including Barbara, in 1901.

'Grandma Keil was very religious, but she was of the old religion, the Waldensians.' They were Christians who followed Jesus's asceticism. Grandma sought to follow this example and gave to anyone in need regardless of personal cost: the homeless, the needy, the hungry – she offered to them all. The Waldensians, at times, suffered persecution from mainstream Catholics for their alternative beliefs. Nevertheless, they were willing to risk all for their faith. On many occasions, Maria, inspired by the Waldensians' stoicism, would soon put her life in danger for her beliefs and values.

Living in a small town, from an early age, Maria developed close friendships with her cousins, especially Willi, local boys Xaver and Wolfgang, and girlfriends Annie, Othelia and Maree. They hung out together every day during school and afterwards the children played, rode their bikes, hiked, swam, collected mushrooms and berries, and got into mischief together. The friends developed a deep bond, born from companionship, faith and culture. Each of them was to need these things more than ever in the years to come.

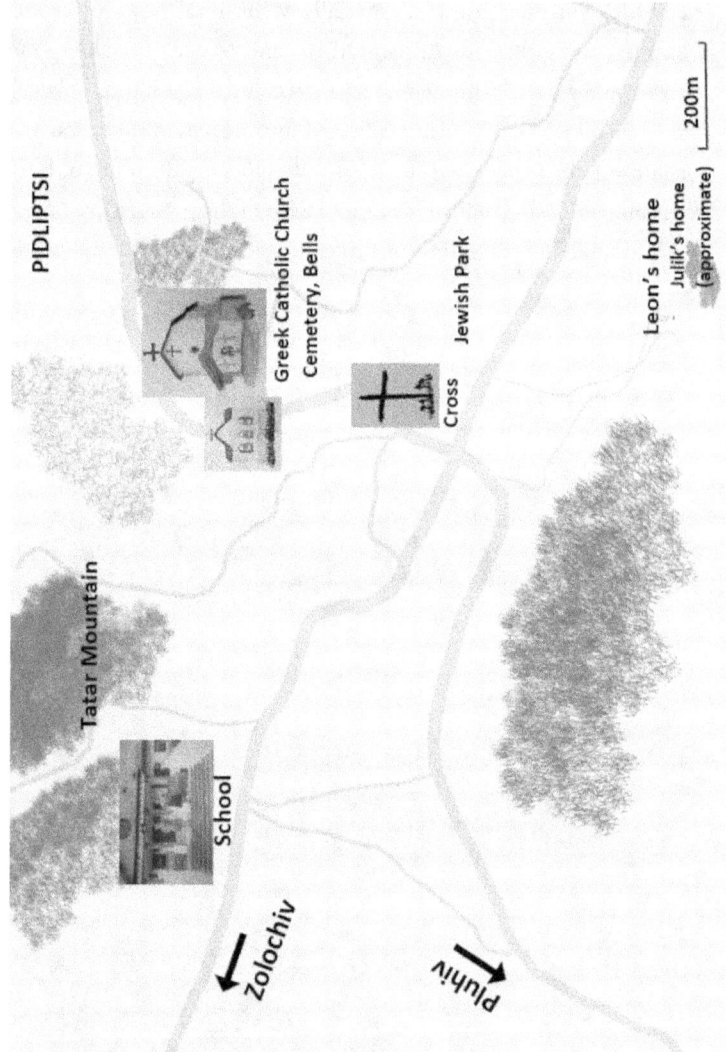

2
Growing up in Ukraine – Leon, 1927–33

> My name is Leon Sokulsky. I was born in Ukraine; I was born 25 February 1927, not far from Zolochiv – that's in Western Ukraine, not far from Lvov, Lviv, I say in Ukrainian now because, in Russia, they called it 'Lvov,' now it's 'Lviv.' That's L-v-i-v.

Leon's self-correction of Lvov to Lviv might not matter to the layperson, but there is significance in Ukranianising Polish and Russian words. The simple act symbolises freedom, independence and defiance of the subjugation of foreign rule.

Leon's mother, born in 1901, was one of five children. The youngest, Wasyl, was only a few years older than Leon, while Zoska, the oldest daughter, was already in her twenties when he was born. The family was part of an extensive network of uncles, aunties, cousins, and friends, most of whom lived in and around Pidlyptsi and Zolochiv.

> I grew up in a village called Pidlyptsi. There was a mother [Marika] Sokulska,[4] and father, Josef Sokulsky. He died when I was four – they told me of pneumonia.

Born just ten years after the Russian Revolution discarded hundreds of years of monarchy, and nine years after the First World War ended, Leon, like Maria, grew up in a period of vast political and social upheaval.

Following the conflict, to correct the past injustices and prevent future conflict, the major victorious powers, England, USA and France, met together in Versailles to formulate a plan for post-war Europe. The victors decided that Germany and Austria must accept total responsi-

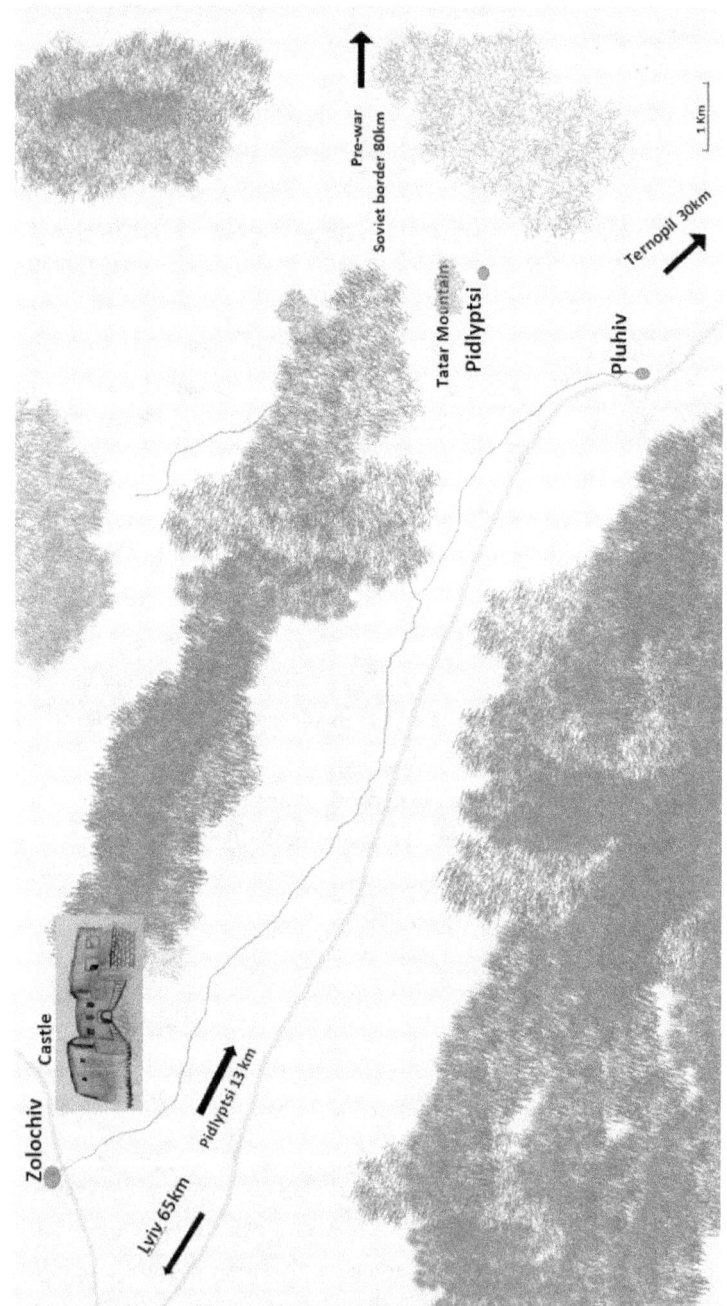

Pidlyptsi and Zolochiv, Lviv Oblast, Ukraine.

bility for the outbreak and cause of the war. Henceforth, they placed severe restrictions on Germany and Austria's capacity to develop its military potential. As a fiscal punishment, they had to pay billions in gold marks in reparations to the victorious nations. Worst of all, for the defeated countries, was their territorial losses.

Germany's significant losses included much of Eastern Prussia to Poland and Alsace/Lorraine to France. The Austro-Hungarian Empire fared far worse. The once-mighty kingdom that had stretched from the Balkans in the south to Ukraine in the north virtually ceased to exist, following the partitioning of her land into several decimated nations. Her great cities, including Budapest, Prague, Belgrade, and Bratislava, became capitals of smaller countries, while Vienna remained Austria's capital. Ostensibly, the arrangement made sense, given that language, culture and geographic location now defined the new nations.

One of the significant outcomes of the treaty was to re-establish Poland as an independent nation. Poland initially existed as an independent country from the mid-sixteenth century, lasting for over two hundred years before being swallowed up by the combined kingdoms of Prussia, Russia and Austro-Hungary. The treaty granted Poland hegemony over Western Ukraine, with Lviv named the capital of the province. Concurrently, Eastern Ukraine, of which Kyiv was the capital, remained under Russian sovereignty. Hence, despite their yearnings and subsequent protestations, one of the most disenfranchised groups stemming from the treaty were Ukrainians. Their plea for independence fell upon deaf ears.

Historically, Ukraine, like Poland, has had a complicated past. In the past millennium, with one or two very brief exceptions, the land had always been under another country's rule. In 1918, in defiance of the judgement, Ukraine declared her independence and decided to fight. Without support, however, the fledgling country was doomed to fail.

> We had a big fight with Poland in November. Every year in November, we have [remembrance]. It's a big day for us. Poland had help from Hungry and from someone else, and they took over that part.

The Russians had the rest of Ukraine. Kyiv was in Eastern Ukraine, and Lviv, the capital of Western Ukraine, still is now.

Leon's family then fell under Polish rule. In general, Ukrainians hated the arrangement, particularly when the government began enforcing the Polish culture, language and religion upon its citizens.

*

On 12 August 2019, the Pilgrims arrived at Kyiv International Airport. The city is beautiful, hectic, progressive and melancholy, all at once. The organised chaos of the inner city streets is something to behold. Cars seemed to be randomly passing into each other's lanes while somehow avoiding collisions. Somehow, it all seemed to work. Everything was relatively cheap; we could live well there. Uber was our preferred mode of transport; we were able to travel at will for barely a dollar.

My football-mad nephews, Michael and James, had the time of their life in Kyiv. In the heart of the city, they at once found a football pub, its interior completely decked out in football jerseys from all over the world. Within an hour, they had made lifelong friends with both the publican and most of the patrons. After that, we saw very little of them for the rest of our stay in the capital.

No visit to Kyiv is complete without a visit to Maidan, the now peaceful Independence Square, in the city centre. There, an angelesque figure sits atop a massive spire as a monument to Ukrainian independence. I stood there without understanding fully what occurred there between November 2013 and February 2014, after what began as peaceful protests against the incumbent government's anti-European/pro-Russian leadership. The scale and scope of the brutality of the government's security force, known as the Berkut, in putting down the protests, at the behest of their tyrannical president, culminated in over 130 deaths. Night after night, Ukranians came out, despite the bitter cold, in peaceful protest regardless of the personal risks as the Berkut took aim at innocent men, women and children, with iron batons, tear gas, stun grenades and even live ammunition. At least when the Nazi jackboots stomped over the Maidanplatz, they knew that their enemy was German. This time it was Ukranians, albeit the worst kind, who murdered and beat them.

After three days in Kyiv, we arrived by plane at Lviv airport, where we were warmly greeted by our cousin Andrii. He knew just a few English words, and we had even less Ukrainian between us, so the conversation was minimal. However, we were all thrilled to see him. He had hired a minibus and driver to take the seven of us to Zolochiv. The trip itself was pure, organised chaos. There seemed to be no road rules; cars and trucks simply overtook at will, at ridiculous speeds, on roads badly in need of maintenance. At one point, we sat behind a police car in front of which travelled a military convoy of several trucks heading east. Suddenly a car sped past not only us and the police car, but the entire convoy in one go. The police car, unperturbed, maintained a steady speed as our driver followed suit. After the shock came the stark realisation that Ukraine is still at war with Russian separatists, who had occupied much of Ukraine's Donbas region. Throughout our travels, we continued to come across photographic memorials dedicated to those Ukrainians who have died thus far in the conflict.

When journeying from west to east, I formed the impression that the closer we got to the old Soviet Union, the more the people walked with their heads down. Perhaps this was because of the history of fear and distrust promulgated by the Soviet regime. In contrast, the European city of Lviv seemed to be a friendlier, more vibrant and happier place.

Having finally reached our destination, Zolochiv, alive and in one piece, we checked into our motel, in a lovely, quiet area on the fringe of town. Soon after, Andrii arrived with our driver to take us to visit his mother, Leon's sister-in-law, Olga Mykulyshyn. Our first objective was to find out more about Leon's biological father, about whom he seldom spoke. We already knew from Leon Junior, who had visited Ukraine in 2010, that our grandfather, Yuzyk (Joseph) Fedortsiv (not

Sokulsky), was, in fact, run out of town, rather than having died of natural causes. We were keen to know what really happened and why the truth might have been covered up.

After an emotional, tear-filled introduction, we settled down in Olga's little lounge room to talk. Through Google translator, Olga explained, together with Andrii, what happened to Leon's father. While in his twenties, Yuzyk had fought for the Austro-Hungarian Empire in the First World War. Although on the losing side, he benefited from the ensuing peace treaty because Poland acquired Western Ukraine. He was one of around two hundred thousand Polish citizens given land and the opportunity to settle in their acquired territory. Yuzyk's property happened to be in Pidlyptsi, next door to the Sokulsky family farm. The people who had previously owned the land, one day mysteriously disappeared. Their departure, in all likelihood, was not by choice.

Marika Sokulska, twenty-one at the time, saw her new neighbour every day. Whether it was love at first sight or a gradual process, no one could tell, but suffice to say, they fell in love and pledged to commit themselves to each other for life. One can imagine their romance blossoming amid the vast Ukrainian fields, amongst beautiful flora, hills and streams. The relationship continued and eventually, at twenty-five, Marika fell pregnant. The young couple, deeply in love, wanted to marry, but as protocol would have it, Yuzyk first needed to seek Marika's parents' blessing for the marriage. Indeed, a formality?

The question on all of our lips was, 'Why did the young couple, so much in love, not marry?' Eagerly we typed our query into the translator and waited while Andrii consulted Olga. Before long, we stared incredulously at her response.

'They did not give permission.'

The parents? 'Why not?' we asked.

Olga's next answer astounded us even more. 'Because he was Roman Catholic, and she was Greek Catholic.'

My sister Elizabeth sought confirmation. 'I want to make this clear,' she asked. 'The family would rather their pregnant daughter have no husband than to marry someone who was Roman but not Greek Catholic?'

The answer came back, 'Yes.'

It seems that after receiving the devastating news that he could not marry his beloved Marika, Yuzyk fled heartbroken, back to his native Poland. In Pidlyptsi, nobody ever heard from him again. As to whether he was run out of town, Yuzyk's departure, it seems, was the opposite of a shotgun wedding. Hence, there may well have been shotguns waiting for him should he ever return. Rather than be told the truth, Olga suggested that Leon grew up thinking that his father had succumbed to a common way to die in those days, pneumonia. It seems that his mother promoted the story to protect him from knowing that his Roman Catholic biological father was likely to be alive and well but unwelcome. To this day, despite our investigations, no one in the family has been able to find out what became of Yuzyk Fedortsiv.

The genesis of Greek Catholicism occurred during Austro-Hungarian rule as a compromise solution that aimed to unite Ukrainian Roman Catholics and Orthodox Catholics under one church. The new religion proved a success, and most of the existing Orthodox and Catholic churches in the area quickly converted to Greek Catholicism. However, the Roman Catholic side of the fledgling church inherited from their Polish overlords remained at odds with Ukrainian orthodoxy. Consequently, Greek Catholics and Roman Catholics often hated each other just as Protestants and Catholics historically did in Ireland. Hence, in practice, rather than the breach, a family would not sanction the marriage of their Greek Catholic daughter to a Roman Catholic son.

*

Ostensibly, Leon was born in Western Ukraine and, therefore, under Polish rule. However, his family never considered themselves as anything other than Ukrainian. As far as Leon was concerned, he always lived in Ukraine while he grew up under Polish sovereignty. 'They ruled us, but they did not own us. We were Ukrainian.'

It was not that Leon disliked the Polish people; he had many Polish friends throughout his life; it was just that he was Ukrainian. When I asked him about this one day, he replied, 'If the Japanese invaded Australia, would you call yourself Japanese?'

I saw his point.

Poland between the world wars was a political, economic and social mess. The country found itself bordered by the Baltic Sea in the north and no less than six countries (seven if you count the Free City of Danzig), and with just about every one of them, there were constant border wars. The biggest problem was trying to unite the assortment of ethnic groups within Poland, who often aligned more with its neighbours than Poland. Consequently, from 1926, Poland unsurprisingly had reverted to a more authoritarian, autocratic rule. The government set about trying to force Ukrainians to convert in name and culture.

> I was born under the Polish government. It was very [much] a dictatorship to us. First of all, we were not allowed, in public, to even sing Ukrainian songs. I remember when we were little boys, and we had on a Ukrainian cap, the policeman came and threw it away, saying, 'You're not allowed to use that.'
>
> I didn't like it because they didn't treat us the same as they treated the Polish people. If you had on a Ukrainian shirt, police told you on the road, 'That's not the right one. Take it off.' We weren't allowed to do the same as the Polish people. Ukrainians couldn't get a good job unless you changed your name to Polish and then change your religion.
>
> Yes, a lot of people were discriminated [against]. You went to the army, but you couldn't be an officer or anything like that, unless you changed your nationality to Polish, and then you'd be all right. You could be a man who looks after the trees, wood, you know, that was all right.

When asked if he considered changing his name, Leon's response was emphatic.

> No, never, ever. They even asked us. Not one of the Sokulsky family would change it to Polish. Just put an 'i' on your name, instead of 'y', and you're Polish – just go to Polish church and change your religion to Roman Catholic. I even speak perfect Polish.

To enforce a cultural conversion, all newspapers and government correspondence had to be in Polish, and limits were placed on when they could speak their native language.

> At home, with my father and mother, everything was in Ukrainian, but once we entered the school, except for one hour a week, we had to speak only Polish.

In defiance, Leon's family privately held onto its cultural and religious traditions, if not publicly. They continued to wear their traditional clothes, sing their Ukrainian songs and dance their cultural dances.

3

Hard Times in Germany – Maria c. 1929–33

By the beginning of the 1930s, the Great Depression, which began in 1929 with the notorious Wall Street Crash in the United States, had started to take hold in Europe. Germany, who relied on US loans to pay her massive First World War debts, suffered even more. Within a matter of months, her stock market had crashed, its banks failed, and millions were out of work. Money and life savings became practically worthless as inflation skyrocketed exponentially. From as early as 1922, however, Germans were already beset by hyperinflation, mainly because of the economic fallout from their defeat in the First World War. Every day, prices went up to ever more ridiculous levels. Where it might cost one mark for a loaf of bread in the morning, by the afternoon, you might need a thousand marks (German currency) to buy that same loaf. There was no point in selling goods because, by the time you took your money to buy more stock, your earnings could be practically worthless. There was little point in working for wages, so people had to rely on what they could produce themselves on their land. Inflation became so out of control that a five-billion-mark note at one point became so worthless that one side was blank. The ink had cost more than the value of the bill.

Corruption soared as the country teetered on economic and political anarchy. These conditions provided the perfect breeding ground for all disillusioned, impoverished, criminal, or even mildly insane persons and groups. From out of the swell of the primordial soup of this dysfunctional political concoction, the burgeoning Nazi Party not only emerged but then also began to thrive.

The Preiße family owned and leased businesses, farms and houses, and had substantial land holdings that employed local workers. Together with sound investing and business acumen, the family was amongst the most affluent in the district. However, the Depression almost crippled them. Inflation took hold so rapidly in the country that if a client paid fifty thousand marks for rent in the morning, it was worthless by the time it got to the bank. Before the crash, the Preiße family loaned large amounts of their cash to friends and acquaintances. Money became so cheap, their clients simply paid back their worthless loans. Paradoxically, some people had no choice but to wait for hours in line for work that paid virtually nothing.

The Keil family and those living off the land were better off than most because they were virtually self-sufficient. They produced their meat from livestock like geese and chickens from their land, which also provided their vegetables, fruit, eggs, butter and milk. Grandma Keil, deeply distressed by the poverty she saw around her, could never turn her back on anyone suffering, so she decided to do something more. She had an idea to run a soup kitchen for the poor people in the area.

To accomplish this, she set up a stall at the intersection of the main road from Döfering to Haschaberg. Every day, she served a free meal for those poor in the district who could not otherwise afford to eat a substantial meal. Initially, she coped quite well, but her altruistic venture quickly became so popular that Grandma soon realised that she could not supply enough food with her limited supplies. To address the shortfall, she enlisted the support of other local farmers. Together with her cousins and friends, Maria volunteered to help by visiting farmers to see if they could spare excess food for hot soup in the winter or sandwiches in the summer. They soon knew the farmers that would help if they could, and the children regularly came back with an adequate supply of food. Maria and her friends then helped Grandma before and after school to prepare, cook and serve people, many of whom they knew to have been well off before the Depression, but were now homeless, starving or destitute. Mental health was a concern, and suicide rates were highest amongst the poor and hungry, especially those who had lost everything. As well as providing for their

*The Family Keil circa 1914, outside their house in Döfering.
L to R: Josef, Margaret, Grandma Keil, Barbara, Michel and Resel.
These were hard times.*

*Keil family descendants outside the Keil house in 2019.
L to R: Chris, Milla, the author, Josephine, Steffany and Michael.*

physical needs, Grandma's kitchen allowed the impoverished to enjoy the therapy of companionship. It was nice to have someone to talk to; to share his or her worries. Word soon spread, and people came from all around, regardless of rain or snow, to Grandma and her little helpers group's stall.

4

Storytime – Leon, c. 1934

Marika Sokulska lived a shattered life after losing her beloved Yuzyk. It was to be a further seven years before she married for the first time, a shoemaker named Stephan Mykulyshyn. Hence, while Leon continued to carry his mother's maiden name, she became Marika Mykulyshyn. By all accounts, Stephan was a good man who treated his new wife with love and respect and instantly connected with his new stepson. 'I grew up very close to him. He treated me like his son. I could never say a word against him.' Stephan was a tall, diligent, resourceful and generous man who was, most notably, Greek Catholic.

Stephan's family, like many Ukrainians, had Cossack lineage. He brought with him many heroic tales of the exploits of his ancestors. The long winter nights spent indoors meant plenty of time for storytelling, and Stephan proved to be an excellent storyteller. Leon's favourite story involved a time when his stepfather personally fought against the Crimean Tatars. It began with a reminder of the many great battles he fought against the Tatars and then described one occasion when an enemy arrow struck him right between the eyes. Years later, when Leon passed the story on to us, wherein he was the Cossack, somehow he had a scar right between his eyes to prove that an arrow struck him in precisely that spot!

During a decisive battle, Stephan captured the Tatars' leader, and, to gather vital information, he tickled him to death under his foot with a feather. Before he died, the Tartar chief laughed so much that he told him everything! Then, his stepfather would always tickle Leon mercilessly to show him exactly how it felt.[5]

Another of Stephan's tales was of the Witch with Potato Teeth. It all began one day when Stephan was a little boy; he was out in the woods one lovely spring day when he got lost. Stumbling through the forest, he found a house in the middle of nowhere; he knocked, and when no one answered, stepped inside. There, he met a witch who captured him and locked him in a cage. Over the next few weeks, she fed him a selection of excellent but fatty food regularly, which Stephan willingly ate.

One day, when he asked the witch why she fed him so much, she replied, 'The only thing I am missing is the taste of human flesh. I am fattening you up so I can eat you!'

On realising the truth, Stephan escaped when the witch fell asleep after leaving the key to his cage on a nearby table. He was able to capture it by throwing a string out with his shoe tied onto it. Unfortunately, Stephan woke the witch while escaping, and she chased after him. In desperation, just before he knew he was about to be captured, he climbed the nearest tree.

The witch arrived and ordered him, 'You come down now!'

Of course, Stephan refused, and so the witch, in her anger, screamed, 'I will chop the tree down!' then ran back into the house to find something to use.

First, she grabbed a knife, with which she tried to hack down the tree, but the blade broke. Then, furious with anger, she ran back to the house and returned this time with a spoon, with which she once more tried to hack down the tree. When that too, bent and became useless, the witch became crazy. She shrieked with so much fury that she attempted to bite down the tree with her teeth in desperation. Of course, all of her teeth broke.

By this time, the witch was utterly beside herself with rage. She was out of control as she ran back into the house, from where after a while, she came back with a fresh set of teeth. There was only one problem: she had made her complete set of teeth out of potato. Once more, she tried to bite down the tree with her potato teeth, but of course, they just squashed into bits of mashed potato, leaving her with only her gums to gnaw harmlessly at the tree trunk.

Finally, with even greater madness, if that were possible, she gave up trying to chop down the tree and instead decided to climb up it herself to bring him down. 'Get down,' she screamed as she ascended, 'I am going to eat you!'

Stephan yelled back, 'No, I won't come down.'

Now, what do you do when a witch is climbing up a tree to get you? Of course, the only thing you can do under such circumstances: you have to wee on her head. That is precisely what Stephan did as the witch got closer. Everyone knows that witches hate water, and that includes wee. She shrieked with pain as the urine burned her skin; she lost her balance and fell to the ground, writhing in agony.

Meanwhile, Stephan climbed down and ran safely back home. That was not quite the end of the story. From that day onward, whenever anyone saw the witch in town, she always had her potato teeth in her mouth.

5

First Memories of Hitler – Maria, 1933

Maria was about to turn thirteen in January 1933, when President Paul von Hindenburg promoted Adolf Hitler to chancellor, the second-highest position in the land. Paradoxically, this occurred even though the Nazis had lost nearly three million votes between 1930 and 1932. With Hitler's power waning and signs of post-Depression economic recovery on the horizon, many people believed the antiestablishment Nazis to be a spent force.

> Before the election, from what I heard, Hitler could not win.

However, they were wrong. Given that no party could gain the majority needed to make the critical decisions necessary to stabilise the government, the Nazis were, paradoxically, actually in a strong position. The major parties, the Communist Party (KPD) and the Social Democratic Party (SPD), fundamentally hated each other, so there was no hope of bipartisan decision-making.

By the late 1920s and early 30s, and with the Great Depression in full swing, the country was close to anarchy. While the KPD continued to be against any form of compromise, Hitler saw an opportunity. He and his Nazi party offered to join forces with the SDP to gain the majority vote needed to pass legislation, to rule the country effectively. Hitler insisted that under the deal, he would have to be chancellor, while Franz von Papen, a former chancellor and the leader of the *Zentrum* (Centre Party), would be his deputy. The compromise convinced the ailing eighty-six-year-old President Hindenburg that only by combining their power could they save Germany from ruin. Hindenburg feared that further instability might be the catalyst for a revolution similar in scope to that which occurred in Russia, still fresh in his memory, just sixteen years earlier. Of course, he was worried that the unstable, outspoken and aggressive Nazis could bring further pain.

Nonetheless, he was convinced that with von Papen as Hitler's deputy, and himself as the president acting as the overall arbitrator, Hitler would be under control. Armed with the knowledge that if worse came to worst, he could, at any time, personally intervene and remove Hitler, the president decided to support the coalition government. On 30 January 1930, two weeks before Maria's thirteenth birthday, he pronounced Adolf Hitler to be, forthwith, the new chancellor of Germany.

However, no sooner had he come to power than Hitler, not one to rest on his laurels, sought total control. Within two months of his taking up the chancellorship, Hitler swooped to evoke an obscure piece of legislation, called the Enabling Act, and thus fulfil his quest to obtain full, unopposed power in Germany. Under the Act, in the event of an extreme emergency, and to keep the peace, the Nazis would enjoy, for up to four years, full dictatorial powers. What they needed, therefore, was an extreme emergency.

There are two versions of what happened next. The first, promulgated by the Nazis, was that a communist named Lubbe somehow breached security at the German house of parliament, the Reichstag, and once inside, he set fire to the building. The heavily biased Nazi courts upheld this version, blaming Lubbe and, by association, the Communist Party, which they argued was trying to initiate a Communist revolution. Given that Lubbe was intellectually disabled, his capacity as the primary perpetrator of the crime is unlikely.

The more likely scenario is that Hitler and his chief crony, ex-fighter pilot ace and now Nazi minister, Herman Goering, conspired to initiate the Reichstag fire and blame the Communists. Thus, they concocted the emergency to provide cause to instigate the Enabling Act. Of course, having lit the fire themselves, they would pretend to be both shocked and furious.

They played their parts well. The plan worked to perfection. The courts charged Lubbe and the Communists with instigating a terrorist attack and for trying to induce anarchy. The indignant Hitler threatened his immediate resignation, which would have plunged Germany into further political chaos, unless given instant provisional power to act decisively and restore the peace. The bold move worked. After that, the Nazis, together with von Papen's SDP, controlled parliament and won the ensuing vote in the Reichstag, thus allowing them the power to take whatever steps were necessary to restore law and order.

On a cold winter's day at the beginning of February 1933, Maria had just attended Mass and was walking alongside the near-frozen Regen River on the way to her mother's house. Suddenly, she heard the sound of a boat's whistle as it pierced the frosty air. She looked to see a largish boat coming upriver. As it came closer, Maria saw that there was a group of rugged-up people on deck. They were leaning out from the boat, waving and calling out something that she could not quite interpret.

Before long, Maria could hear what they were joyfully shouting: 'Hitler is on the throne! Tell everyone! Hitler is on the throne!'[6]

When later she passed on the news to her family in Döfering, she was disappointed to realise that they never shared the people's enthusiasm on the boat. 'My people, from the start, were not with Hitler.'

While the Enabling Act may have brought stability of sorts, it was all too good to be true. The Nazis initially promised that this was to be short-term, to establish proper law and order. The inference relied on the Nazis' goodwill to reinstate the democratic processes as soon as they achieved political and economic stability. In hindsight, that was never going to happen. There was no chance of a democratic process hindering Hitler's megalomaniac ambitions.

The Enabling Act officially signalled the temporary end of all forms of opposition, including other political parties, the free press and any media, forum, or person who might be anti-government. In short, it signalled the day that free speech in Germany died.

> There was a lot of fear. The first thing I remember was, 'Shh, don't say anything any more, You'll be arrested; sent to a concentration camp.

The Nazis tried to quash internal resistance and were quick to silence their critics. The propaganda poster reads, 'Durch Kampf und Arbeit siegen wir...nich durch Gerüchtetratsch! Through battle and work we will win...not through gossip!'

By 1934, thanks mainly to the changing global economic climate, the worst of the Depression had passed. In Germany, the Nazi-controlled press claimed that the Führer, Adolf Hitler, was the sole reason for turning the economic tide in Germany. In truth, much of his success was due to good fortune. Nevertheless, Hitler deserves credit for supporting existing, and commissioning new, massive public works that employed hundreds of thousands of Germans and included the famous autobahns that connected cities and towns throughout Germany as never before. Despite the restrictions imposed by the Treaty of Versailles, tens of thousands more found employment in hitherto banned armaments manufacturing industries and vastly growing Wehrmacht (the combined armed forces of army, navy and air force). That, added to the fact that Hitler outright refused to pay for war reparations, meant that Germany found itself dragged out from the economic doldrums of the Great Depression. There was, however, a catch. To justify the continual increases in expenditure, especially in armaments and the armed forces, Hitler would eventually need to use them.

At first, the positive changes ensured that most people were better off under Hitler, and his popularity increased. Some of his critics argued, however, that it was all too good to be true. Soon, rumours began to spread about Nazi-built concentration camps for nonconformists, especially anyone who spoke against the Nazis. Together with hardened criminals, life in the camps was often short-lived.

On 2 August 1934, much to the delight of Adolf Hitler, President Paul Von Hindenburg died aged eighty-six.

Maria was less enthusiastic.

> There was a lot of mourning, and every day for one week afterward, the church bells had to ring for one hour at noon.

Hindenburg's death gave Hitler the opportunity he craved. Soon afterwards, he called another election to combine the roles of president and chancellor and, he hoped, to instal himself as Führer.[7] This time, he took no chances. To ensure success, he had to not out-campaign but eliminate the opposition.

At the time, most of the children at Maria's school enjoyed falling under the auspices of the region's leading political party, the Bavarian Peoples' Party (BVP). The party often arranged weekend camps for the children to promote their ideals of Christian values, daily prayer and healthy living. Maria and her friends loved these camps because they liked the balance of developing their social, moral and spiritual wellbeing while participating in healthy outdoor activities.

For the moment, the Nazis continued to tolerate Catholics, primarily because there were so many of them. One-third of the entire population was Catholic, with numbers much higher in Bavaria. Hence, their support was still significant. Regardless, by 1939, restrictions on religious lessons in German schools continued to alienate many Catholics who might otherwise have been supporters. No one was exempt from Nazi scrutiny.

The BVP openly and actively opposed the Nazis, seeing them as an egregious threat to their religious, political and social freedoms. The Nazis, now in complete control, saw the danger of BVP anti-Nazi propaganda as provocative and destabilising. They used this premise to dismantle and illegalise the BVP and any other opposition, especially their hated nemesis, the Communists. The Nazis banned any sort of defamatory anti-Nazi publication, closed down the printers and arrested their leaders.

Maria recalled the perceived impact.

> My Aunty Resel came outside [at the] weir – white, like a sheet – saying, 'Hitler is on the throne, Hitler is on the throne, Hitler is on the throne… What happens now? Now, there will be war. There will be a war!'

*

The weir that Maria mentioned is on the Regan River, close to where her mother lived. Eighty-three years later, our group of pilgrims planned to explore the river. We purchased floats and, starting upstream on a perfectly hot summer's day, began to drift slowly downstream, cooly observing the idyllic views from the water. Eventually, the river forked and, to the right, we could see the same weir where Aunty Resel prophesied the coming cataclysm. Nephew Michael and I stopped and sat for a while within a small but glorious waterfall, allowing the water to cascade over us while enjoying the spectacular scenery. It was an extraordinary feeling to acknowledge some of the histories that passed this point.

Eventually, we continued our downstream journey. We passed by Cham museum, once a hospital for the Black Plague victims, and further along, we passed beneath Florian Geyer Brücke, the iconic bridge used in the Second World War movie *The Bridge*. In the film, seven youths fruitlessly attempted to hold the bridge, defending the town against the oncoming American army. Their zeal caused all but one to lose their lives fighting a long-lost cause. Our journey over, we soon found ourselves alongside our hotel, the Reganbogen.

*

Following Hitler's rise to absolute power, It soon became apparent that the Nazis subjugated the local populations by coercion and fear.

> They said, 'Do not say anything any more. You will be arrested. They will send you to Dachau.'

Located near Munich, Dachau concentration camp, built in 1933, evolved into the worst kind of prison. To create a deterrent, the Nazis sometimes allowed visitors and occasionally released inmates, knowing that they would spread the word about the terrible conditions.

> We didn't know what happened there to the people, but we knew it was bad, what they did.

The Nazi tactic of intimidation did not entirely work, instead forcing some critics to operate secretly. Maria recalled that she had collected anti-Nazi leaflets handed out surreptitiously by children.[8]

> There were two sorts of leaflets, and I still know them today. I wish I could just *hept auf* [kept them]. I hid them for long years. Later, when Hitler came, I had to *verschwinden lassen* [make them disappear]. Otherwise, they would kill you. Before the election, I found the leaflets still that they gave the kids to give out. I found [them] some years later. The same leaflets were still here.

Maria recalled, more than fifty years later, word for word, its prophetic message.

> 'So est zum Dritten Reich gegehen. [So, this is how it will be, in the Third Empire.]' Hitler made the *Dritten Reich*. There wasn't a *Dritten Reich* in the moment, before that. 'Wo Kopfe rollen, Galgen stehen. Galgen zum aufhänge. [Where heads will roll, gallows will stand. Hanging Gallows.][9]
> This is really true. This is what one leaflet had on.

The use of the term Third Reich on the leaflet was surprising given that it was far too soon to compare Hitler's Nazis to previous empires.

The First Reich referred to the Holy Roman Empire and the reign of Germanic King Charlemagne. It lasted from the tenth to the nineteenth century. The Second Reich was much shorter, lasting just forty-seven years, from Bismarck's unification of Germany in 1871 to the end of the First World War in 1918. Hitler, wanting to go one better than the previous empires, was soon referring to his Nazi Germany as the Thousand-Year Reich.

> Hitler made the *Dritten Reich*; there wasn't the *Dritten Reich* at that moment, before the war.

The authors of Maria's leaflet predicted both pessimistically and accurately the rise of the next great empire.

A second leaflet, equally foreboding, predicted future generations of Germans would suffer because of their ancestors' sins. Maria recalled the words.

> Kinder and Children's Kinder they will one day curse those in the grave that voted for Hitler.

An underground movement arose, in which people risked their lives to post anti-Hitler literature. Some were captured and executed. Some went into hiding, where they continued to seek ways of undermining the Nazis in any way possible.

6
Calm Before the Storm – Leon, c. 1935

> We weren't bad off either. We had two cows, we had horses. The horses did all the work. We had geese, we had pigs, we had loads of chickens, I don't even know how many – stacks of them. We had a fantastic, big garden, loads of garden where we grew plums and cherries, and things like that. Big nuts you know, big walnuts, great big massive ones.
>
> Oh, I was happy enough, you know running about, running barefoot to school. You name it, we had it. We used to buy soap and salt and vinegar. The rest, everything, we made our own. We made butter ourselves, we sold butter, our own eggs, and we sold to the rich, and he sold to someone else to make a profit.

The key to survival was self-sufficiency; get a plentiful summer crop, and use it to endure the harsh, freezing winter when nothing could grow.

> We had dried fruit all year round, you know. We had dried apples. We had cucumbers all year round. Everybody prepared for the winter. [We] used to grow cabbage and had a special machine that cut it very fine. We had big barrels. You fill it into barrels, and you put a bit of weight on it, with big stones, so it gets sour, salt, you can put a bit of carrot, cut to make sauerkraut for the winter. Same as cucumber.

Given that harvest time was only a small window in summer, they would also have to prepare enough food to last them until the following year, which meant leaving food to ferment throughout the winter.

> We used to pickle a big barrel of cucumbers. Seal it up, dump it in

the water right through the winter. In the spring, when you open it, it's all fresh.

His mother was a superb cook. She happily taught her recipes to Leon, who knew how to make all of the Ukrainian staple dishes, like vareniki (potato-filled dumplings), holopchi (cabbage rolls with meat) and borscht (beetroot soup). The fertile soil and their ability to preserve food for the winter effectively meant that they always had something nutritious to eat.

When Leon was very young, his mother made a large, delicious, piping-hot cherry pie for the family. While she was attending to her other chores, she left Leon alone. At first, he resisted the temptation, but soon, he ate a tiny piece of the pie. Then, still thinking his mother might not notice, he cut off another small slice. One thing led to another, and before long, Leon had eaten half of the pie. When his mother returned, she was angry but did not show it. She pretended she had not noticed and, instead, offered him a whole bowl full of cherries. Not wanting to tell his mother that he was already full, Leon proceeded to eat from the bowl. When he said he had had enough, his mother insisted that he finish the whole bowl. Leon, not wanting to admit the truth, kept eating. He never forgot the terrible stomach ache he had because of his dishonesty and learned a valuable lesson about honesty.

Despite the frustration, Ukrainians in the west may not have been aware of how fortunate they were, compared to their counterparts in Soviet-held Eastern Ukraine. Three years before Leon's birth, the first Soviet leader after the Revolution, Vladimir Lenin, died. His successor, Joseph Stalin, disliked Ukrainians and their persistent demands for independence. By the winter of 1932, Stalin decided to wipe out all resistance. He ordered his troops to systematically isolate hundreds of Ukrainian villages and towns before removing all livestock and harvests from their farms. Thus he left the residents with nothing to sustain them through the winter. Systematic starvation ensued, and, while estimates vary, within two years, he had, by conservative estimates, murdered about five million, approximately one fifth of the entire population.

News of Stalin's attempted genocide soon spread to the West. Thanks to their eastern brothers and sisters, Leon and his family, who lived close to the border, knew better than most the terrors that pervaded. Facing starvation, many there tried desperately to flee westwards. However, Stalin warned them that to leave was a criminal act. He placed Russian soldiers along the border and issued orders to shoot anyone trying to cross into Poland.

Despite the risks, some did manage to escape. Some did so in the hope of returning with food for their families. They would raid farms west of the border for food, stealing chickens, digging the soil with their bare hands for vegetables and taking fruit from trees. Marika and Stephan did not mind helping out until word spread that some were crossing the border to steal young children for food. Henceforth, Leon had to stay inside at night for fear of abduction and cannibalism.

Later in life, Leon sometimes joked about eating nail soup. We did not overthink the joke at the time, but there is truth in the story in hindsight. Metals or metal filings added to soups provided an essential addition for those starved of iron, which is necessary for energy and cellular respiration. This knowledge, famously used in prisoner of war camps, undoubtedly saved lives.

Despite the worries, Leon was a much-loved child who enjoyed his childhood and had plenty of positive role models and an extensive support network of relatives and friends whose homes were always open.

While not wealthy, the family was sufficiently affluent to be one of the first in the area to purchase a crystal radio. It required the owner to use headphones, meaning that only one person could listen at a time. After dinner, the family would sit and listen to music or the latest news from Warsaw. While nobody could understand how the technology worked, the ability to connect to the outside world brought a good deal of joy to the family. Typically, Stephan would usually listen to the news, and then relay the messages to everyone else. Sometimes, friends and relatives would visit to enjoy the novel technology. When Leon had a turn with the headphones, he was astonished to hear voices and music. As a little boy, he had a theory about how it worked.

> I thought that there must be little men inside the box.

7

Did You Join the Hitler Youth? – Maria, c. 1935

It was evident to teachers and schoolchildren alike that education in the Third Reich was quite different. The new, Nazi-driven curriculum elevated Adolf Hitler to a godlike status. Children heard that only the Führer would save Germany from the terrible threats both outside and within the country. The children knew, according to the curriculum, that Hitler was their friend and only he could ensure their safety and prosperity.

The Nazi-based curriculum emphasised the ideology of the superiority of the Germanic/Aryan race over all others. By logical extension, therefore, all other races must be inferior. While this notion is not unique to the Germanic race, many citizens embraced the idea. In 1841, Heinrich Hoffman added lyrics promoting German superiority to Joseph Haydn's *Deutschlandlied*. From the moment he penned the opening line, *Deutschland, Deutschland über alles, über alles in der Welt* (Germany, Germany over everything, over everything in the world), he set the tone for the theme behind the lyrics. Eighty-one years later, in 1922, its impact still resonated, such that the German government at the time adopted the song as their national anthem.

The Nazis simply used the notion of Aryan superiority for the basis of their political and cultural platform. Hence, all people, their worth and potential, could be measured by their degree of Aryanism. It was this mentality that the Nazis applied particularly to the Jewish race. The controlled press broadcast the most insulting and derogatory claims that Jews were responsible for virtually every problem. Lessons in Maria's class mandatorily proclaimed the notion of social Darwinism; that the fittest and healthiest races become more potent due to the passing down of superior genetics. Additionally, they learned that to maintain superiority, the strong must either subjugate, dominate or eradicate the inferior races.

At the same time as Maria was listening to this in the classroom, a black American athlete by the name of Jesse Owens turned that theory on its head when he won four gold medals at the 1936 Olympic games in Berlin. Embarrassingly for Hitler, he was in the stands to witness Owens's dominant victory in the hundred-metres sprint. No doubt, had a German won (Erich Borchmeyer, Germany's best, finished fifth), he would have been there to congratulate him in person. Instead, the result caused Hitler to turn away in disgust, and he left without staying for the medal celebrations. One Nazi commentator, in empathy for Hitler's attitude, disparagingly chose a different tact. Rather than acknowledging Owens's superiority, he expressed his view that the victory was unfair because black men were more comparable in genetics to racehorses than humans.

Of course, the Nazi press ignored Owens's victory, and in the classroom, Maria only heard about German successes. However, despite the Nazi mandate on education, one of Maria's teachers embraced the curriculum unenthusiastically.

> Our teacher had to put something in his lessons about Hitler, but he wasn't for Hitler.

Religious intolerance was evident in the new curriculum, causing Maria, her teacher, and the Catholic community great concern. Some unsympathetic Nazis, however, took matters into their own hands.

> Somebody else came in the school. We had prayer every morning in school, and before we came home from school, and somebody came and took the cross. We were very religious. The school, the Lehrer [teacher] played the organ in the church and every day in the masses, and we had singsongs in the school. So we had no cross any more to pray.

The removal of the cross had a profound symbolic impact on Maria and the other children. If the Nazis sought to eliminate competition between state and religion, the strategy failed for Maria. The decision only served to strengthen her faith, and she became even more anti-Nazi, especially when a large photo of Hitler now stood in place of the cross. It is little wonder that many felt disconnected from the Nazis' world.

> After a time, the Nazis knew that our village was not for Hitler. They had Nazis in the area who told the authorities.

Increasingly, outspoken Catholics, like everyone else who voiced contrary political views, found themselves in danger of arrest and extradition to concentration camps. One day, Maria arrived at school to find a new teacher at the school. She took an instant dislike to the pro-Nazi woman, who promulgated the Nazi idea of racial hierarchy. The theory held that pure-bred Aryan Germanics, typically tall and muscular with blue eyes and blond hair, stood at the top level. At the bottom were Slavs and Russians, who they labelled *Untermensch* (subhuman), together with Jehovah's Witnesses, dark-skinned Africans and African Americans, Roma, homosexuals and Jews. Maria began to hate school.

Paradoxically, almost all of the top Nazi leaders lacked the qualities required to be at the top of the racial hierarchy. None of them sported the quintessential blond hair and blue eyes. Goebbels had a club foot and walked with a limp. Himmler was stubby, dark and perpetually ill, Goering was obese and suffering from heroin addiction, and Röhm, the SA commander, was a homosexual, overweight and alcoholic. Even Hitler himself had the wrong colour eyes and hair. Moreover, both Hitler and Himmler forcefully suppressed evidence that they almost certainly had Jewish grand- or great-grandparents.

Beyond the classroom, young boys joined the Hitler Youth, while the girls joined the equivalent Bund Deutscher Mädel (BDM). The groups usually met on weekends, with attendance being compulsory. The Hitler Youth boys' education focused primarily on military training, work and sport. In contrast, the girls' education focused on the *Weltanschauungsgemeinschaft* (worldview) and included child-rearing, exercise, obedience and domestic sciences. Necessarily, this education provided girls with the requisite skills to nurture the next generation of the Master Race.

At fifteen, Maria found the BDM to be intolerably dull. She hated having to give the Hitler salute and laughed at the idea of conformity.

> Yes, I would have joined the Hitler Youth. Ha, ha, ha! We had to go and join the Hitler Youth, the BDM: the Bund Deutscher Mädel. One Sunday I went, the next Sunday, I thought to myself, 'I'm not going any more.' You just go marching all the time, and you had to give them, every time, five pfennige [pennies]. I didn't want to give them five pfennige. I could buy some sweets for that. Five pfennige was a lot of money in those days.

The next Sunday, true to her convictions, Maria stayed at home.

The next day, when she arrived at school, her teacher called her out: 'Keil, why did you not go on Sunday to *Appell*?'[10]

Maria stuck to her plan.

> I said, 'I've got no money.'
> I'll never forget what the teacher said to me.
> My mam wanted to go to Cham [to work] just before she was married. Three hours to walk is too far and cost too much money [to catch a train]. She bought herself a second-hand bicycle, and it was fifteen marks. Somehow, the teacher had *das kennt* [known that].
> 'You said you have no money! Your mother has the money to buy that bicycle.'
> She put that on me, in the school, that my mother had the money to buy that bicycle. And then, I said nothing.

The inference was that if her mother could afford to buy a bicycle then she could surely afford to pay for her daughter's attendance. Her teacher may have been concerned that she would be accountable if attendance rates at the camps fell. 'Next time, you *will* go,' she demanded, not wanting a precedent set whereby students could arbitrarily opt out.

The following weekend, after much deliberation, Maria defied the order and did not attend for the second time running.

A poster promoting the BDM. While many young girls may have been impressed, Maria was not interested in their antics.

The next time, I had to get up from my chair. I was sent outside.

Her teacher, who presumed that Maria might not have acted alone in her decision, decided to take a different approach. 'Who told you not to go?'

I didn't understand it. It was a godsend, because if I said somebody told me I shouldn't go to Appell, they would be arrested.

The teacher tried again. 'Keil, you're a good girl. Who told you not to go? Was it your mother?'

Maria's heart was racing, but she could see the trap. The circumstances brought out her stubborn nature.

I said nothing. Then it came into my head, this horrible thought came into my mind, what should I say to make the teacher angry? I wanted to make the teacher angry. Whatever she said, it didn't matter what she said, I never said a word.

The teacher yelled and, at one point, threatened to have the whole family arrested. Maria stood defiant.

She went round and round, she would have stoned me, if she could, but she had to let me go.

After the incident, Maria never went to another BDM meeting, nor did the teacher follow up on her threat to have her arrested. For the moment, she was safe, but her love of learning at school subsided after that. At fifteen, Maria happily left school forever. She missed her friends, but by the summer of 1935, they too had moved on.

8
School and the Doctor's Car – Leon, c. 1935

Leon's school had two classrooms and two teachers. Miss Serben, a beautiful, dark-haired woman in her early twenties, wore red lipstick and taught the younger children, while Mr Jutka, a short, stocky Jewish man, still in his thirties, taught Leon and the other older children. Leon liked them both.

One day, the children were outside in the playground when they witnessed the strangest sight. A peculiar wagon appeared right up the driveway in front of the school and drove up to the school. Leon was amazed to see an ordinary, well-dressed man alighting from the vehicle. Mr Jutka and Miss Serben came out to find out what all the excitement was all about, and bravely, Leon thought, approached the man who, to Leon's surprise, seemed friendly.

> He was looking for a house; I remember it like today. It was the summertime, and this woman, she was having a problem having a baby. They got in touch with the doctor, and the doctor came by car. We didn't know what's going on, what's that thing coming along?
>
> Afterwards, when he finished with that lady, you know it was a dusty road, and this car was going away, with the doctor, and we were running after it, all the dirt all over our face.
>
> I came home, and Mum said, 'Where have you been, Leon?'
>
> I said, 'This thing coming, this big one without horses. There were no horses pulling it, and it's going on its own, and we were running after it.'
>
> 'How many of you?'
>
> I said, 'Maybe ten boys.'
>
> She said, 'Don't be stupid. That's a car. I've seen it once in town. There are quite a few we get now, not many, but there are some who have them: doctors and top policemen, and so on.'

*Leon's school. Above: c. 1940. The women are unknown but the one on the right fits Leon's description of Miss Serben.
Below: the Pilgrims on the same steps, 2019.*

The next day, Mr Jutka and Miss Serben brought all of the children together to talk about cars. They predicted everyone could, one day, have one. It seemed impossible, but Leon believed them. Some of the children doubted that that could ever happen.

*

The following morning, the Pilgrims travelled to Pydlyptsi, Leon's birth town, to visit Leon's sister, our Aunty Anna, and her family, who had inherited the family farm. On the way, we asked Andrii if we could visit the site of Leon's school. He had spoken highly of his teachers and of how much he had loved school, and of the first time he had seen a car. I wanted to see where he played and learned as a child. Andrii knew the location and soon we arrived along a dusty road in a lovely wooded area, where a relatively modern building now stood, nestled in the forest.

Sadly, Leon's school building no longer exists. The Communists demolished it some time around the Cold War era, replacing it with a Soviet administration building whose unattractive façade lacked aesthetic quality. Its soullessness and ugliness is symbolic of the period itself. If

Leon kept this photo, c. 1936, all of his life. It is his oldest photo and shows him, third from the right, with his classmates and Mr Jutka. His best friend, Julik, and Mikel are likely to be among the children.

the Communist revolution intended to develop thriving communities, they failed in this instance. The building now looks totally out of place amongst the natural, green, wooded surrounds that probably looked no different than they would have before the 1950s. It is easy to imagine the children who played merrily on these grounds so many years before. Surrounded by lush foliage, a single home-made football goal remains alone at one end of the field. Perhaps children still sometimes come here to play.

About a hundred metres in front of the building, seemingly in the middle of nowhere, we were delighted to find the original concrete steps that once led to the original school building. There, we took photos where the doctor's car stopped. It was a beautiful place to sit and ponder. I stared down the tree-lined path the vehicle had come down on its way to school. It was a picture-perfect scene. At the end of the driveway, about a hundred meters up, and amongst the greenery, you can just make out the main road. I imagined what Leon would have witnessed, seventy-eight years before, when the Germany army, with its tanks, artillery and troop carriers, made its way down that same road.

9

Die Jude Eisfeld – Maria, 1936

By 1936, as the global Depression was nearing its end, Hitler began to ride the wave of economic prosperity that swept not only through Germany, but throughout Europe, America and most of the rest of the world. The construction of the autobahns and other national works campaigns not only provided work for millions of Germany's unemployed, but it improved transport efficiency that would soon prove crucial in mobilising his growing armies and create further economic and social growth. In violation of the Treaty of Versailles, Hitler, at first covertly and then with increasing impunity, exponentially increased Germany's armaments manufacturing. Together with rapid increases in personnel in all areas – Heer (army), Kriegsmarine (navy) and Luftwaffe (air force) – he swiftly built up a formidable military and provided employment for millions.

It was against this backdrop that Hitler took perhaps his most significant gamble to date. In the aftermath of the First World War, another condition of the Treaty of Versailles was to create a demilitarised zone in the Rhineland, between the Rhine River and the French border. Yet, in March of 1936, Hitler defied the stipulation, claiming that Germany was fulfilling her entitlement as a sovereign nation when he ordered his troops to occupy the demilitarised area. Despite protestations from France and her allies, no one undertook to take decisive action to stop Germany, when evidence suggests that had they reacted aggressively, the Wehrmacht would have capitulated, with the probable end of Hitler's power then and there. It was a decision that they were later to regret.

At that time, Germany was still militarily weak, yet France, vulnerable and fearing the consequences of another conflict, misread Germany's strength and backed off. Additionally, at the time, many sympathetic politicians and observers tacitly agreed that Hitler had the right to arm his sovereign territory.

Most Germans saw the remilitarisation of the Rhineland as a resounding success. However, many in Maria's village, especially the older ones whose memories of the last war were fresh, feared another global conflict and continued to distrust Hitler.

Meanwhile, as the economy thrived, the Nazis stepped up their persecution of Jews and other minority groups in society. In 1936, they introduced laws that excluded them from economic, social and cultural prosperity by denying their rights in education, employment, marriage equality and property ownership.

Nazi propaganda used Jews as a scapegoat for virtually all of Germany's woes. In all media, newspapers, magazines, radio and cinemas, the Nazis fed the public a steady diet of anti-Semitism. What began as verbal propaganda soon escalated into physical abuse, violence, incarceration and, finally, murder. No wonder many Jews and other minority groups fled the country for more friendly lands.

Of the pre-war German Jewish population of about half a million, none lived in Döfering. However, Maria regularly travelled to the much larger town of Cham. From a population of five thousand, some seventy-two, or about two per cent, were Jewish, many of whom owned Cham's flourishing businesses.[11] Maria had, until then, limited exposure to anti-Semitism and racial discrimination.

On Sunday, 20 December 1936, Maria arrived by train at Cham station and made the short walk to the Klosterkirche,[12] where she attended mass. It was an important celebration in the lead up to Christmas. Afterwards, she walked down to see her mother at the Neue Post Gasthaus.

> When I came to Cham, one Sunday, I came down from the church, from the Klosterkirche, and when I went down the street – in the Platz there, suddenly, there is a big, big shopping centre – there were al-

ways a lot of Jews there. The special ones I remember because they were the Jews we always bought shoes from; when we were children. Their name was *Die Jude Eisfeld* (the Eisfeld Jews).[13]

Maria arrived to witness that the Nazis had trashed the shop. Shoes were everywhere; people could come and take, free of charge, whatever they wanted. As a further insult, on the facade of the shop, in big white words, someone had painted a sign with a caption that Maria could recite more than sixty years later: '*Palästina, mach die Türen auf; die Jude Eisfeld kommt in daur Land.* Palestine open your doors; the Eisfeld Jews are coming to your land.'

> When I came to my mam, I asked her what happened here with the Jews.
> She said, 'I don't know. They took them out. The people said that it was wrong! They took them in their nightdress, and they [smashed] the windows.'

The infamous *Kristallnacht* (Crystal Night), when the Nazis sponsored the systematic arrest and destruction of Jewish people and property on a national scale, was not to occur for another two years. However, in Cham, that night came early. That night and the following day, police arrested Jews in Cham without charge. For many, including the Eisfeld family, the arrests were temporary, and later, they were able to return home. However, that was only a short-term reprieve. Perhaps the people were not aware, but the long-term goal was for nothing less than the extermination of all Jews, wiped from the face of the earth.

Along with many others, Maria was understandably anxious about the Eisfelds, a hitherto respected family within the community. A group of angry residents had gathered around the shop.

> Some police officers came over to appease the crowd. They said to all of the people, 'They're going to Palestine, so they will not get killed.'

They tried to tell the crowd that the forcible eviction of the Eisfeld family during the night was for their protection.

> In the moment, they believed it. People didn't know anything about what happened in the concentration camps in those days. They didn't know anything.

It was a flimsy premise. The only thing the Jews needed protection from was the Nazis themselves.

> This was really awful what they'd done, and the people was really upset they [were] shouting and screaming…and then they said, 'Where'd you put the Jews? You leave them here…'

A Nazi sympathiser joined in and said that the Jews deserved it because they were so greedy. Maria replied, appealing to their sense of decency.

> 'If you think they have so much money' – they had all sorts of excuses – 'then increase their tax or something, but don't do that to people you know.'
> 'Don't worry about it. They are going all to Palestine.' That is what they told me.

To complain further might have been risky. The Nazis routinely spread fear to control the masses, and to protest too loudly not only put you in danger but also your family.

> And that's what I saw. The people were quiet. They could do nothing any more.

*

Eighty-three years later, a week after we left Ukraine, I stood in Cham's quiet and beautiful Altstadt, old town centre, called Marktplatzbrunnen. While Allied bombing destroyed many throughout Germany, Cham's Altstadt survived intact. The place, filled with old-world German charm, looks as though it came out of a fairy tale. As I stood by St Jacob's Kirche, I imagined what it would have been like when jackboots marched down this very place in the centre of town.

I wanted to find where the eviction of the Eisfeld family occurred.

I had a strange feeling that they would have owned the shop directly across the road, and on a whim, went inside to tentatively ask one of the shop assistants if they knew if the family Eisfeld had owned the shop at some point. The girl was nice and polite and replied that she did believe that the Eisfelds were, in fact, previous owners.

Then I went back across the cobbled road to St Jacobs, the lovely church where my parents married. There, outside the church, stood an elderly gentleman enjoying his early morning cigarette. After some small talk, I asked him if he knew anything about the Eisfeld shoe shop. Amazingly, he recalled the Eisfeld Jews and that the family had once owned that same shop, but they had moved elsewhere before the war. He told me about the Jewish Rambach[14] brothers who were tailors who owned the shop next door, and spoke highly of them: *'Nicht teuer and immer ehrlich.* Not expensive, always honest.' He recalled that they all disappeared before the war and never came back.[15]

My next stop was at the Rathaus (town hall), where I hoped to gather further information about the Eisfeld Jews and Cham's history during the war. The helpful staff arranged for me to meet with Timo Bullemer, the person in charge of the town's archives. An hour later, together with the rest of the Pilgrims, we met at the office of a tall, warm and friendly man whose youthful appearance belied his knowledge of the history of Cham. He surprised me when he instantly recalled the Eisfeld Jews and went straight to his bookshelf to extract a tattered book. He flicked straight to a page that confirmed the Eisfelds once owned that same shop in the Altstadt. My intuition was correct. However, by 1936, they had moved, not far away, to another shop.

Before we left, Timo asked for my email address in case he found some further information. To our surprise, as he typed in my address, we realised that he already had it in his mailbox. Then the penny dropped! During my research in Australia, I had found a document confirming the existence of the Eisfeld Jews in Cham. I had emailed the author, who provided some additional information. It was then that I realised the author of that document was the man who sat before me.

The next day, I followed Timo's directions and found the former Eisfeld shop. Remarkably, next door stood the Neue Post Gasthof, where my grandmother worked. That is why Maria would have gone there – to visit her mother. It was surreal to stand there at that same spot and imagine myself surrounded by shoes when Nazis trashed the store. I imagined the indignities and humiliation the Eisfelds experienced during their eviction and arrest the previous night. The Nazis even had a name for this forcible removal of Jews: *'Nacht and Nebel.* Night and fog.' Their crime? Their religion.

Nazi persecution of Jews culminated two years later, in November 1938, in what is infamously known as *Kristallnacht* (Crystal Night). It was then that the systematic oppression of the Jews became a sanctioned national event. It was a free for all; anything Jewish was fair game. Haters shamelessly attacked Jews everywhere, waking them from their sleep to be dragged from their beds, to be bashed, abused, humiliated and even murdered in some cases. Concurrently, Nazi thugs desecrated Jewish property, including their sacred places of worship, the synagogues. Rarely were the perpetrators ever held to account. They committed their crimes with impunity.

Eisfeld advertisement, courtesy of Timo Bullemer, Dates from the Jewish History of Cham. The caption reads, 'Shoe warehouse, own workshop. The widest choice in all types of shoe goods from the simplest to the most elegant.' Maria was there the day after their arrest.

The Eisfeld shop as it is today. One can imagine the shoes strewn across the road, the windows smashed and the painted message that the family were heading to Palestine. Appropriately, Jewish people purchased it after the war and called it the Victory Café. Next door is Klara Vogl's Gasthof Hotel.

The Neue Post Gasthof is still in the heart of Cham. I took the photo unaware that the jewellery shop next door used to belong to Eisfelds.

In Cham by 1938, the Jewish shop owners were gone, and just twenty-four Jews remained in the town. The evictions continued, and by mid-1942, only one Jew, a woman, remained. She had married a Christian man, and that most likely saved her life. The idea promulgated by the authorities that Jews would be cared for was a lie, and most Jews desperately wanted to leave the country. However, it became increasingly difficult to do so as demand for visas increased. Fortunately for the Eisfelds, they did manage to secure safe passage to Palestine, just in time.

10

Milestones – Leon, 1937

Among his many hobbies, Leon loved to dance – and then, as always, he did love an audience. Punctuated by high kicks and floor tricks requiring great upper and lower body strength and stamina, Ukrainian boys typically emulated the Cossack warriors' dance. The girls, beautiful, attired in colourfully embroidered traditional Ukrainian patterns, danced skilfully, with grace and poise. Sometimes they danced in gender, but then they came together with open and closed holds, to dance charmingly as couples.

Nearly the whole village would turn up to sing hymns and dance with the grace of ribbons and flowers. They would watch the young boys and girls celebrate with traditional Ukrainian dances, which would end with the presentation of bread. A young child presented the village with a loaf of bread, symbolising the importance of food and of sharing food. Leon would watch and breathe in the fresh air with not a single care in the world. He wore the finest clothes that his mother saved for special occasions. With his freshly pressed blue pants (loose and baggy, and bound at the hips and legs) and white shirt, decorated with a traditional blue/gold pattern, and his red boots always polished, Leon was ready to show off happily to the rest of the village.[16]

On 25 February 1937, Leon had two extra-special reasons to celebrate his tenth birthday. The first occurred when Stephan and his heavily pregnant wife woke him and insisting that he leave the warmth and comfort of his bed. They led him outside to the stables, where, to Leon's great surprise, a beautiful young horse stood shivering in the cold. Leon took an instant liking to the colt, who sported a white, black and grey coat. The conversation that followed went something like this.

'What will you call him?' asked Stephan.

'I don't know,' replied Leon incredulously.

'He looks like *shimmel*,' laughed his mother.

Marika jokingly used the German word for mould, *schimmel*,[17] to describe his mottled appearance. Leon had nothing against the mould that grew in certain places inside and outside of the house. It sounded just right, so he named his horse Shimmel. From the first touch, the two formed a connection that was only to grow stronger in time.

The second reason occurred later that night, exactly ten years to the day after he was born, when his mother gave birth to her second son, Mykhas. Leon was instantly devoted to his helpless baby brother.

Leon's life became hectic. He learned that caring for his little brother and Shimmel, on top of everything else he had to do, made for a full life. Mykhas was to be Leon's only brother, and Shimmel his only horse. His dancing days were about to end.

*

After leaving the school with Andrii and our driver, we travelled to Pidlyptsi and the place of Leon's childhood. Amid the summer backdrop of endless golden wheat fields that complemented the pure blue skies to make a most welcoming and beautiful sight, it was easy to see what attracted Leon in his youth to the area.

We continued to Aunty Anna's house. If the village had a centre, we did not see it. Punctuated by the yellow and lavender purple flowers, Pidlyptsi seemed to consist of a series of farms nestled in a green valley.

Finally, we bounced up a long, driveway and entered Anna's front yard. There she was, with her husband, absolutely delighted to see us all. The day before, Andrii stopped to buy a large bag of fancy sweets, apparently Anna's favourites, which she accepted gratefully. After tearful greetings, we stepped inside to meet her son, Igor, who immediately began plying us with vodka, and was clearly enjoying the opportunity for celebration.

We arrived at the kitchen, where there lay a banquet. Anna and her family had spent several hours preparing a vast array of traditional

Ukrainian foods that, together with the vodka that Igor, proclaiming toast after toast, passed around with great regularity, all went down very well. The conversation was difficult; we had no phone reception and, therefore, no Google translator. However, appreciation, laughter, gestures of affection and sign language are universal. We had a wonderful time.

After lunch, we went outside for a walk. Out the back, there were two large stables, detached from the main house. I looked inside to see two enormous pigs side by side, huddled somewhat forlornly in the mud. I was to learn these buildings were built by Marika and Stephan, with the intention that they would one day belong one to each of their two sons.

Crocheting is a popular pastime in Ukrainian culture. Aunty Anna kept this beautiful 600 x 300 mm creation of Marika Sokulska amongst others in perfect condition in her attic for over fifty years. She gave them to Milla when she visited in 2011.

11

Brückls, Stepfather, Referendum – Maria, 1937–38

In sleepy Döfering parish, everybody knew everybody. The Brückls were churchgoing Christians who owned a medium-sized farm just a few kilometres away in the nearby village of Haschaberg. Frau Brückl became a close childhood friend of Barbara Keil and provided support when she fell pregnant. She loved little Maria and became an aunty of sorts. During the Depression, the Brückl family was one of the most reliable donors to Grandma's soup kitchen. Naturally, when she heard that Maria was keen to acquire employment, Frau Brückl hatched a plan. There was little work for her on her farm, especially given that they already employed a full-time farmhand. However, Frau Brückl knew that her neighbours, the Bösls, could use help from time to time and, especially since all of them had young children, perhaps Maria could alternate her services between farms.

As it transpired, her neighbours agreed that between the farms, she could be offered employment. Maria was happy to leave school together with its Nazi curriculum and fanatical teacher and settled quickly to very busy days.

Brückl's farm had hundreds of pigs, as well as cows and horses, and large fields for vegetables and hay. Maria did not mind the hard work and long hours, and loved working with children. Her pay, while barely enough per month to buy a dress, was enough to give her a sense of pride and independence. Most importantly, she always had lots to eat and the wives of the farmers, while sometimes demanding, were welcoming and appreciative of having Maria there to lighten their load.

To the right of the backyard of Brückl's farm stood Bleschenburg

Georg Brückl and his wife Maria on their wedding day.

(Bleeding Mountain). Often, when she had a break, Maria would travel, either by herself or with the children, up a well-established trail to the top of the mountain, where, nestled in amongst the trees, was a quaint little chapel. It was an idyllic place and Maria's favourite for prayer and solitude.

All was not smooth sailing, however, and one day, after a disagreement, Maria announced that she was leaving. Herr Bösl quoted a new Nazi law that forbade it. Essentially, the law stated, 'Those needed at their place of work, they cannot leave.'

Maria, not to be intimidated, never returned for work there the next day. Both families were sad to see her leave. However, after the authorities heard, via a third party, that Maria had walked out, she suddenly found herself in a perilous situation.

> He went to the *Arbeitsamt* [Employment Department] to Cham – to some bigger Nazis from the next town. They were so strict in the *Landwirtschaf* [Department of Agriculture], because Hitler knew that they needed people to work in the field. Brückl's friend then went to the *Arbeitsamt* in Cham [and came back with the ultimatum]. If I left, I'd leave straight away [for] Sachsenhausen.[18]

Maria had no choice. Now, she was trapped. She had to stay or face imprisonment.

*

While she continued to work long hours at the Gasthof Hotel, Barbara also volunteered her services as a cleaner at the Franziskaner Kloster church, located a stone's throw from her house. Occasionally, Maria joined her mother for Mass there and in time, knew all of the parishioners, including a drunkard named Johann Kolnhoffer, who attended Mass with his wife and three children. Maria never liked the man. She found him to be rude and abusive, especially towards his wife and children, and because he turned up at Mass smelling of alcohol. Fortunately, he worked with his father and brother, who owned a successful butcher shop in Cham. Having survived the economic meltdown of the Depression, the business was beginning to thrive in the increasingly prosperous Cham community.

Johann was a dark, bristly haired man with a bushy and curling moustache. His sunken eye sockets and sallow appearance may have been related to his traumatic experience in the First World War, where he served on the Western Front, and were further accentuated by his addiction to alcohol. The death of his wife, while giving birth to twin boys only served to make Kolnhoffer's addiction even worse.

Barbara felt pity for Johann after the loss of his wife, and offered to help him out with the children. One thing led to another and before long, the two decided to marry. It was an opportunistic union that suited both couples.

The relationship worked, at least ostensibly, and in 1937, much to Maria's dismay, Barbara Keil, thirteen years his junior, married Johann Kolnhoffer.

> She was very upset. She had nowhere to go. She was getting older and things like that. She married him. His wife died – she had five or six kids already, and she died [giving birth to] twin boys. To help them out, she helped the kids, and it just didn't work. He had already [fought] in the First World War.

The wedding photo shows Barbara dressed in black, and with neither partner looking particularly happy. Perhaps it was a sign of things

Barbara and Johann on their wedding day in 1937.

to come. Not long afterwards, Johann asked Maria to join the family and live with them. Maybe he had had too much to drink at the time, or perhaps he just wanted an extra pair of hands to help with the children and the kitchen. Truth be told, however, Maria, who disliked Johann even more after they married, wanted nothing of the sort.

> I liked it more growing up in Döfering. In Döfering, I loved it. While in Cham, I didn't like my [step]father very much. He was always laughing, and like he was always making a fool, a joke out of me.

Cracks soon appeared. Kolnhoffer's drinking worsened and restricted his ability to work. Thus, Barbara had to continue to work long hours. While she was away, Johann could not cope with rearing two infants. With limited support, it was decided to place the children into foster care.

Maria, meanwhile, had to fend for herself.

> My parents had money, but my stepfather spent all of his money on

beer, and who knows what else? He never gave any to my mother, and he never gave anything to me.

Maria saw Kolnhoffer as a liar who took advantage of her gullible mother:

She, my mam, she was very stupid, really. She believed everything he said.

The comment may or may not have been fair. On one hand, she married a man who was damaged by war and personal loss. Perhaps she felt sorry for him. While the relationship was one of mutual benefit, one point of contention was that Barbara was anti-Nazi while her husband was pro-Nazi.

Less than a year later, in March 1938, Hitler made the first of his international conquests, when he forced the annexation (*Anschluss*) of Austria. In a coordinated combination of political and social agitation, the Nazis were able to stir up a nationalistic fervour to convince many Austrians that they would be better off ensconced within the auspices of the Third Reich. They succeeded, in part due to Goebbels and his propaganda campaign that facilitated the infiltration of fanatical Nazis into all aspects of political, military and social life in Austria. Nevertheless, many were not convinced and they abhorred the idea of losing their independence to throw in their lot with the Nazis. Hitler, in his ruthlessness, stopped at nothing to have his way. His strategy of threats, coercion and even assassination eventually did enough to complete the *Anschluss*.

A month later, in April 1938, following criticism both internationally and nationally, Hitler ordered a referendum to prove that the people collectively of both Germany and Austria supported the *Anschluss*. Hitler, together with his cronies, desperate to guarantee a resounding victory, decided to make sure by rigging the vote.

He achieved this through several strategies. Firstly, the Nazis ran the only legal campaign. Thus, any other opposition campaigning was illegal and its perpetrators subject to arrest. Secondly, they posted guards at every electoral booth to intimidate and beat up anyone who chose not to vote *Ja* (Yes). Thirdly, to make it blatantly obvious, and to yield a psychological advantage, they made the *Ja* circle much bigger than the *Nein* (No) option.

Objective observer and American journalist William L. Shirer witnessed first-hand the rigged ballot.

> As it was, it took a very brave Austrian to vote 'No'. As in Germany, and not without reason, voters feared that their failure to cast an affirmative ballot might be found out. Wide slits in the corner of the election booths gave the Nazis, sitting a few feet away, a good view of how one voted.[19]

On the day of the plebiscite, Barbara decided to vote *Nein*. Maria, not yet eligible to vote, accompanied her mother to the polling booth in Cham on the Sunday after Mass.[20]

Upon arrival, however, after seeing armed guards patrolling the booths, Barbara hesitated.

'I can't do it,' she whispered to Maria as they waited in line.

Shortly afterwards, one of the soldiers caught Maria's eye.

She whispered to her mother, 'It's Wolfgang! He won't say anything. Go to that one!'

When Barbara's turn came, Wolfgang's booth was free, so she headed straight over. Barbara picked up the pencil and quickly crossed the *Nein* option. If Wolfgang saw her vote, as was his job, he said nothing as Barbara placed her ballot in the box. The two left nervously, half expecting to hear a shout.

The final vote nationally was unsurprising: a resounding 99.75% voted *Ja* in favour of the *Anschluss*. This meant that out of every 10,000 voters, only twenty-five voted against Adolf Hitler. Even though the Nazis were enjoying unprecedented popularity at the time, the extent to which the Nazis influenced the outcome is debatable. Nevertheless, despite the overwhelming success, the Nazis were not impressed with the Cham booths, where a few too many voted *Nein*. A subsequent enquiry as to the identity of the rebel voters yielded no results but the Nazis noted the anomaly. Later, they would have their revenge.

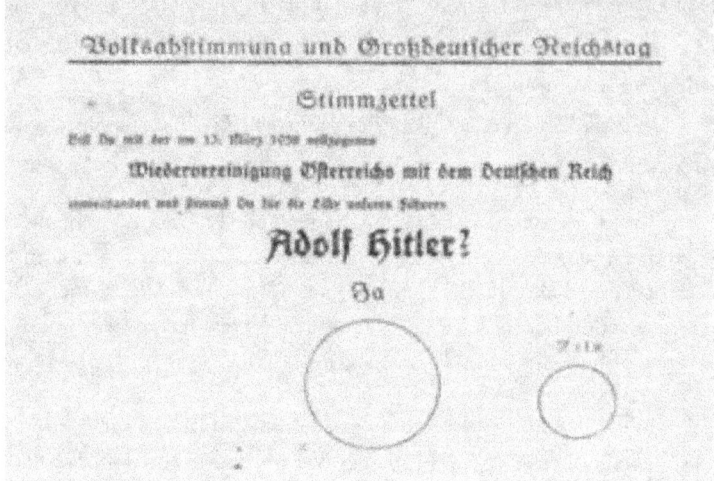

The ballot sheet similar to that filled out by Barbara Keil. Note the much larger 'Ja' option. It was one of several strategies used by the Nazis to influence the vote.

Following the *Anschluss*, the nation continued to flourish in post-Depression Europe. In comparison to the volatile past, peace and stability seemed plausible to optimistic Germans, buoyed by Hitler's promise that this was to be his last territorial demand. Provided you were not racially inferior, if you followed the rules, you would be all right.

Those who thought it all too good to be true were right.

12
Julik – Leon, 1938–39

Leon's best friend was a Jewish boy whose family lived on a farm just up the road.

His name was Julik Hershki, Her-shki. Oh, they were very rich, very rich people. They had a big garden and people working for them as well for nearly nothing. I used to go there and get the white rolls; because we never had white bread, except for Easter and Christmas, when Mam baked it. They regularly had white bread rolls; they had everything goodness [whispered], so he used to give me a little bit.

Leon used to visit the family house to deliver farm produce.

I was there regularly. I used to take them the buttermilk.

The process of making buttermilk, the most expensive and sought-after part of the milk, involved skimming the full cream milk from the rest of the milk and mixing in a small amount of lemon.

The rich people drank the buttermilk, and we used to drink the skim milk.

Julik was Leon's age and size. He had a lovely smile and soft green eyes. The boys soon became great friends. In wintertime, they trudged through the deep snow and rode their sleds down the hills, between the snow-topped pines.[21] In the summertime, they ran barefoot to school along dirt tracks, through lush, green forests and golden trees.

Oh, we played games. We [would] go down to the garden, his garden, we used to play with the horses, they had horses, you know with the little horses they had there, go into the woods and look for bird's nests.

When they found a nest, the boys would climb the tree and take the eggs. Then they would take them home for their parents to cook together with other vegetables from the garden, Leon's buttermilk, and Julik's bread rolls, to make into a delicious meal.

Their days were idyllic and full of adventure. Leon on Shimmel and Julik on his horse, together with their other friends in the village, became the fierce Cossack warriors, fighting the fearful Tatars. Over the mountains, across streams, and through the woods and across the fields, they would battle, using sticks for swords.

Julik's sister Edith was not your typical, play-with-dolls girl. About two years younger than Julik, she broke the young Jewish lady gender stereotype, preferring to play with the boys; fighting imaginary battles, and getting herself just as dirty and dishevelled.

Some days, when the weather was warm, Leon and Julik rode their horses up and down the pathways, along golden meadows and up the hills. On longer trips, they stopped for a picnic lunch. In the winter, they made snowmen, and had snow fights, ducking behind trees and firing at their pretend enemies.

Every day was an adventure. When not riding their horses, the boys had access to other modes of transport.

> We had a bicycle, when I was a kid. We used to go [to school] in wintertime with a sled and in the summertime, we just used to run... If you took a shortcut through the cemetery, it was about a half hour's walk to school, but if you took the main road, it was a little bit longer.

It did not matter whose house they stopped at for a meal to greet them on their return home. There was no teasing and no inequality. Nobody cared about race or religion.

Occasionally, Leon arrived at the Hershkis' house to witness Julik and his parents participating in what seemed to him to be a bizarre ritual.

> They used to have a piece of wood on their head, like a square, tied around their heads and praying... [Julik] had to do it, yeah.

The 'piece of wood' was a small black leather box, about three-square centimetres in diameter called Tefillin. They contain scripture readings.

Leon's family's religious tolerance may have stemmed from his mother's experience in losing her first love and the father of her child due to religious prejudice. Unlike much of the rest of Europe at the time, she did not want to foster that attitude in her sons.

13

What Happened With the Czechs? – Maria, 1938

No sooner had the political dust settled following annexation of Austria than Hitler made his next territorial demand, the annexation of the Sudetenland.

The background to the conflict had its roots in the aftermath of the First World War, when the victorious powers, England, Russia, France, and the USA, met at St Germain to decide on the fate of the Austro-Hungarian empire. They chose to split the multicultural empire into smaller, independent nations. By merging the Czechs, the Slovaks, the Bohemians and the German-speaking Sudetens, who lived on a stretch of land bordering Germany, the Allies created Czechloslovakia. Hitler's argument was simple. The victors were wrong. Sudetens were German and Germans belonged with Germans.

Maria lived and worked just a few kilometres from the Czech border, and the area that was occupied primarily by Sudeten Germans. Hence, she lived exactly where, in the event of conflict, a German invasion would likely occur.

> That is where all the trouble started in 1938.

To support his claim, Hitler's idea of reuniting the Sudetenland with Germany was based on several flimsy premises, one of which was that the Czechoslovakian government systematically persecuted Sudeten Germans, who made up most of the population in the disputed area. He argued that Sudeten Germans wanted reunification with the homeland because of their shared culture and language. The fact that many Czechs lived there did not matter. They would have to leave.

The Nazis argued that Czechoslovakia should never have existed in the first place. That its existence as a hodgepodge of disparate races was delivered up by illegal decisions of 1919. Hitler spoke with such contempt about the government and its leaders that he spat out rather than said the word Czechoslovakia when referring to the country. He and his press expressed outrage that Germans had to live against their will in a cruel, bastardised society. No doubt, there was some validity to the claim, especially for many poorer Sudetens who eyed unification with their prosperous neighbours.

> Over the border, there were lots of our people living there. Oh yeah, they wanted to get out. The Czechs weren't good to them either.

Maria lived just a short walk from the forest that separated the countries. With frequent contact with her neighbours across the border, where Germans and Sudeten Germans came and went as they pleased, she could see first-hand what was happening in the disputed area. On one hand she saw destitute Sudetens, who were forced to beg for German charity.

> So poor the people were. The kids, they were sending little kids, say a bit older than Andrew.[22] They already came to sing, they sent them to us over the border, to sing, and then they got some money to bring home. [I remember] two girls and a boy, they were singing, in Deutsch [German].

Maria then began to sing:

> *Teuer Schwalben, auf Frankreich Auen grunen; der Heimat gern zu schauen.* Precious sparrows flying over France's green fields, how I would love to see my homeland. Little kids were singing this.

This sad lament was most likely written from the perspective of French soldiers, imprisoned within the Austro-Hungarian empire following their defeat in the Franco-Prussian War of 1870.

German propaganda played a significant role in creating a rift between the Czechs and the Sudeten Germans and public sentiment in

Germany began to support the cause to free the oppressed Sudetens from their tyrannical Czechoslovakian overlords. However, Maria knew, in this case, that the Nazis were lying.

> We would say, 'It must be terrible, what we heard that happened there last week,' and so on. They were shocked. 'What are you talking about? That didn't happen,' they said.

While some poorer Sudetens may have wanted out of Czechoslovakia, many of the more affluent ones wanted to stay. For example, there were many Sudeten-owned hotels in the area, where you could relax in the hot springs that reportedly cured all sorts of illnesses.[23] Given the economic benefits, many were nervous about losing their wealth and property to the Nazis.

> Some were very rich ones. All the hot wells [health spas] were here in Bohemia,[24] from us not far. One of the hot wells is Marienbad [Mariánské Lázně], and the other is Karlsbad [Karlovy Vary]. There came from the whole world, the people here. There was a lot of money here, for the cures.

For them, life was good, especially when the government allowed Sudetens to retain their lands, language, traditions and culture. Moreover, after the disaster of the First World War, a large percentage of the population appreciated the opportunity to live in their new, smaller, multicultural and independent homeland.

Nevertheless, according to the Nazis, the Czechoslovaks were belligerent criminals who refused to negotiate. Repeatedly, stories about their cruelty to the persecuted minority Sudetens abounded. The outraged message was clear. Germany was not going to tolerate it. If the Czechs would not yield peaceably, then Germany would use force to repatriate its people.

The truth was that Czechoslovakia had good cause to not negotiate with the Nazis. Not only did they know the Nazis were lying, but they risked losing a significant part of their military defensive capacity, were they to lose the Sudetenland. They also knew that other hungry eyes were watching, ready to lay claims to the remaining carcass of Czechloslovakia were the Nazis to prove successful. The door for the complete dismemberment of their country would be open.

Maria was not fooled.

> He was a liar! How could you trust what he said? We knew that the stories were wrong.

There was an added fear. If Germany and Czechoslovakia were to go to war, the entire region was going to be slap bang in the middle of the opening battle. These were nervous times, especially when locals began to witness the rapid build-up and movement of German military along the border. The writing had been on the wall for some time. Now, almost everyone expected war to break out at any moment.

> In 1933, most people in our village thought that by 1939, there would be a war. Before, we had so many horse riders and army here all the time; they went over to the border.

Hitler's biggest concern, however, was that Czechoslovakia was allied to England and France, who guaranteed Czech independence. Were Hitler to take the Sudetenland by force, then he might find himself stuck in a two-front war. Hitler, though, remained defiant, insisting that he would free the Sudetens from the villainous Czechs.

Then, on the brink of war, to everyone's surprise, they had peace again. Hitler took the full credit as far as the Nazi press was concerned but in truth, Hitler's Italian ally, Benito Mussolini, stepped in to broker a deal with Germany, Italy, France and England, to sacrifice the Sudetenland to ensure peace. The English and French desperately wanted to avoid war, even if it meant sacrificing the Czechs completely. The infamous 'piece of paper' that the English prime minister, Neville Chamberlain, waved triumphantly upon his return to England included both his and Hitler's signatures guaranteeing peace between the nations.

Appeasement, in what became known as the Munich Agreement, may have averted war, but many observers, including the bitter and overlooked Czechs, who were not even invited to the negotiations, saw this as only a temporary respite. As far as they were concerned, the Czechs were sold out for a piece of paper that would soon symbolise the abject failure of the policy of appeasement.

Some wondered why the Czechs did not choose to go on alone to fight the Germans. They had an extensive army and the heavily wooded and elevated Sudeten region provided excellent defensive capabilities in their version of the Maginot Line. In truth, they had no real choice. Had they resisted, they would have been totally without allies, and Germany was too strong to fight alone. To rub salt in the wounds, government and military personnel were given barely a week to leave the region. They had to leave their defences and businesses behind intact.

Czechoslovakia, now far too weak to resist, was ready to be torn apart. Nazi-backed Slovakia was the next to claim independence and, as the government collapsed, Hungry and Poland got in for their share by extending their borders into the crippled nation. The final death throe occurred in March 1939, when the Nazis, ostensibly to protect the Bohemians and Moravians, rolled into the Czech part of Czechoslovakia. They pronounced the region 'The Nazi protectorate of Bohemia and Moravia'. Hitler had his way. Czechoslovakia ceased to exist.

For the Allied powers, who hitherto stood by mute, this was the final straw. They knew that Hitler could not be reasoned with. To be fair, the result did allow Britain and France, who were unprepared for war at the time, much-needed breathing space to prepare for what now seemed to be an inevitable conflict. Meanwhile, Hitler, while stepping up his own military might once again, assured everyone that that was his last territorial demand.

In truth, Hitler had no genuine interest in the negotiation and was secretly disappointed that Chamberlain and Mussolini interfered to prevent conflict in 1938. He needed war to justify armaments expenditure and to satisfy his lust for conquest. Like a spoiled child, he would have it.

The wave of nationalistic fervour that swept Germany in the aftermath of the Munich Agreement was shared by the Kolnhoffers, who were thrilled to announce the birth of their first child, a boy. It was the husband who traditionally chose the name of the child, and Johann was perhaps so impressed with Hitler that he chose to name his first child after him. There was great cause for optimism all around and Johann may have foreseen the benefits of so openly professing his loyalty to the Nazis by naming his first son Adolf; and what a great thing for young Adolf to grow up in a brave world, carrying the name of the greatest man in the whole history of Germany.

Maria hated the choice. Her mother said that Adolf was simply a popular name.

No sooner had the dust settled with Czechoslovakia than the German newspapers and radio were at it again. At Hitler's behest, the Nazis, full of righteous indignation, aimed their fury at Poland. Under the Treaty of Versailles, the independent but mainly German free city of Danzig, located on the northern coast of Poland, could only be reached via the Baltic Sea. The Nazis demanded that the Polish government allow them to build a road through Poland to Danzig. When the Polish government refused, Hitler was outraged.

14

First, Came the Russians – Leon, September 1939

Why did Poland not avoid conflict and accept Germany's quite legitimate demand to build a simple road? If they had, their fate would almost certainly have mirrored that of Czechoslovakia. Hitler would then have made his next demand, possibly Poland's western fringe, which before the First World War, was part of the German state of Prussia. This would have been followed by another claim, and then another. Ukraine, no doubt, would at least temporarily have claimed her independence, and Germany would, at least temporarily, have supported it as an excuse to invade.

Hitler had no love for Russia, and, in fact, planned not even in secret, as promulgated in his bestselling book, compulsory reading for all Nazis, *Mein Kampf* (My Struggle), to annihilate its people. He realised, however, that he needed a temporary truce to ensure a one-front battle if England and France fulfilled their obligation to support Poland. Therefore, a few days before the invasion, Hitler had to manipulate peace with his sworn enemy.

> Molotov and Ribbentrop [the Soviet and German foreign ministers] signed an agreement that there would be no war between the two [nations]. They said, you take all of Poland, we take all of our Ukraine and we make peace.

The Soviets should have been suspicious of Hitler's intent. In *Mein Kampf*, he first postulated his theory of *Lebensraum* (living room) in the east, and predicted, in a survival of the fittest ideology, the inevitable struggle to the death between communism and fascism. The racial superiority of the Aryan Germans, he argued, would ensure success and their reward would be abundant *Lebensraum* for his people to allow for future growth and advancement. Meanwhile, the *Untermensch* former inhabitants of the land would be removed, liquidated or enslaved.

On the morning of 1 September 1939, Germany invaded Poland. As was his wont, Hitler had to fabricate a reason that at least ostensibly, would make it look like it was someone else's fault. Hence, a select group of Nazis created evidence that Polish paratroopers had, without provocation, crossed the border and attacked German outposts, including a radio station. It was all a lie, of course. The Nazis rounded up and murdered a group of concentration camp inmates, dressed them in German and Polish uniforms and staged an artificial scene inside the German border. They recorded the incident as evidence that Poland were the aggressors. While most impartial observers doubted the truth, Hitler had his story, and he was sticking to it.

From the start, the Polish army fought bravely but never stood a chance against overwhelming firepower. Additionally, the Wehrmacht incorporated a new military strategy known as Blitzkreig (lightning war) in which a coordinated combination of tanks and air support followed by infantry and artillery made sudden and decisive (lightning) thrusts into enemy territory, before mopping up the flanks. The tactic created a level of chaos and disorganisation that demoralised and confused the defenders. Resistance was passionate but futile. Within two weeks, the Polish army was a shambles and well on the way to total defeat.

Despite their agreement with the Nazis, the Soviet Union moved tentatively, perhaps first wanting to be sure that Poland was defeated. Sixteen days after the invasion, with the cream of Poland's forces destroyed, they moved into eastern Poland.

> So the next morning I saw them all, Russians singing and walking and riding their horses as they came and took us over.

The Soviets' job was relatively easy. Poland, with nearly all of its military resources in the west, had virtually nothing with which to defend its eastern border. Within a day or so, they had reached Pidlyptsi.

> There was no fighting whatsoever in Ukraine. The Polish more or less just gave themselves up. There was no war where we lived… there was nothing you could say about it.

Within six weeks, it was all over, as what was left of the Polish resistance crumbled before the irrepressible onslaught of the Wehrmacht forces. The Nazi–Soviet Pact of 1939 and the ensuing invasion meant that a unification of sorts existed between east and west Ukraine. Western Poland had become the easternmost province of the German Reich, and east Poland, which included the western part of Ukraine, became the westernmost province of the Soviet Union. The problem, however, was that Ukraine, far from independent, was now a province of the Soviet Union.

Many locals were initially optimistic. Leon's parents believed that things would be better now that the Poles had gone.

> We thought that the Russians would move out after peace and leave us to ourselves. They preferred the Russians to the Polish. They thought well, the Russians we speak the same language, and eventually, they would go out and give us a free Ukraine.[25] That's what they said: 'We'll only stay to make peace all around, then we'll move out, and you can have the whole Ukraine back.' That was all propaganda.[26]

Regardless of the false promises, Leon and his family were lucky. Stalin was not ignorant of Hitler's long-term aims of *Lebensraum* in the Soviet Union. Therefore, with the perceived future conflict inevitable, he decided, rather than to use coercion, to win over the Ukrainian people with compromise. While he promoted communism, together with its ideals, as the way to a utopian society, Stalin allowed Ukrainians to enjoy a certain amount of freedom of religion, and promised independence to the would-be nation in return for the acceptance of soviet ideals. The strategy seemed to work.

> The Russians never did me any harm. In school, after the invasion,

> we had to learn Russian, of course, and we didn't have to speak Polish any more. Naturally, we were happy about that... Everybody had to be well educated, and we shared everything. It was all right for people who were not very rich. If I have lots of money and you have nothing, I have to give you half.

Consequently, life went on as it usually did. Had things transpired differently, Western Ukrainians might have been on the receiving end of a *holodomor* (man-made famine) similar to that in Eastern Ukraine a few years earlier.

However, certain groups were not so fortunate.

> The next thing, everything was all right. There was just get rid of the rich people, the Russians, you know. They took them away, the very rich, to make everybody equal. Say you have too much milk – you have nothing, I have something – they used to take part of mine and give it to you... The rich people, they sent them away to Siberia. I knew that perfectly well.

Polish government officials, aristocrats and military officers also fared very badly under Soviet rule. Depending on their rank, many were executed immediately, while others were sent to horrible deaths east of the Ural Mountains, in the vast, desolate wastelands of Siberia. Sparsely populated and freezing for most of the year, Siberia housed most of the infamous gulag (hard labour) camps in the Soviet Union. Similar to the Nazi concentration camps, anti-government or criminal activity, either real or imagined, almost always resulted in a one-way trip.

> Some of the clever ones, they just got out before the Russians came in. Some of them went to Poland[27] or England if they could manage it.[28] Regardless, if you complained enough, they sent you to Siberia. They were very strict.

Just when I thought I understood, and nodded my understanding, my father left me thinking that I did not know the half of it.

> People don't realise. People like you, you were born in a free country. You don't even notice what happened there. People would not be-

lieve what you tell them, the stories. They say, 'That's impossible, that's a lie, how could it be that?'

Leon continued to explain the Communist manifesto.

If I have two cows and our neighbour had none, then we must give that cow over, because you don't need two...[if you only have one cow and you neighbour has none, that is a problem]. Eventually, they wanted to have it all in one collective farm. So you just work on a collective farm and you have nothing at all: just your garden.

Soon there was barely anyone left to complain. Most people, ostensibly at least, appeared not to mind. Sharing everything seemed OK, and prospects remained positive.

They told us that they would only be staying for a while to establish the peace and then they promised that they would leave us alone to rule ourselves.

Ironically, the Soviets did, as promised, leave within two years, but it was not a decision made of their own volition.

Poles under Nazi occupation fared just as badly. No sooner had they arrived than the Nazis began systematically, brutally, murdering thousands upon thousands of their citizens.

15

War Begins – Maria, 1 September 1939

People said, 'This will be a bad year.'

Over two million Germans perished in the First World War. Nearly every family lost loved ones. The memories were still fresh for many people. One can imagine how terrified the less optimistic Germans felt about the growing prospect of another global conflict.

> Then came 1939, it was September, the beginning of September. I remember still we were in the field outside, and we were putting hay on the wagon, and the Brückl Ludwig[29] [picked up a pile of hay and] put it on the wagon. He said, 'Now listen...there will be war now because the whole of nature is in mourning.'
>
> This is true. In this time in September, at the beginning, there was so many birds singing at this time of year. Now, at that moment, there was not a bit of sound anywhere. I swear it was like a dead house...really, and this is true. The whole nature *trauert* [mourns], the whole nature is mourning while there comes war.

It seemed as if the whole of the natural world could sense it. Something terrible was afoot. Since 1933, there had been so many false alarms. When the news actually came, it was not on their doorstep as they had expected. Nevertheless, the atmosphere was surreal.

> Then about a week later, all of a sudden, we heard it in the morning, on the wireless, we had no television, nothing like that, just a wireless and not everybody, just the next-door neighbour, had one.

Sixty years later, Maria's recollection of Hitler's speech on that day remained fixed in her memory.

Then Hitler said, I remember his words…this morning… *'Heute hat Poland zum ersten mal auf meinen lieben Soldaten geschossen.'* That's what he said. *'And er sagt, Ich selbe ziel ein Waffenrock an… und sehe nicht mehr aus bis der Zieg ist unter. Und wen wir nicht ziegen dan, wird ein anderer Krieg kommen, aber der letzte Regiment im feld, das wird ein Deutsches zein.* Today, Poland fired first at my beloved soldiers… I will put on a uniform, and I will do nothing else until this war is won. If we lose this war, then there will come another war, and the last regiment in the field will be German.'

So it was to be a fight to the death if need be. If Hitler used himself to mean the whole of Germany, then his words were to be prophetic. His intent that Germany would fight to the death was to be played out within the next six years, but only after another fifty million lives were lost.

Maria, on reflection, could only repeat one single word: 'Horrible… Horrible!'

Following the invasion, all eyes were on England and France given that they had collectively promised to support Poland in the event of attack from Germany. The overriding question was, would they honour their pledge? Hitler, who had called their bluff, half expected them to back down. Instead, England and France stayed true to their commitment to support Poland, and, three days after the invasion, following an ultimatum that Hitler ignored, the countries simultaneously declared war on Germany. By extension, other allied countries like Australia and Canada immediately followed suit.

True to form, the Nazis blamed Poland for the war. In Döfering, however, the locals were skeptical about Germany's innocence, despite what the media insisted. Many people, even if they would not openly admit to it, strongly suspected that Hitler had started the fighting. They had been through the lies before in the 1914–18 conflict, and the memories were all too clear. Maria, like most Germans, had relatives who died or suffered from acute post-traumatic stress, and desperately did not want to live through that again. Others, perhaps more stoic, remained bitter in the aftermath of the last war and now relished the opportunity for Germany to have her revenge for the injustices of 1914–18.

Poland, despite fighting bravely, suffered a series of catastrophic defeats against the far superior Wehrmacht, and within just five weeks it was all over. Despite any pessimism the German populace may have had, the rapidity with which Poland was defeated surprised almost everyone. Some of Hitler's harshest critics, no doubt, changed their mind at this point, thinking that perhaps Hitler was, after all, a great leader, one in whom they could faithfully trust. Indeed, for the next six months, apart from a few minor skirmishes, so little happened in the conflict that many started to believe that the war would be resolved without further bloodshed.

One or two of the local boys were conscripted into the Wehrmacht but there were no fatalities in the Döfering parish district during the Polish campaign, and life in the villages continued as usual. Hence, the Phoney War was the phrase coined for the lack of action following the initial outbreak of war. As the days, weeks and months passed, people increasingly believed that it was only a matter of time before peace talks resolved the conflict.

Then, about six months after Poland's capitulation, Germany suddenly took the initiative with an all-out attack that first saw the invasion and defeat of Norway. Inside a month, on 10 May, the Wehrmacht had launched its invasion of Holland and Belgium. A few days later, they had overpowered the Lowlands and crossed the French border. France and her allies, relatively speaking, had plenty of time to prepare for the onslaught and most observers felt that at the very least, a drawn-out conflict, similar to that which occurred in the First World War, would ensue. However, any optimism that France, her more than two million armed forces and her supposedly impenetrable Maginot Line might overcome the Nazi onslaught were quickly dispelled. Similarly to Poland, the French army proved to be vastly inferior and disorganised against the Nazi Blitzkrieg that simply went around the Maginot Line. To trounce the French so easily, in just six weeks, exceeded the wildest dreams of the most ardent advocates of Germany's military capacity. At that point, anyone who had their doubts had to admit that they got it wrong.

So strong was Germany at the time that, on 10 June, they had the resources necessary to successfully invade North Africa. Hitler's favourite general, Erwin Rommel, soon won early victories that threatened to give Germany complete control of the whole of north Africa and the Mediterranean. Only sparse resistance in Cyprus, Malta and Egypt ensued.

Perhaps the only saving grace in what otherwise was a total defeat in Europe occurred when the cream of the English army, consisting of nearly 300,000 troops, found themselves hopelessly trapped and surrounded in an ever-decreasing pocket of resistance with their backs to the sea at the port of Dunkirk. With the situation seemingly hopeless, capitulation at that point would have resulted in the most significant defeat in British military history, and almost certainly have spelled the end for Winston Churchill, the newly appointed prime minister, and his anti-appeasement government. Had this occurred, there is little doubt that the ensuing government, led by Nazi sympathisers like Lord Halifax and Fascist leader Oswald Mosley, would have sued for peace, reducing England to little more than a Nazi puppet state.

However, on the brink of total disaster, Churchill, struggling to gain the support of parliament, and in what was probably his last throw of the dice, initiated a hastily organised massive flotilla of every available hodgepodge sea craft, each tasked to 'bring the boys back home'. Even though the mission proved a resounding success, pessimists still saw the subsequent rescue of over 300,000 British and French troops in the context of a defeated army returning with the proverbial tail between their legs. Optimists, on the other hand, saw it as a decisive psychological and military success. The soldiers had made it home. They would fight again.

Thus England and her allies, many of whom were in exile, now stood defiant against the Nazis. Hitler was unperturbed. He was sure that his Luftwaffe would finish off the stubborn English in due course. If not, Germany would invade the island and take her by force.

Annoyed as he was with England's futile resistance, Hitler's plan was simple. First, destroy Russia before the end of 1941; then defeat the stubborn English.

16

Germany Invades Russia – Leon, June 1941

After a wonderful day, we said emotional goodbyes to Aunty Anna and her family and continued with Andrii and our driver on our journey.

As we sat back for our trip back to Zolochiv, the darkness began to gather around us.

Milla exclaimed, 'There it is! The cross, the cross.'

I glanced out from the window and there it stood.

'Slow down, she cried,' but our driver did not comprehend and carried on.

*

In the summer, Leon always got up very early, often to get in a few hours riding in before the day became too hot. It was just a little after five a.m. on 22 June 1941 when Leon rode out with Shimmel towards Tatar Mountain. He carried no watch, but Leon had developed a good sense of time based loosely on the rising sun but mostly on instinct. He planned to ride to the top of what the locals called Tatar Mountain, and return home in time for Mass.

Mindful not to push his young horse too hard, Leon zigzagged Shimmel up the grassy incline, carefully avoiding potholes and sticking to well-worn paths. Tatar Mountain was not overly steep, and Shimmel managed the ascent easily. When they finally reached the summit, the horse and rider gazed down below at the most splendid views of the valley below.

A few dark clouds fought with the first of the sun's rays in what was clearly a losing battle. It was going to be a beautiful day. Yellow fields of wheat stretched out below as far as the eye could see, caressed by the early morning breeze, in blissful solitude. It was nearly harvest time, and the coming months would bring longer days, and shorter nights, as the workers tirelessly scythed and baled hay for winter feed. Trees, many carrying ripening plums, lined parts of the landscape. Only the cherry trees were bare of fruit, their season having come and gone. This year, the rains fell at just the right time, and the warm days were perfect for growing. As Leon peered over the splendid valley, he knew that they would have more than enough for when the cold season arrives.

Suddenly, the distant sound of gunfire jolted Leon from his reverie. He instinctively pricked his ears to sense the direction, and instantly had a strong sense of its source, close to his home. It was not the first time he had heard the blast of rifles discharging their deadly cargo. Fortunately, Shimmel remained calm beneath Leon's touch and followed his directions as the pair journeyed back towards the location of sporadic gunfire. Soon, when they verged upon a fork in the road, just a few hundred metres away from his home, Leon had his suspicion confirmed.

There stood an old wooden cross about twelve feet high. It had been there for as long as anyone could remember. To Leon's left, there on a grassy knoll that overlooked the cross, lay a group of Russian soldiers. Leon knew that they were using it for target practice. It was not the first time, and, although their actions incensed the deeply religious locals, they did not seem to care. The Russians were probably drunk or hungover from the night before. Occasionally, they struck bunches of freshly picked flowers that had been left at the base of the cross by worshippers the day before. They guffawed with laughter as the petals flew indiscriminately awry.

Leon slowly, cautiously, steered around the soldiers, being both fascinated and annoyed that they could wantonly show such sacrilege. Suddenly, uncharacteristically, Shimmel began to blow out through his nose and bray in agitation. 'Settle, settle,' cooed Leon, pressing his face close to his horse's ear, both to calm his horse, and so as not to alert the soldiers to their presence. At first, Leon thought it was the sniper fire

The cross, pictured left, as it stands today. It has stood at this place for at least eighty years. Holes from the sniper's bullets are still visible today. This is where the Russian soldiers lay dying.

from the soldiers that had frightened Shimmel, but then he detected something else, a faint, unusual buzzing in the sky.

Leon looked to the west as the fading darkness began to give way to the bright glow of the rising dawn. As his eyes strained against the skyline, he became aware of what looked like a dark cloud approaching from some distance away. Before long, the cloud morphed into what at first he thought was a large flock of birds flying toward him. Then, Leon realised that what he was seeing was something surreal. Suddenly, above him were hundreds of airplanes heading eastward into the Soviet Union.

Leon had recently seen a single airplane flying over Pidlyptsi. Perhaps it was a German reconnaissance plane, operating secretly to assess enemy strength and potential targets.

This was vastly different; there were hundreds of them. The entire sky was so thick with aircraft that they negated the impact of the rising sun and almost blocked out the sky. Leon turned away from the sounds of strafing and immediately found himself in the thick of it all as bullets fired all around him. Leon feared for his life.

Unsure of how to get to safety, Leon spared a glance towards the Russian soldiers who were now standing in the open, firing simultaneously at a German plane that had swooped low to strafe them. The soldiers stood no chance.

> The next thing I remember as clearly as I sit here, there was this plane coming over, shooting everything…du, du, du, du, shooting everybody, all the Russians, shooting [them] down.

Rather than take down the German plane, Leon watched as the plane passed and rose, continuing its flight and leaving in its wake soldiers dead or dying on the ground. The aircraft flew so close that Leon could see the black and white trimmed Swastika symbol on the tail wing and the black Luftwaffe cross on the underwing of the plane.[30]

The Russian soldiers lay on the ground; two of them were writhing in agony and pleading for help. A third soldier lay silent, face down, spreadeagled on the dry earth beside the cross upon which he had so recently taken aim.

Leon, ignoring their pleas, rode home, where he found his relieved parents. Leon struggled to get the words out to explain that the injured soldiers needed help but his mother was not listening.

> She explained that the Russians are atheists and blasphemers. They fired at the cross of Jesus Christ, and we will not help.[31]

Meanwhile, the Luftwaffe continued its flight over Pidlyptsi on its mission to destroy Ternopil's airport, which lay about thirty kilometres southeast of Leon's village. On arrival, to their great delight, they found most of the Soviet planes stood idle on the ground ripe for the picking.

Joseph Stalin, the Soviet supreme commander, for whatever reason, initially refused to believe his intelligence agents who, for some time, had warned him of the likelihood of a German attack. Instead, he ordered his forces not to mobilise. When the Soviet pilots at Ternopil finally received the call to counter-attack, it was too late. Most of their aircraft never made it off the ground before the Luftwaffe had reduced them to flames. The few Russian planes that did manage to get off the ground found themselves in a one-sided battle against the superior Luftwaffe aircraft and their battle-hardened pilots. The cream of the Soviet air force soon lay destroyed, with minimal losses to the German planes.

Over a million Wehrmacht soldiers crossed the border that morning, completely overwhelming the Soviet forces in Poland. Within a few days, they had advanced deep into Western Ukraine.

The Sokulsky family knew the German invasion had begun but heard nothing about it when they checked for news on the radio. It was not until later that evening that news was broadcast confirming Germany's unprovoked attack on the Soviet Union. Stalin himself assured his listeners that the Motherland would defend herself with all of her power and that ultimately the Soviet Union would prevail and crush her enemy.

Meanwhile, the cries of the dying soldiers were heard late into the night. Their plaintive shrieks rattled the family as they settled into their nightly routine. When Leon begged his parents to make the screaming stop, Marika countered that it was too dangerous to help the blasphemers because the Germans would be there soon and they would shoot anyone who helped them.

The cries continued throughout the night. Nobody could sleep. Eventually, Leon's stepfather rose from his seat and quietly walked out into the night. After a while, the screaming stopped.

The dejected Russian army continued to collapse along the eastern front. Many might have resisted for longer but readily surrendered because they despised communism. Despite some resistance around the city of Lviv, the Wehrmacht poured through Ukraine virtually unopposed. On 2 July, just ten days after the invasion, the German army marched through Pidlyptsi without resistance. With only minor battles, Zolochiv and Ternopil fell at about the same time.

> Where I was, there was not much of a fight.

Leon sat at the end of his driveway as the army came past. He watched them travel eastward to where the ever-increasing frontline lay, while the remnants of Russian armies moved westward following their mass-surrenders.

> …and the Russians used to come, millions, just free walk, they just gave up…prisoners of war without fight… They thought…well, some of them didn't like communism, you see, because they had it for [twenty]-five years. They even told us, 'You'll find out how bad it is when they stay a bit longer here…' They all went to prisoner of war camps.

While surrender seemed like their best option, had the prisoners realised the horrible fate that awaited them under German imprisonment, they indeed would not have chosen to surrender.

> They went right [to] the next stop Kyiv. There was a big battle at Kyiv. Russia sent Mongols to Kyiv, where they had a really big fight, but they did no good in the end.

It is unknown how many died in those first few weeks against the might of the Wehrmacht. Initially, it was a very one-sided battle as German forces repeatedly cut through the Soviet lines. The Blitzkrieg tactics once again worked and resulted in the surrender of hundreds of thousands of Soviet soldiers.

When they arrived, Leon was impressed.

> Then the Germans came. That was fantastic! I remember it as clearly as I am sitting here. It was on a Sunday. I know that is was Sunday because we were going to church on Sunday. One day I was playing in the fields, and the next day the Germans were marching down past my house. They just walked into our village, as you would walk in here. I was not worried at all.

The arrival of the Wehrmacht initially allayed Leon's fears about the appearance of the invaders. He had no idea how they would physically appear. 'I thought they would have two horns on their heads.' Instead, he was impressed to see their smart uniforms, beneath which they looked just like ordinary people.

> I was happy…to see the motorbikes and the cars coming along. Then, when the soldiers marched past us, on their belts was *Gott Mit Uns*.

Leon stood by unafraid and in awe as General Stülpnagel's 17th Army passed by his village. He noted his mother's optimism.

> I said, 'What's all the writing about?'
> She told me. She knew what it said because she learned from my grandmother. Austria was occupying Ukraine before Poland,[32] and all the older people spoke German. She said, 'They must be Christian people. They all have *God Mit Uns*, that means God is with us, on their belts. They mustn't be so bad, they must all be good.' They already promised to give us an independent Ukraine.

The infantry marching along with mechanised vehicles from motorbikes to tanks impressed Leon.

> The whole army passed through our village just like the Russians did two years earlier, but these Germans were smart and well dressed in their uniforms.

The Blitzkrieg continued throughout the initial Russian campaign, and with complete control of the air, the Wehrmacht continued to make rapid gains into Soviet territory. The plan was to take Moscow before the winter arrived.

The Soviets had closed their churches in the east and enforced a policy of atheism amongst its citizens. Ukrainians in the west knew that religious worship had no future under Soviet rule. It is not surprising that they embraced the Christian soldiers who, until recently, shared the same language.

> We had three or four hundred years of Austrian rule. They had conquered all those countries from the Volga River; they had Hungary and Galicia,[33] where I came from. You see, when my grandmother

was born, Ukraine was a part of the Austro-Hungarian empire, and she spoke German. Most of the older Ukrainians spoke German and Ukrainian.

If the Russian prisoners of war had cause for optimism, their hopes soon evaporated in the most terrible of ways.

> We saw miles and miles of Russian soldiers marching through our village to prison camps. They all got killed!

The Nazis, who saw the Russians as *Untermensch*, did not entertain the idea of keeping them alive. The Soviet Union never signed the Geneva Convention, which mandated the humane treatment of prisoners of war. Consequently, the Nazis had an excuse to ignore rules regarding the proper treatment of Soviet prisoners. With no concern for their welfare, pain or suffering, the death toll for Russian prisoners of war numbered a staggering ten million plus by the end of the war. The Nazis murdered them in many ways – starvation, shooting, bombing – nothing was off the table; they disposed of their bodies in mass graves or burned in crematoria or pits. Sometimes, they just left them in the open to rot, where they died. The Germans often placed their prisoners into large holding pens with no food or water. When the winter came, those still alive were too weak to do anything, and nature simply did the rest as they perished in the snow.

Word of Nazi atrocities inevitably made its way back to Russia, and beyond, that surrender meant certain death. Understandably, after that, mass escapes became commonplace amongst Russian soldiers.

> The way the Germans were treating them once they were in prison, they escaped into the woods. They all went partisan after that.

Knowing their fate, many soldiers took matters into their own hands and at least died fighting rather than face capture and horrible death.

> Say there is a hundred going or two hundred. There's bound to be maybe a hundred get shot, but a hundred escape. They can't get

them all. They're not Jewish people, they're Russian people. They said to the other prisoners, 'Don't be stupid! Don't go there.' They said, 'I'd rather die in a war and not in the camps here.'

Ultimately, many fought to the death. They attacked the German soldiers, often in a suicide charge, where, at the least, they used up German bullets. If possible, someone would steal a rifle and at least die fighting.

However, some in the German High Command saw value using Ukrainians to fight along with the Wehrmacht against their common enemy. The Stalinist pogroms against Ukraine in the 1920s and '30s and the subsequent hatred many locals had acquired in seeing their own family and friends starved to death made the decision easy.

Some of the young boys joined the German army. They didn't mind getting killed against Russia. Nearly every nationality wanted to fight. They were sick and tired of the Russians. Nearly every nationality went with the Germans because they wanted to fight against the Communists.

To rally the masses, the Nazis initially allowed the Ukrainian people to have their hero.

Our leader was a man named Stepan Bandera, and nine days after the invasion, he declared independence.

Many people revered Bandera, who, in support of the Nazis, helped to raise Ukrainian armies to fight the communists, giving them hope in the belief of independence.

We had about twelve divisions fighting in Brody [about fifty kilometres north of Pidlyptsi]. So in 1941, the German authorities pronounced an independent Western Ukraine; and they proclaimed Lviv as the capital.

Once again, Ukrainians misjudged the motives of their conquerors. If they learned from history, they should have known better than raise their hopes.

However, some Ukrainians continued to fight alongside Germans during the war, hoping that eventually they would either get their independence or become firm allies of the Nazis. Rather than utilise Ukrainians into a discrete fighting force, 'instead, they split our armies up and took over their command'. They might have been more cohesive had they been allowed to fight as one.

The truth was that Hitler, like many before him, never intended to grant Ukrainians their freedom. His ultimate plan was for Ukraine to become a Nazi state, with the indigenous population reduced to slavery. In truth, Hitler simply used them as he did Romanians, Bulgarians and anyone else who wanted to sacrifice themselves as the fodder of sorts for the Nazi cause.

However, Bandera insisted that it had to be an autonomous Ukraine that existed in partnership with, rather than servitude to, the Nazis. It was not long before he fell victim to their wrath.

> Then in about three weeks, their leader, Stepan Bandera, they took him to Germany to Sachsenhausen concentration camp because he didn't do what Hitler asked him to do. He had to come under German rule, and he didn't accept German rule. He said we don't want to fight anybody else, we just want to fight Russian soldiers, not the Western world.

As far as Hitler was concerned, Bandera was a puppet, similar to Pétain in France.[34] If he was going to make trouble, then he had served his purpose. Later, when the war had turned, the Nazis released him, hoping he could rally support for Ukraine against the communists. Bandera survived the war only to be assassinated by the KGB in Munich in 1959. He remains a controversial figure in history. Some see him as the champion for Ukrainian independence. In contrast, others see him as a villain who supported the anti-Jewish pogroms and the subsequent murder of so many innocent victims.

The Germans were good at first, but as time went on, the people came to understand they were as bad as the Russians, if not worse.

If you were in the German army and your family had one cow, and the Germans came to take that cow, you would not be so keen to fight for them. A lot of them went partisan after that. Whatever they wanted, they took. They just came and took it, and nobody could say or do anything about it.

Worse was to come. No sooner had the Wehrmacht conquered Ukraine than the Einsatzgruppen (commando units)[35] ordered the Jewish population's complete round-up. Before the war, Zolochiv contained one of the highest per capita Jewish populations anywhere in Europe. On 3 July, just one day after the town fell, the Nazis ordered that the entire Jewish community, numbering over three and a half thousand, or one-third of the total population, report to Zolochiv Castle the following morning, ostensibly to attend some kind of community meeting.

17

Why Did We Attack Russia? – Maria, 1941

Following Dunkirk, Operation Sealion, Germany's expected invasion of Great Britain, never occurred. Hitler decided instead to bomb England into submission, rather than embark on a more risky channel crossing. From July to October 1940, German planes prioritised attacks on English airfields. England retaliated with small hit-and-run missions along the coast of Norway and France. Still, it was the bombing of Berlin in August 1940 that had more far-reaching repercussions. While not overly destructive, the attack created a psychological blow given that the Luftwaffe commander Herman Goering famously jibed that if any English bomber ever reached Berlin, 'You can call me Meyer.' The result catalysed Hitler to switch focus from English airfields to English cities. Over the ensuing months, London, Coventry, Birmingham and Sheffield were among the hardest hit. However, as a military strategy, it failed to meet its objective of bombing the country into submission. Instead, it strengthened British resolve and provided crucial respite for the hitherto decimated air force to recoup their losses. Churchill's famous 'We will fight them on the beaches' speech additionally helped to galvanise a nation that threw every resource into increasing their military offensive and defensive capacity.

England's early successes occurred more by deception rather than military might. Often with assistance from the fledgling underground organisations on the mainland, her commandos wreaked havoc by targeting areas of vulnerability such as blowing up ships, sabotaging rail lines, and assassinating unsuspecting Nazis.

The Battle of Britain proved a significant inconvenience to the German war effort. By the end of the year, Hitler, perhaps frustratingly, switched his attention to follow his favourite plan. He turned his eyes to the vast lands of the Slavs, Russians and Mongols, in the east. The annihilation of his most hated enemy, the Bolshevik Soviet Union, was his ideological battle to the death.

Most Germans, including Maria, had no idea that Germany would attack Russia. It was never in the news; as far as everyone knew, the war was all but over. Their boys would come home. Hitherto, of the fifty or so men of fighting age in the parish, three had perished in battle before April 1941. That was bad enough. Hopes were high that another generation did not needlessly have to die. Technically, Germany was still at war with England, but according to the propaganda, Goering's Luftwaffe had mercilessly bombed her airports, and her cities lay in ruins.

Many Germans who initially opposed Hitler had to admit that they got it wrong. The simultaneous outstretched salute of the massive crowds who turned up to be a part of the Hitler-mania that swept the land confirmed Hitler's acquired god-like status throughout the land.[36]

In Döfering, less than two years after Hitler announced that Poland had attacked Germany, Germans heard the news that Germany had no option but to invade Russia. They were assured that it was all Russia's fault and that Germany acted in self-defence. It was surreal; the boys would need to return to the front.

> There was no one that I know of in my village who wanted to fight. No one!

Eventually, they all had to go.

18

The Schutzstaffel (SS) Arrive – Leon, 1941

Throughout his life, Leon never considered Jews any differently. Regardless of wealth, religion or status, he never felt inferior or superior to anyone, and until 1941, he had lived a sheltered life. His parents taught him to respect all people. Julik's family may have had some strange customs and traditions, but none of that mattered at all. Earlier in the year, the Hershki family welcomed their newest member, Sarah, a beautiful little girl, and a sister for Julik. Naturally, they would have doted on their little sister, as would Mykhas and Leon.

Within a day or so after the army's arrival, Leon returned from his morning ride to see a black car come racing towards him down the dusty, potholed road. It slowed down and stopped near where he stood. Leon was curious more than worried, thinking how important the man must be to travel in such an impressive vehicle.

The car carried a driver and a passenger, who got out and approached Leon. He was about twenty-five or thirty years old and looked very smart in his impeccable black uniform. Leon began to worry about what such a significant man might want with him. When the man spoke, it was not in German, but Ukrainian.

The best way is to ask young boys like myself.

'How are you? Have you ever tried chocolate before?'

Leon shook his head as the man reached deep inside his jacket pocket to reveal a pistol in its case around his waist. Instead, he took out a shiny silver wrapper and handed it to Leon. 'Try some. Don't worry, there's nothing wrong with it.' He took a block and put it in his mouth. 'See? That's a good boy.'

At this, Leon took a bite of the mysterious substance. Its sweetness tantalised him. It was better than anything he had ever tasted before.[37]

The man continued to engage Leon in small talk, about beautiful Pidlyptsi and their love of horses. Leon began to feel comfortable and asked him about his uniform and his skull-capped hat. The man explained that he was an officer and that his cap meant bravery.

As Leon ate some more chocolate, the man casually asked, 'Do you know any Jewish people here?'

Leon never saw the harm in the question and answered that there were.

'Have you got any friends [who are] Jewish?'
And I knew nothing about that they were killing Jews, you know.

Completely unaware where the conversation was heading, Leon answered honestly.

'Oh yeah, I've got my best friend is living down there,'
'Where is he living?'

Leon pointed out to the officer where Julik lived. Leon asked the officer if he was going to give him some chocolate as well.

The man grinned widely and nodded. 'Yes, I will make sure he gets plenty of chocolate.'[38]

Before he left, the officer had one more question: 'And what about the other Jews in the area? Can you tell me where they live?'

I said, 'There and there,' you know.
He gave me a bar of chocolate. You tell them everything. I didn't know what he asked for.

Leon had never heard or Einsatzgruppen or Death Squad, or SS.

The next morning he awoke to a loud cry. Knowing that something terrible had happened, he leapt up from his bed and raced to the kitchen. There sat his mother weeping.

I was told they were all dead.

Leon sprinted across the field and up the hill towards the Hershki house, his heart pounding in his chest, barely able to process how terrible he felt. With each breath he drew in, his panic rose. He kept thinking that it must be a mistake.

When he arrived, he knocked heavily on the door, but there was no answer. He half-expected Mr Hershki to open it, still wearing the block on his head. Leon found the door unlocked and cautiously entered the house. At first, everything looked normal. Leon called Julik's name. The house was empty. Then he noticed something strange. The home was always immaculate inside, but now there was mud and dirt on the carpet.

Leon gazed around; he sensed that something was very wrong. He reached the window to the backyard and peered outside. The image nearly knocked him off his feet; his eyes glued to the sight that would remain forever imprinted on his soul.

They were all dead. They were all in the garden.

Five bodies were lying on the ground. Leon ran outside and stared into the distant eyes of his best friend, Julik. Beside him was his family, their faces pale and colour-stricken.

A dark red patch of blood highlighted Julik's sister Edith's pink dress. His father's broken glasses lay on the ground beside his shattered body. A little further along lay his mother on the cold, wet ground. A matted bloody mass covered the back of her head.

The shock of the sight caused his heart to constrict in his throat, blocking his breath. Then he felt like vomiting as he looked at the tiny body [Sarah] that lay bloodied and mangled against a nearby tree, bashed to death by savages.[39]

The sight of her head smashed haunted him throughout his days.

Leon noticed that a truck began reversing its way into the backyard. Two people got out and looked solemnly at Leon. He knew them to be farmhands from neighbouring farms. They began loading the bodies onto the back of the truck. Leon stared in disbelief. Two days ago, he was here, playing together with Julik and his sisters in the garden. Now they tossed their lifeless bodies as if they were rubbish.

Leon, numb with shock, walked home, not knowing what to do or how to feel. His mother and grandmother were there waiting for him at the top of the driveway. They wrapped their arms around him as they all cried. How could they do this to them?

The Nazi directive in the towns usually, issued by obliging local Ukrainians, was for all Jews to report with one packed bag at a given place for resettlement. The punishment for those failing to follow the instructions was execution. The Hershkis were a proud family. The Nazis or their Ukrainian sympathisers may have murdered them at their own home because they refused instructions to leave, or simply to save time.

Later, Leon heard that German soldiers had taken over the place.

The impressive Hershki family home would have made an ideal headquarters for German operations. Leon was heartbroken by the loss of his friend. He never went to that house again.

19

Two Heinrichs – Maria, 1941

In 2008, Milla and her husband Peter visited Cham. The only accommodation they could find was a room at the Neue Post Gasthof. Milla, typically loquacious, mentioned to the owner that her grandmother, Barbara, had lived in Cham. In a fantastic coincidence, the owner instantly recalled Barbara because she had worked there for over twenty years from the late 1920s onwards. I was keen to meet with her and in 2019, without knowing if the elderly woman was still alive, we walked into the Neue Post, where Milla embraced the first person she saw. It was the owner, Klara Vogl. The two remembered one another from eleven years before.

That evening, the Pilgrims sat at one of the long quaint wooden tables in the hotel restaurant and ordered meals.

Now eighty-eight, Klara joined us for a pleasant dinner. Klara explained that she was a child when Barbara worked there. She remembered our grandmother fondly, and recalled her work ethic: *'Sie war immer putzin, immer putzin.* She was always cleaning, always cleaning.'

However, when we mentioned Johann, Klara shook her head in anger, describing him as a violent drunkard with whom Barbara should never have stayed.

'Barbara would sometimes knock on her door late at night,' she told us, 'to get away from his violence.'

When I asked Klara whether he was a Hitler supporter, she replied, *'Zu dumm. Er wollte nur besoffen sein.* He was too dumb. He just wanted to be drunk.'

*

On the morning of 22 June 1941, Germany began its mission to destroy the Soviet Union. Time was of the essence. Those operating within the German High Command who had an appreciation of military history knew that to avoid a potential Napoleonic-style failure, Russia must capitulate before the winter set in. However, the invasion, codenamed Operation Barbarossa, initially planned for 15 May, was delayed for five weeks because Hitler ordered first the overthrow of Yugoslavia. There, a military coup had taken over the incumbent Nazi-backed government. Hitler, infuriated, and believing it to be backed by the British, insisted on dealing first with Yugoslavia. The five-week delay was to prove crucial.

Initially, Germans had good cause to be optimistic. The logic was simple. It took five weeks to beat Poland, six to defeat France, and two to overrun Yugoslavia. Hence, the battle-trained Wehrmacht anticipated that six weeks would be enough to overcome the Russians. While Churchill was understandably thrilled when Germany attacked Russia, creating a two-front war, the respite looked to be a temporary one. Within three days of the onset of the invasion, the Soviet Union's outlook was already looking bleak.

Three million Wehrmacht soldiers and their military hardware Blitzkrieged their way across the vast Ukrainian plains, destroying more than half of the Soviet air force. Whole Russian armies, in their tens of thousands, had to surrender en masse. It was hard to fathom that Russia could provide more than token resistance. Harold Nicolson, an eminent British politician and political commentator, on 24 June noted the extreme pessimism in his diary.

> Eighty per cent of the War Office experts think that Russia will be knocked out in ten days.[40]

Russia was different, however. The sheer distances to travel meant that the war would probably last longer than six weeks. Almost on schedule, Army Group South reached the critical city of Stalingrad, and Army Group Centre, who had overrun Kyiv and met the most resistance, were well on the way to Moscow, with over two months to spare before winter. Meanwhile, Army Group North eliminated Leningrad effectively as a fighting force when they surrounded the city in a siege that would last for over 800 days. Despite Stalin's decree that the Soviets were not to be captured alive, by October, the number of Soviet prisoners had already exceeded three million.[41]

Anticipating the fall of the nation's capital, Stalin ordered a scorched earth policy whereby nothing useable was to fall into the Nazis' hands. Instead, they moved whole factories, together with massive amounts of military and cultural valuables, to locations east of the Ural Mountains, where they began to prepare their final lines of resistance.

Hot on the heels of the invading Wehrmacht came the Einsatzgruppen, Hitler's extermination squad, tasked with the job of eliminating Jews and other so-called *Untermensch*.

At this time, amid great optimism, Barbara and Johann became parents again. If their first child, Adolf's birth coincided with Hitler's rise to power, then their second son's birth in late 1941 coincided with the peak of Nazi hegemony.

Johann again took responsibility for choosing his child's name. This time, he decided that Heinrich would be the most appropriate choice to go with his brother, Adolf. Johann decided Heinrich either because he liked the name, or wanted to pay homage to Hitler's notorious henchman, the man most responsible for carrying out Hitler's plan for the murder of over six million Jews and other *Untermensch*, Heinrich Himmler.[42]

Maria, as with Adolf, remained unimpressed with her new brother's name; it added to Maria's sense of abandonment and disconnection from her family. Barbara, having just taken a significant risk by showing the lack of allegiance to Hitler in the plebiscite, may not have preferred the name that Johann chose. However, given that an investigation was under way as to who voted *Nein*, perhaps the name showed a sign of loyalty that may have put the otherwise under suspicion family in the clear.

*

The next day, we visited the former Kolnhoffer home. We had learned from Klara that the lower and upper floors of the three-storey building had been requisitioned by the SS during the war. The building is unusual and appealing. It is rectangular, with a half-round cylindrical-shaped addition at the end facing into town. The white rendered façade has three or four tiny windows per floor, designed hundreds of years ago to repel invaders. Maria, loathing the Nazis, had another reason to avoid the place.

At the time, the building provided cheap rent for the family. However, the building has much popularity today. When Pilgrim Josephine picked up a Cham tourist brochure, she was surprised to see the former Kolnhoffer/SS lodgings identified as one of the town's iconic buildings.

We tried the front door, but no one seemed to live there. We stood and imagined what day-to-day life would have been like for the family, with the SS coming and going every day. Outside the house, we noticed a tree with a single, enormous green apple hanging upon a sagging branch. Feeling mischievous, we decided to pinch it and eat it later.

A few days later, we agreed in a nostalgic ceremony in our hotel to eat it. The apple tasted awful. It was so sour that one bite was as much as anyone could manage. The bulk of the apple found its way into the bin. That night, I composed a poem to commemorate the occasion.

> The tree once produced only the sweetest of fruit,
> But for all it had witnessed, it could only stand mute.
> While the SS committed heinous crimes of abuse,
> Now only the sourest of fruits can the mute tree produce.

Heinrich's birth coincided with great success for the Wehrmacht on the battlefield. The wave of optimism that Germany rode looked like getting even higher when on 7 December 1941, Japan, Germany's Axis ally, attacked and destroyed the cream of the American fleet stationed at the naval base at Pearl Harbour. Japan, like Germany in Europe, was already a proven military success in Asia. Within a few months, her Imperial forces controlled most of the Pacific region, including much of China, the Philippines and Burma. Having reached Papua New Guinea, the Japanese army was heading down the Kokoda Trail on her way to Port Moresby and then on to Australia.

The day after Pearl Harbour, the USA unsurprisingly declared war on Japan, and four days later, Germany declared war on the USA. Now with her U-boats, Germany could readily attack her shipping convoys that had hitherto been supplying Britain with all manner of goods. The plan was that Japan would annihilate the USA, while Germany finished off the Soviets. Then, with England impotent and alone, the two countries could control the entire world at their leisure. Nobody else could stand in the way. The Thousand-Year Reich was about to become a reality.

20

Holocaust – Leon, June/July 1942

The German army under the command of General Stülpnagel occupied Zolochiv on 2 July 1941. Immediately following them, the SS Einsatzgruppen began their pogrom against their local Jewish population, including those in surrounding towns and villages. Some local Ukrainians gathered to help enforce the Nazi directive, forcing all Jews to be easily identifiable by wearing the international symbol for Judaism, a yellow band with a black outlined Star of David on their arms or a yellow star sewn to their chest.

The following Nazi directive ordered that all Jews must report to various locations for resettlement. Most Jews by now knew the consequence of non-compliance was execution, and therefore most, with the exception of the Hershki family, followed the directive, arriving at the correct time and place. There, the Nazis ordered the Jews to walk, not in the direction of Zolochiv but towards the small neighbouring town of Pluhiv, about three kilometres south-west of Pidlyptsi. They promised that transport would be waiting there to take them to their resettlement destination.

One particular Jewish group had been rounded up from all over the district. Leon watched as a long line, marched along the road past his farm. They did not know the fate that awaited.

> They just came along in their line with their badges there around their arms. They just went marching moving along as if they were happy. They didn't try to run away.

Leon wanted to see where they were going, so he followed at a distance. Some other boys from the villages had the same idea and came along. As the procession went along the winding track towards Pluhiv,

Leon noticed that the German soldiers accompanying them carried their guns with them the whole time. That was strange for a group that was about to be peacefully resettled. Even stranger when they arrived not at Pluhiv, but at a clearing in the forest.

> The Russians dug a trench, a big trench, with big machinery, trying to see if they could find some coal up there. It was not far from my house at a place called Pluhiv. They left [in a hurry] because the Germans were chasing them.

The Germans hurried the Jews along with some urgency, as if there was some mutually beneficial consequence to their combined expediency, then forced them to line up along the whole length of the trench, which was 'about the length of a swimming pool'. Each of the Jews wore the compulsory Star of David.

> The next thing, they were bringing all the Jews in with their badges around their arms, standing all in a row. They didn't mind. The next thing, du, du, du, du [Leon made the sound of a machine gun firing].
> There were hundreds of them in a big line.

Just a few German soldiers guarded them all. Leon watched from a nearby hill.

> We used to watch them; they [the German soldiers] didn't mind. Then, one bloke was standing there with a machine gun, and he wiped the lot out.
> It was a terrible thing.
> They fell into the trench. Then, German soldiers fired into the pit.
> Then, the next thing, another Jew came. They put some sort of white powder, I don't know what sort of white powder, on them.[43] Then the next load and then the next load. Some of them were probably still alive.[44]
> Then, they brought the next lot in.
> Never did anyone try to escape. You think to yourself afterwards, you could not kill them all. Why don't they run away? Why do they all want to die? I never, ever saw the Jews fight or try to escape or anything like that.[45]

The killing continued throughout the day until the Jews were all dead. They may have been compliant because they did not know they were about to be killed. However, when they knew the truth that they were going to their deaths, they accepted their fate and chose to die with dignity with their families.

To make a point, Leon recalled a story about a Jewish man who was about to be executed.

> The German officer came over to him. He recognised him and wanted to help him. He came over and said, 'You are not Jewish. I know you. I know your parents. Why are you here?'
> The man answered, 'I am Jewish.'
> He gave him a chance. He could have saved himself, but he preferred to die with his people.

Not everybody, however, accepted his or her fate. Simultaneously, as the round-ups occurred, Mr Jutka disappeared, leaving Miss Serben to run the school by herself. He must have known what fate awaited him if he stayed.

> He and his wife ran away. I never heard what happened to them. They knew, they were clever. They ran away. Some of them might have come back afterwards, but I was already gone by that time.

Soon, word began to spread around that the Germans were killing all the Jews.

> Some of the men and older boys joined the resistance, and some Jewish people tried to get away or hide.

Jews were not the only victims of Nazi cruelty. One day on the way to school, Leon came across something hanging from the bell. As he got closer, he recognised the outline of her body, the colour of her hair and the dress she often wore.

> They hanged her at the church, underneath the bells. Outside every church, inside but outside they've got what the Germans call *Glocken*. Bells.

> There was a big sign there [around her neck]: 'If you hide anybody, you will get caught, and the same will happen to you.'
> They hanged the teacher, a young Ukrainian teacher, Helena. She was hanged because she tried to save her Jewish friend. She kept her somewhere at her place, and they, the Germans, found her.

Helena Serben had a life and death choice to make. She was aware that the Nazis would have murdered her friend if she reported her. She knew what the SS did at Pluhiv and to Julik and his family. She must have known that her own life would be forfeit if they caught her harbouring a Jew.

Despite the risk, Helena chose her friend over her safety, and the Nazis found out. Perhaps an informant told them, or a random search of Helena's home uncovered her presence. Regardless of the circumstances, Helena Serben, the beautiful, caring person she was, paid the ultimate price for her loyalty.

It must have been a terrible week for the whole community, especially as the Nazis forbade them from taking down her body.

> I felt horrible then afterwards. She had to hang there for days.

Some took her murder very seriously.

> It was horrible! After that, I think that many of the people turned against the Germans. Some of our older boys even ran away to join the resistance.

There was no more school after that in Pidlyptsi. The Nazis had no interest in educating *Untermensch*. According to them, Ukrainians were, after all, just servants, called to serve the Master Race.

The Zolochiv Jews fared as poorly as those in Pidlyptsi. Their fate was made worse by the heinous crimes of some of their fellow townspeople, many of whom, for whatever reason, embraced anti-Semitism. Not only did they aid, but they very much abetted the Nazis to implement what the world came to know as the Holocaust, the systematic murder of millions of Jews, amongst others, during the Second World

Another key stop on our Pilgrimage was the visit to Leon's church in Pidlyptsi. There outside the church, amongst the first things we saw was the same bell where the Nazis hanged Miss Serben for hiding a Jewish girl in 1942. One cannot imagine the horror that young woman felt as they forced her to step up on the narrow ledge at the base of the arches. Then, after tying the noose around her neck, they would have pushed her off the ledge. They placed the warning around her neck to discourage anyone who might try to do the same as she did.

War. Some Ukrainians were passionately anti-Semitic and readily joined in for the cause. Still others joined in the slaughter to please their sadistic bloodlust or simply please their Nazi overlords.

*

We were fortunate to discover that our cousin, Victor, is the current director of Zolochiv Castle, now a museum. We visited on 13 July, and on that day, the weather, which had been uncomfortably warm, was now perfect; the skies were clear, and a lovely breeze swept over the castle. Victor met us there and, with an interpreter, took us on a tour of the museum.

The castle served first as a Soviet prison and then as a Nazi prison during the war. A few days before the Germans arrived, Ukrainians executed over 700 prisoners who might have been released by the Nazis. They were worried that the Nazis might embrace some prisoners who might seek vengeance. The Ukrainian militia then blamed the Jews for the crime and forced them to dig up the bodies with their bare hands. A few days later, the Jewish dead overfilled those same pits.

There were many interesting artefacts to observe in many splendidly restored rooms. Once an operational castle, the museum still has the large central courtyard, about the size of a football field, that it had in 1941.

We then learned that Einsatzgruppen (SS), with help from the Ukrainian National Committee (volunteer Ukrainian militia), executed the approximately 3,500 Jews who gathered there that morning at the castle. It was a very sobering feeling to know that the courtyard, now surrounded by beds of beautifully arranged flowers, was the scene of the massacre.

The volunteer Ukrainians readily herded together as many Jews as they could muster.[46] Hundreds of members helped to force the Jewish population from their homes towards the castle. So brutal and zealous were some of the volunteers that many Jews did not even reach their destination. The Ukrainian militia beat and even killed defenceless Jews at will on their way to the castle.

So packed was the castle courtyard that awful day that only half of the three and a half thousand Jews who arrived that morning could fit within the enclosure. It is hard to imagine the scale and brutality of the ensuing massacre that took place where we stood.

Einsatzgruppen, armed with machine guns, mowed down row after row of helpless Jews, while outside the castle, the rest, about 1,700, were murdered in a flat area with their backs to the castle wall. Following the initial machine-gun bursts, the Ukrainian militia moved in. Their methods were unbelievably heartless. They simply hacked into the dead and dying crowd with whatever weapons they could muster, including picks, spikes and rifles. It is almost unfathomable that these were, in many cases, neighbours and fellow townspeople, many of whom they would have known personally. Occasionally, an SS soldier would throw in a grenade.

The Zolochiv massacre. German soldiers stand behind piles of the dead. The building to the right can also be seen on the right in the photo below of Zolochiv Castle as it is today.

Typically, during such massacres, the murderers were heavily intoxicated, numbing their senses to their terrible task. Some, nevertheless, enjoyed their work. Two huge pits, one inside and one outside the castle, became their graves. Their bodies still lie there in unmarked graves.[47]

Wild looting of Jewish homes occurred in the city; neighbours robbed and beat their neighbours.[48]

However, not all of the locals had a vendetta against the Jews. Not all Ukrainians were wicked. Fortunately, some showed compassion and decency and refused to condone or take part in the pogroms. Others, like Helena Serben, went further and took a considerable personal risk to save Jews.

> There were other Ukrainians: Mykola Dyuk would hide for eighteen months in the school annex the family of the very young Roald, the future world-famous scientist and Nobel Prize winner.[49]

However, the Zolochiv pogrom and the massacre at Pluhiv were typical of those that occurred throughout the conquered lands of eastern Europe. For convenience, the murderers used any natural or human-made grave, trench, or ravine to bury the dead, usually within walking distance from where the victims lived.

> Most died in situ, rounded up, shot, and buried in ravines outside their own hometowns.[50]

By the end of the war, Nazis had murdered an estimated 2.2 million Ukrainian Jews. This astonishing figure amounts to more than a third of the accepted total of around six million Jews killed throughout Europe during the entire Holocaust.

Despite his summation of witnessing the massacre at Pluhiv and their willingness to accept their fate, Leon knew, of course, that the Jewish people did not want to die. History attests that Jews in some places resisted the Nazis as vehemently as anybody did. In April 1943, for example, a group of poorly equipped Jewish inmates in the Warsaw Ghetto decided to defy their imminent death by forming a resistance group. Over time, they resourcefully amassed weaponry including self-made items, especially Molotov cocktails. Rather than lie down and submit to the Nazis, they fought them from house to house and street to street, holding out against Wehrmacht troops for over a month. The Wehrmacht had to call on reinforcements needed elsewhere. Eventually, it took over two thousand SS and regular soldiers, at the cost of hundreds of casualties, to clear the Warsaw Ghetto.

Zolochiv today is like stepping back in time. Charming as they were, every fourth car looked as though it had just driven out of the Cold War. A short walk away from our hotel, we were shocked as we passed a construction site that the scaffolding was of timber pieces crudely tied together with rope. Each piece looked as though someone had hacked it from the tree rather than being created in a sawmill.

There were deep holes in the footpaths, and buildings everywhere were in disrepair. Exposed rusted steel reinforcements made us think that parts of buildings were ready to give way. We passed by long-abandoned construction projects and wondered when they might recommence work. There were promising signs; the whole town centre was a construction zone that should become a beautiful and vibrant hub for commerce, leisure, and tourism.

One night, some of the Pilgrims watched the town's premier football team, FC Zokil, play a pre-season friendly. The club management treated them like royalty; their names were called out over the loudspeaker and introduced to the cheering crowd.

Our last night in Zolochiv was memorable. Victor, Andrii and their families joined us for a meal at the restaurant at our hotel. A most

The Pilgrims with our Ukrainian family.
Andrii is far right, with wife Oksana third from right.
Victor is second from left, with wife Maria far left.
On the same night, we were joined by a group of young people in singing the Ukrainian national anthem.

touching moment occurred when my sisters Milla, Elizabeth and Josie began singing the Ukrainian national anthem.

Soon, we were all at least attempting to join in. As we sang, about twenty or so young people, who were celebrating a birthday at the tables adjacent to us, began to sing along with us. Soon, the beautifully yearning strains of Ukraine's anthem filled the entire outdoor area. We shared with these, the next generation of Ukrainians, a strong emotion of optimism and connection to the country.

21

Fatalities, Women in War – Maria, 1942

The Soviet Union initially suffered massive losses. No other country in Europe could have withstood such decimation to their military, but the Soviet Union was a different kettle of fish. What saved them was the vast wealth of human and non-human resources that spread over land more than twice as big as the rest of Europe combined. Huge factories, some formerly located in the west and moved east, began churning out vast quantities of high-tech armaments, including Soviet T34 tanks, the Ilyushin Il-2 aircraft and the terrifying rocket launches colloquially known as the 'Stalin Organ'. Additionally, massive armies, some highly trained, others relatively untrained, were created almost daily, from all over the Soviet Union, and sent into battle. Germans knew nothing of this. The only news they heard via the newsreels was success after success. However, the propaganda could not lie about the death toll, and as it kept rising back home, people began to realise the truth.

In 1935, in defiance of the Treaty of Versailles, the Germans introduced conscription. Along with hundreds of thousands of volunteers, this ensured that Germany had a consistently growing army. Before Russia's invasion, their numbers were plentiful, with only small losses incurred in conquests thus far.

Soviet population and ideology differed from that in Germany, giving an advantage that played out as the war progressed. Hitler insisted that a woman's role was child-rearing and domestic work. However, Stalin mandated that nobody was exempt from the war effort, including armed combat, provided it killed Germans. Thus while Germany had about sixty million inhabitants, most of whom were exempt from military duties, in contrast, the Soviets, with no such restrictions, potentially had an army of over two hundred million. Everybody had to be prepared to do whatever was necessary to ensure ultimate victory. Later in the war, Goebbels coined the phrase 'total war' but by then it was too late.

Inevitably, there were fatalities. Döfering parish suffered its first, when an early conscript from Rhan, Joseph Stangl, died during France's invasion in 1940. A steady trickle of parish men followed, another in France and one in North Africa. Each time, the community mourned. Each time, they hoped and prayed that it would be the last.

It was a terrible time for all of the villages in the close-knit parish community, where everybody knew everybody. Every death resurfaced memories of the last war. When the first bodies arrived home, the whole district, from Rhan, Haschaberg, Lixendöfering, Flischberg, Almoosmühle and Döfering, joined the funeral processions. Eventually, the deaths became too frequent, and the bodies seldom arrived.

Gradually, following Russia's invasion, people started to realise that, like the last war, this war would drag on well into the future. Unlike in the First World War, when enlisting seemed like an adventure, and all the young men wanted to join in the excitement of battle, this time, at least in Döfering, no one volunteered to fight.

As casualties began to rise, the Wehrmacht needed many more men to make up the shortfall. Authorities searching for recruits may have noticed that there were still quite a few men left in the Döfering region who had not joined. Perhaps they remembered that this parish showed less support to the Nazis in previous elections.

> They sent all of our boys to the Russian Front because they knew we were not for Hitler.

22

The Pilot – Leon, 20 April 1942

Paradoxically, throughout July and August, following Operation Barbarossa,[51] life in Pidlyptsi returned to relative normality. Meanwhile, the Wehrmacht continued to make rapid progress into Russian territory. By that winter of 1941, they had all but achieved their objectives. Army Group North was confident that its siege of Leningrad and its more than three million citizens would soon bring about the city's capitulation. Thousands starved to death every day and together with the Luftwaffe's constant indiscriminate bombing of the defenceless city, over 1.5 million men, women and children would die by the time the siege ended more than two years later. For Army Group Centre, the capital, Moscow, was literally within sight and seemingly about to fall, and for Army Group South, the battle for Stalingrad raged. The High Command expected the city, named after the Soviet leader, to capitulate at any time. Its demise probably would have signalled the end to the war.

Then the snow fell.

So confident was the German High Command that the Soviet Union would fall before Christmas that they did not prepare soldiers adequately for the harsh Russian winter. The realisation that they were in for a much longer campaign than first anticipated came as a severe blow to Germany's chances. Crucially, this provided England and her Allies with breathing space to develop her defensive and offensive capacities. England used her time wisely.

Having failed in 1941 to deal the decisive blow, and as temperatures plummeted to as low as -50º below, Germany had to dig in for the winter. While the Wehrmacht had to make do with makeshift, inadequate clothing, the Soviets were far better prepared to survive in sub-zero temperatures. By the end of the winter, one of the coldest on record, hundreds of thousands of German soldiers lay dead, frozen solid into the Russian snow.

By mid-1942, the Russian forces had restocked and replenished, ready for the spring offensives. In contrast, while reinforced, German armies had suffered a momentous blow and could not adequately replace their losses. By now, everyone knew that the war was not going to end any time soon. The Soviets had made the most progress in rearming their troops and counterattacking Wehrmacht forces along the eastern front.

England's military infrastructure, meanwhile, continued to suffer under relentless Luftwaffe air raids. However, when Goering decided to switch to bombing cities, with the aim of destroying English morale, he allowed England's air force much-needed respite, during which she recouped most of her losses. By the end of 1940, the Battle of Britain was effectively over. England had forged ahead with armaments production and recruitment. In 1941, her scientists cracked the German Enigma codes, allowing British intelligence to track German military movements. In the air, and on the seas, the advantage proved to be decisive. Not long after, the US codebreakers achieved similar success just before the significant battle of Midway in the Pacific. Consequently, the Japanese suffered a considerable defeat. The war had shifted in favour of the Allies.

Despite hostilities, the Nazi hierarchy ordered that Hitler's birthday on 20 April had to be celebrated throughout Germany and her conquered lands. The SS Einsatzgruppen, who had murdered almost the entire Jewish population of Zolochiv, ironically chose a place called the Jewish Park to host 'a fantastic big celebration'.

> After they cleared the Jews out, there was a very big party. Everyone had chocolate. There was drinking, dancing. There was beer. They invited all the young girls. Naturally, we young boys went there too, you know. They didn't mind the young boys like me going along.

All of a sudden, this Russian plane came down very low and started shooting at everyone. It killed a lot of civilians and a lot of German soldiers.

After passing once, the Russian plane turned and returned for a second sweep as Leon and most of the party ducked for cover.

The German soldiers, straight away, went after that plane, and they shot back at it, and they got it, and the plane went down in the woods and landed not far from where I was born in the forest. Everybody ran after it. There weren't big trees, but there was bush everywhere. Actually, it was not far from the place where they buried all the Jewish people [near Pluhiv].
I ran too with the German soldiers. I ran to see what happened.

The plane was still intact when Leon and the others arrived on the scene. The pilot had managed to get out and fled into nearby bushes. German soldiers, however, followed quickly and soon dragged the pilot out into a clearing. Leon got a surprise when he saw their prisoner.

Eventually, they caught that pilot – a Russian, a woman pilot. There were no men, just one woman. She did a lot of damage.

Over the years, Leon relived this story to me on several occasions and always cringed when he described what followed.

Of course, they were cranky because she did so much damage, you know. Terrible, terrible things happened. They tore off her clothes, so she was standing completely naked.
She screamed at them while four German soldiers held her, one on each arm and one on each leg. Then, one of the soldiers came forward, and with a bayonet, he split her stomach completely open. Then he pulled out her insides and let them fall to the ground.

Leon had seen pigs and cows slaughtered, but never a living person. When the Germans let her go, she stumbled around, bleeding everywhere with her insides out.

One of the German soldiers then came forward. With a machine gun, he started firing. He shot her completely in half.

One German soldier then took her arms while the other took her legs and dragged apart her body's two halves.

> Where there was one woman before, two bodies were lying there – horrible!
> She was doing her job, fighting for her country.
> Of course, she shot anyone who was there, Ukrainians as well.
> She thought they were just Germans celebrating.

German or Ukrainian, it made no difference, according to Stalinist doctrine. Anyone fraternising with the enemy was a traitor and deserved what they got.

There were many women pilots in the Russian air force. This pilot was probably on a one-way flight.

> Some of them went to commit suicide as well – to kill some of the Germans.

When Leon returned to the park, bodies were lying here and there, dead and dying. Tables and chairs lay upturned with drinks and food lying all over the ground. Leon never found out how many others died that day. He never wanted to know; he just went home.

23

Xaver – Maria, 1942

Farms were stereotypically family affairs. Men worked tirelessly with manual labour in and around the farm and women cooked and tended to the children, and helped with the chores as soon as possible. Everyone had to be a Jack of all trades, so Maria's daily tasks also included collecting the eggs, milking the cows, sowing and harvesting vegetables, cleaning out the stables, fixing the fence, and so forth. She did whatever work was needed.

Maria worked up to sixteen hours per day, six days a week. The wage was meagre but included food and lodgings. At week's end, she could afford to go to Cham and buy herself something from the markets. Sometimes, Maria went home to the Keil House to visit family, especially her grandma, who had become bedridden. After they had eaten, Grandma would lead the family in prayer and Bible studies before bed. Often struggling to stay awake, Maria loved Grandma's stories of Waldensians, who sacrificed everything for their faith. She had no trouble falling asleep.

Maria looked forward to her Sunday, day of rest. Now that her best friends had all left school, meeting them on a Sunday became significant. All of the girls had boyfriends. Maree and Wolfgang became an item. Annie began seeing a soldier named Heinz, Othelia also had a boyfriend, and Maria and Xaver had become an item.

Xaver lived not far from the road between Hascherberg and Döfering, and he would meet Maria on her way to work or church. Before long, they saw each other almost daily. On Sundays, Maria often met with Xaver to celebrate Mass at St Adagios. Sometimes, the group might meet and travel by train, wagon or bicycle to Cham for the day. Depending on the time of year, after Mass, they might go for a swim in the Regan, or go bushwalking, where they arranged for a picnic lunch. In the winter, probably outside the Keil house, they skated or skied down and around the stunningly picturesque mountains.

Along with exercise and fresh air, Maria's friendship group loved to sing. Wherever they were, they made a great choir. Their favourite song was perhaps 'Tief drin im Böhmerwald' ('Deep in the Bohemian forest'). Maria acknowledged the beautiful, uncontrived relationships she had, particularly with Xaver.

> He was my boyfriend. We never had to say anything. We were happy just to sit together and say nothing.

Life was idyllic, but by 1942, everything was changing. Most of the boys, while coerced into the Hitler Youth, thus far had avoided conscription into the country's armed forces. However, there was no way that the Nazi warlords, with their rapidly mounting loss of men, were going to overlook the district's boys any longer.

The Pilgrims and the Brückl family enjoy a meal together. Oliver is second from left with wife Claudia, and daughter Eva in the foreground, followed by Markus, Marille, Sepp, Selina, Daniela, Simon and the Pilgrims.

24

The Bomb – Leon, April 1942

Easter was Leon's favourite time of the year. He would rush to church at the break of dawn, ready to receive his coloured eggs. The mothers would slowly boil the eggs until they were soft and warm, and then with a piece of wax, they would create the most beautiful patterns by dipping them into pots of beautiful, coloured dye. The colouring was fine art, made from centuries of tradition. Marika created the curls, stripes, and crosses along with the delicate shell with perfection.[52]

13 April 1942, was a gloriously warm spring day. The entire community arrived to celebrate Easter mass. Leon, his one-year-younger cousin Mikal, and a group of other boys, had other things on their minds. As soon as Mass finished, they bade their parents farewell. They would be back for lunch.

> The church was packed that morning. It was Easter Sunday, there was a big school, and a big park and the Russians had left a tank and loads of ammunition.

The boys had found the tank left behind by the Russians and had opened the hatch to explore inside. It was quite an adventure to pretend to be part of the crew, playing war games with the controls. The tank was kaput, of course; it would not start, otherwise, the boys would long since have taken it for a ride. Still, it was an excellent find for the boys, who found a use for the ammunition left in and around the tank.

> Someone had the idea that if they could detonate a bomb, it would make a fantastic explosion. In Ukraine, we had a tradition: on Easter Sunday, the boys used to do anything to start shooting, you know, with powder or shooting guns: to have something go bang.

It was not the first time. The boys discovered that the bullets were in two parts, the body and the tip. The tip screwed into the body and served as a detonator. With careful effort, they were able to unscrew it from the main section. Then they would bring the caps to the cemetery where, with plenty of cover from the tombstones, they could safely detonate the small amount of gunpowder inside the lids to make an impressive fireworks display. The explosions blew high and loud, sending a stream of fire and sparks into the air. It was all over within a few seconds, with only the scorched cap and a scorched mark on the gravestone left. The pyrotechnics display was such fun that the boys were keen to go back for some more.

> We went after the big bullets. Get the end off, and bring them to the cemetery, give them a bang and [get] a big explosion.

Near the end of Mass that day, Mikal sidled over to Leon as a dozen or so boys snuck out through the back door.

> Mikal asked me, 'Can you and me go down there to see what they're doing?'
> So we went there, and there were all young boys there, and they were trying to get the ends off the bullets. The bullets were like the end of a bottle, and you undo that. Sometimes you tap it a little bit, and it comes off, and you put them in your pocket. You take them to the cemetery, near the Jewish park, you put them on a stone grave, light it with something, and you blow it up. I already had two of them in my pocket.

The cemetery was right beside the church, so the children collected their bomb tips and began to make their way back. As they were leaving, Leon noticed that one of the boys struggled to remove the top off his bomb. The boy was wearing a new beanie with a Tryzub that his mother had made and presented it to him that morning for his Easter present.[53]

The other boys gathered around to watch.

> This bloke, this little fellow, he had a stone, and he kept hammering. I said, 'Don't do it any more. You can explode it when you hit it hard.'

The little boy had no interest in listening. He said, 'Ah, what do you know about it?'
There were about a dozen boys there.

Leon could see the risk but was powerless to stop him, so he focused on the others.

I just told [them] to keep away.
'Oh, you're too weak,' the boy answered, 'you're too scared of everything.'
I said to Mikal, 'Come on, let's get out of here.'

Then they began to walk back to the cemetery.

As soon as I said it, he hit it again with a rock, and she blew up.

The blast knocked both Mikal and Leon to the ground, rendering them unconscious for several seconds, then confused, temporarily deaf and terrified all at once as they began to assess the situation. Fortunately, by the time the bomb exploded, the boys had ascended about two metres higher, and onto a ledge, so the hill itself shielded them, absorbing the main force of the blast. Leon remembered as he regained consciousness. He was on his back, looking up at a tree branch from which hung the hat that the little boy was wearing – the one his mother had given him that day. 'Why is it in the tree?' thought Leon. The next thing he heard was Mikal groaning with pain. Leon struggled to help him to his feet. Then they glanced over the ridge, where they took in a truly macabre sight.

And all the kids hanging on the trees, bodies everywhere.

The boys, who had crowded around the bomb, took the brunt of the blast, providing further cover for Leon and Mikal, but blowing themselves to pieces.

There were survivors.

Everybody screaming and I grabbed hold of Mikal, and I said, 'Come on, let's clear off,' and we ran over the mountain. What we called

Tatar's Hill. Somebody else was alive. Not everybody got killed. About seven or eight got killed. Some of them you couldn't recognise the body.'

Mikal was wounded in the leg. He still has the scar; he couldn't run. Just a piece of meat, [the bomb] took it out. A lot of bleeding, yeah, a lot of bleeding.

I said, 'Come on, it's not very far away.'

We came to our house, they all were in church, and Grandma was at home. Ah, but Grandma wrapped it up to stop the blood flowing.

I think she put some leaf, I can't remember it properly, wrapped it up with cabbage leaf or something, and tied a bandage over it. That's how they did it, the old people, and then his father came and took him with a horse to the doctor, who bandaged it properly. He healed all right, but it left a big scar there.

There followed the worst of times for the entire community. Those who heard the blast rushed to see something akin to the most gruesome that war could offer. Some arrived to find only pieces of their children.

The victims' families came to identify and collect their deceased children, but the task was not easy.

Parents recognised them by their clothes, only by what they wore.

The grimmest task was to match body parts with the rest of their corpse.

There were body parts up in trees. Half a body was here and half a body there.

In the next few weeks, funerals took place for the dead boys. Neither Leon nor Mikal attended. It was unlikely that they would have been welcome, especially Leon.

Everybody in the village said, 'Oh, Leon is the oldest. He is their leader.'

They blamed me. Everybody blamed me. They blamed me for everything.

I didn't feel very good. My mam didn't feel very good, and nobody in the family felt very good.

Leon was barely fourteen at the time. Fortunately for his mental health, he never blamed himself.

> I didn't do anything wrong. I didn't ask them to come there. I warned them, 'If you hammer it, it could explode.' But they didn't take any notice of me. They just tapped a little bit further. Yeah, I didn't hammer it. I just tapped it a little bit. It's not a bomb, just a bullet from the tank. We wanted just the end of the bullet. Once you get the end off, nothing will happen to it. It won't do any harm.

Of course, the event traumatised Leon.

> I felt awful. I've seen all this flesh, arms hanging from the trees and everything. I was too scared to ask anybody.

The weeks that followed were terrible for everyone, especially the families of the deceased children. There was at least one person to whose survival Leon may have contributed.

> One of them must have run the other way, and we ran down towards our house.

Perhaps he survived because he heeded Leon's warning and tried to leave the area. Regardless, many people continued to blame Leon, and the ensuing weeks and months were terrible.

> They said I was the leader.

For the remainder of his time in Ukraine, Leon lived in fear of physical reprisal. He and Mikal lay very low over the next few months. Leon never knew how many or who perished that Easter Sunday in 1942.

> We left the church. We should have stayed at the church, but we wanted to get the bullets.

Leon showed no animosity towards the families.

> I told them not to do it. I don't blame them [for hating me]. You would do it too if that would be your son.

The hill where the boys may have died. Leon and Mikal reached the flats on the top of the ridge before the bomb exploded, saving their lives.

The heartbreak that befell the people of Pidlyptsi that Easter Sunday was not the last. In the ensuing years, unexploded bombs and mines continued to take a savage toll.

> When I went there in 1990, I said, where is so and so? Oh, he got killed by a mine exploding or picking up the big bullets like we were doing and mucking about, and it exploded. Stacks that I knew that I used to go with to school, they died afterwards because everything was lying about, you know, mines and bullets. The Russians left, the Germans left – I was very lucky.

*

After visiting Aunty Anna, the Pilgrims, along with Andrii, followed the now tarred road to visit his church, the Greek Catholic church in Pidlyptsi. The first thing that stood out was the white, three-arched bell structure upon which the Nazis murdered Helena Serben.

To the back of the church lies a cemetery where we visited the graves of our grandparents and great-grandparents. It was here, no doubt, that

Leon's friends enjoyed their fireworks. It was here, no doubt, that the bodies of his friends now lie.

The church stands about halfway up a hill that is about a hundred metres high. Along the top runs the flattish ridge. We noticed a distinct depression and an unprecedented change in the colour and type of vegetation that grows within eyesight. We wondered if that was where the explosion occurred. Impulsively, I ran up the hill, through the scrub, scratching my legs to reach the exact spot where the depression lay. Whether or not the boys died there that Easter Sunday, is of course, not known. However, it was there that I stood to pay my respects to them; and their lives that they never lived.

25

Arrests – Maria, 1942

> There were two friends, the priest [Father Eigat] and another one [name unknown], a relation or whatever. One ran away and was in hiding, and the other one, they caught him, and he was arrested. They were very worried about him.

In Maria's region, the Nazis routinely arrested people because they spoke out against Hitler's regime. No one was safe, including the clergy, as two local priests, Pader (Father) Rockermann and Pader Eigat, were about to discover. Pader Eigat incurred the Nazis' wrath when he criticised them from St Adagio's pulpit. Somehow, the authorities found out; perhaps one or more parishioners had Nazi sympathies and complained to the Gestapo, who swooped to arrest him. However, Eigat managed to escape after a tip-off from one of his supporters. Unable to apprehend him, they took his friend. He would spend the rest of his short life at the infamous Dachau concentration camp, where horrendous atrocities occurred, including the infliction of slow and painful deaths due to medical experiments.

26

One From Each Family Must Go/The Journey – Leon, Mid-1942

Increasing casualties, especially on the eastern front, meant that the Wehrmacht began to experience an acute shortage of fighting men. As far as Hitler was concerned, Germany's life and death struggle required every able-bodied man to do their duty, leaving a large hole in workers' availability in German factories, construction and farming. The conquered lands containing millions of young men, women, boys and girls provided the perfect solution. They would become the new, almost unlimited, expendable workforce, at the same time releasing hundreds of thousands of German men to replace those lost in battle.

The great advantage of this new multimillion workforce was that it involved virtually no financial outlay. It was free labour; you did not have to pay anything. All you had to do was feed and provide rudimentary shelter for it, much as you might do for a horse or a cow. All you had to do was maintain it, and it would do its job. It had no rights, and if it no longer served a purpose, you could dispose of it in the same manner as you would any farm animal.

Soon after the bomb killed the boys, Leon was outside when a German soldier on a motorbike rode up to his farmhouse. His mother opened the door. In his hand, the soldier carried a 'stick', a thin, flat piece of timber from which he read aloud a message to the household.[54] The soldier announced that each family was to select one person to be designated to work in Germany. That person must report the following Monday at precisely eight a.m. to the *Bürgermeister* (mayor) at Zolochiv train station. Failure to obey this directive would result in imprisonment or execution. The person, however, need not fear. Moreover, the message stated that at the cessation of work duties, estimated to be approximately one year, the individual could return home. The announcement came via the authority of the German High Command.

For Leon's family, there was only one choice. His little brother, Mykhas, at five years old, was not a viable option and his stepfather, Stephan, in his forties, needed to be there to work the farm.

> I didn't choose to go, but one of us had to go. They chose me to go. They said you've got to leave someone [Stephan] there to work on the farm. I was fifteen at the time.

The idea of leaving his beloved home to head into the complete unknown left Leon feeling understandably apprehensive. However, living in a shattered community, who blamed him for causing so many deaths, left him more optimistic about his future.

> When it happened, they told me I had to go, but then I thought to myself, 'That's a good idea to get out of the road in case somebody did some harm to me…' I didn't want to go.

With such a tragedy, it was natural to seek a scapegoat for the loss of their children. 'Did they threaten you?' I asked.

> Oh, yeah. When I went to church or on the street, people, they said, 'He's the one who did all the damage. He is the master of the gang, [that killed our boys].' I never told any of the boys to go, seven, eight, nine [year-olds].

Otherwise, Leon did not want to leave the farm to live amongst the Nazis. In his short life, he had witnessed, at their hands, atrocities of torture, execution and mass murder. How could anyone trust them? The week leading up to his departure was full of anxiety and foreboding.

> They didn't know what they were [going to do] with the people.

They knew not to trust the Germans, but they also knew that failure to show up on the day could mean his execution. Of course, Leon could leave, run up into the mountains, and try to link up with the resistance to fight the Germans. At just fifteen, his life expectancy there could be very limited. Either way, his family would pay the price. Stephan would have to leave the farm and take his place, and the Germans would punish them for allowing Leon to flee. In the end, there was only one viable option.

> We never knew what they would do to us. They tell us one thing, but then they do something else, but I knew I had to go.

Mikal also had to go. It had been a few months since the shrapnel from the bomb had torn his calf apart, but while he walked with a slight limp, he was capable of work. Another cousin, Zophia, ten years Leon's senior, was among other relatives who had to go. Born in Pidlyptsi in 1917, Zophia, at twenty-five, was the eldest of three daughters. Her biological father died fighting in the First World War, leaving his wife Olga pregnant with Zophia.

Eighty years later, daughter Helina explained,

> She was going to marry my mum's father, but he went to war and was killed. Olga then married a man named Michael Jarosz, who adopted my mum. He also had two other daughters, and when the Germans came around to take people to labour camps, he gave them my mum [the inference being that Zophia was chosen because she was not his biological daughter].

The conquered lands were a godsend to the Nazis. All told, over the next two or so years, they were to supply more than three million boys and girls as slaves for the German Reich. Like livestock, they became the possession of their owner and provided they were fed and kept in reasonable condition, they could serve a purpose as needed. They had no rights and could be worked to death, with impunity if their master desired.

On 25 May 1942, when Leon and a group of his peers arrived at Zolochiv station, they had no idea of the fate that awaited them, nor the conditions in which they would have to exist.

Meanwhile, all across all of Germany's conquered lands, similar transports were occurring. The Nazis permitted only one suitcase per person for the thousand-plus-kilometre journey. Leon's mother packed a change of clothes for him and filled the rest of his luggage with food and water. Zolochiv's mayor was there to greet them together with an unusually large group of German soldiers who lined them up and took down their names.

> There was about, that I know, eighteen of us, the same age as me. All had to go. There were fourteen boys and four or five girls.

They first needed to be examined by an optimistic doctor.

> Then there was a doctor, who walked down the line, checking us to see if we were healthy. When my turn came, he had a good look at me, especially my teeth and in my ears; and then he said, 'You're a strong young boy. You come and work in Germany for a year or two until we win the war then you can come home.'

Having passed, Leon worried that Mikal, having lost a significant portion of his calf, would be excluded, although that might not be such a bad thing if he could turn round and go home. No one, however, failed.

> That is all they said. 'Oh, you'll be back again. You'll learn the language, you'll have a good job and all this. We'll look after you over there.' Naturally, they thought they would win the war in a year, and then everything would be in order again.

One can imagine the mayor taking the limelight with an optimistic speech. It all must have sounded straightforward enough.

After each of the conscripts received a clean bill of health, the group walked with their families, escorted by German soldiers, to the tracks, where they waited for their train. When it finally arrived, everyone was surprised to see that it was not a regular seated train, but a cattle truck. German soldiers stepped forward to slide open the doors. Instead of seeing cattle inside, the carriage contained the peering and anguished eyes of a large group of boys and girls, just like themselves. The soldiers gave them no time to process their thoughts. *'Schnell, schnell, einsteigen.*

Zolochiv station. The façade has remained virtually unchanged since the 1870s. Leon and the others arrived here on 25 May 1942. The Bürgermeister was there to bid them farewell. They were to be gone for a year. What a surreal feeling it was to stand there and imagine that extraordinary moment in history when the children, with Nazis at the watch, stood there with their families and awaited their fate.

Quickly, quickly, get in,' they cried, as the children scrambled on board, squeezing in with those already there, and with barely time to say a proper goodbye.

Leon quickly embraced his family.

As his mother hugged him, she whispered, 'Tell them you are fourteen, not fifteen.'

Why she chose, impulsively, perhaps, to offer that advice is unknown. Maybe she had insights, or perhaps it was just a gut feeling; either way, the repercussions of that advice changed everything. Meanwhile, little Mykhas had become inconsolable and would not let go of Leon's hand, so that he could not board the train. Just in time, Leon and Stephan forced Mykhas's grip to break as an angry soldier approached, ready to strike with the butt of his rifle. Then, with all children on board, soldiers abruptly slammed shut the carriage doors. The families struggled for a final glimpse of their loved ones while those inside scrambled for the air slots to see their loved ones one last time.

With a huge groan, the train jolted from its inertia to begin its long journey. It didn't take long for the children to realise that this was not a pleasant trip.

> Then they took us just like cattle, you know. We were close together, you see, you had no room to…there was no toilet, there was nothing at all in there. If you want to piss, you do it in your trousers. It was for two days.

Two days without a toilet meant that everyone in that train at least had to urinate and probably defecate as well during the journey. When they peed, they tried to go near the edges so the urine would run out through the cracks down the sides. Inevitably, however, in the middle of summer, the environment soon became extremely foul. It was incredibly demeaning for the occupants, who had arrived clean, well dressed and hopeful.

From Zolochiv, the train proceeded slowly westward, occasionally stopping to pick up more passengers. Within hours, they reached the city of Lviv, where they stopped for several hours before taking on more passengers.

The train then crossed into Poland and stopped at the city of Krakow. Leon peered through the cracks to see that they were unloading a group of older men and women from one of the front carriages and replacing them with much younger ones. The following morning, after a sleepless night, they finally opened the doors, not to let anyone out, but to force another group of Polish youth into the already overcrowded cattle carts. When they opened the doors to let them in, the pungent smell of piss and shit completely overwhelmed the startled youth.

> Inside you would do whatever you want to do. The stink everywhere was terrible.

They would not have entered the cattle carts of their own volition.

At first, the Polish children concluded that all Ukrainians stank. However, it was not long before nature called, and they realised the stench had nothing to do with Ukrainian hygiene. Before long, they all got used to the smell, and whenever fresh passengers got on, they went through a similar process.[55]

From Krakow, the train travelled west into Germany.

> Then they stopped first at Dresden and then at Leipzig, to take some people out, mostly men and older boys and girls.

At Dresden, a German officer stepped forward and, not wanting to get too close to the stench, called out that all boys fifteen and older were to get out there. Leon badly wanted to get off the train, but he remembered his mother's words: 'Tell them you're fourteen.' He stayed silent.

Unknown to Leon, most of the *Ostarbeiter* (eastern workers),[56] who got off in Nazi Germany's industrial north (formerly Prussia), perished within a few months. Often, they dumped them in temporary camps, where many starved or died of diseases like cholera or typhus. Others were forced to work in perilous occupations with no regard to health and safety. Life expectancy was short.

Ostarbeiter Katarina was one of the lucky ones who lived to tell her story. Initially, she had to work in a factory where they turned molten metal into parts for tanks and planes. Katarina worked up to eighteen hours a day with no breaks or food, other than a bowl of foul, watery stew soup and a piece of bread before and after the shift. The heat and the flames were unbearable. Fumes penetrated deep into her lungs and burned into her eyes. There was no protective equipment issued and no consideration for the person as a human being. At night, she would lie in agony, her respiratory system clogged with dust and ash; she coughed up coal-black phlegm throughout the night and day. Her eyes felt like sandpaper and burned like fire.

Others died from starvation or endured severe, often life-ending beatings. Arbitrary murder and executions were commonplace. Rights? What rights? Eventually, the fumes and the heat had rendered Katarina all but blind and with chronic emphysema. As soon as the Nazis realised that she could no longer be productive, they would undoubtedly have killed her.

Katarina's lifeline occurred when a new doctor arrived at her foundry. His job was not to medicate but to assess. Those deemed fit could return to work, while those deemed unfit suffered death in various ways, including gassing, lethal injection, shooting, being beaten or starved to death. Occasionally, the doctor might send someone considered saveable to the infirmary. Many died there regardless, but at least they had a chance.

The doctor who reviewed Katarina should have sent her to her death. Still, he took pity on her and, after a week in the infirmary, insisted on her transfer to 'light duties' where she spent the rest of the war in the tailor's department, repairing and making clothing for soldiers and officers. The move undoubtedly saved her life; she survived the war and eventually moved to Australia.[57]

> The train went on and on. We didn't know what's going on. The next thing, the train stopped, took some people out, mostly boys, men. The train goes a bit further. Then it stopped again, take some more off. I thought, 'What the hell are they going to do with us?' You know, everybody was scared. But they were taking the oldest, older, growing up people, but we were only kids. I don't know where they took them – maybe different work, different factories, you know, so they can look after them. Maybe they already trained to be soldiers. We were only boys. What can a fifteen-year-old boy do?

Some of the older boys had to join the Wehrmacht. However, they fought not as equals but as virtual cannon fodder. For example, if there were a minefield to cross, the *Untermensch* had to go first.

The young, pretty girls suffered severely as well. Often the Nazis forced them to work as sex slaves, and rape and murder were commonplace. They eliminated without mercy any worker falling pregnant or contracting a sexually transmitted disease. Sadly, that was the inevitable consequence for almost all of the victims.

The young Ukrainians, including Leon, Mikal and Zophia, knew nothing of this. Their journey continued.

Fortunately, their loved ones had packed food and water into their travel bags for most of them on the long journey.

> Mam gave me something in my bag, you know, we used to eat at night, a little. I used to give Mikal a little bit.

Despite their rationing, by the time they headed south-east into Czechoslovakia, everyone had run out of food and was starving. However, the biggest problem was dehydration. It is common knowledge that people can live for weeks without food but only a few days without water. The oppressive heat and cramped, poorly ventilation quarters served to exacerbate their thirst.

By the time they stopped in the Czech capital city of Prague, the heat and stale air had created almost unbearable conditions. Severe dehydration typically causes increased lethargy and weakness, headaches, hallucinations and, finally, death. One desperate boy noticed that the Germans were loading water onto the train and took matters into his own hands.

> It was packed, the train was packed, there was no water on it. I remember one boy about my age; somehow, he opened the [sliding] door because it was a cattle train and not the kind of train where you can sit down, a cattle train, and he was very thirsty and they were pumping water into the, filling up, the train, you know. Every train has to have water. They were filling up, they ran out of water, and he ran out, and the German [soldier] shouted to him, 'Stop,' and he didn't understand…and they shot him. He was only a young boy.

Leon and some of the others began to follow but instantly clambered back inside as the boy, killed by a single bullet, fell to the ground.

> I thought what a horrible people these Germans are. Fancy shooting a boy like that. He didn't do anything wrong he just wanted a drink of water. Everybody was scared.

Eventually, they were under way again, but the journey had become a nightmare. Fortunately, the carriages' occupants were young and fit, but the heat and dehydration sapped their energy.

> Some people couldn't stand it any longer.

Then, just as they were nearing the end of their endurance,

> We stopped at a place called Pilzen, where they gave us something to drink, water, just to keep us alive.

It was highly unlikely for the Nazis to have given them water out of kindness. Their cargo of slaves served an essential purpose for the Third Reich war machine. They could not afford to be the suppliers of damaged goods.

The train was still packed and stiflingly hot with little ventilation and no sanitation. Still, the respite at Pilzen was a godsend on the way to their destinations.

> [Finally], we stopped at the border with Germany; they [still] wouldn't let us go out. Everybody was [still] thirsty, you know…and then the next morning, we landed in Bavaria.
>
> Then they took us, oh about a hundred boys, into Bavaria to a place called Cham. The train stopped. That was where Mikal and I got off.

The doors to the cattle truck opened, and the bright sunshine temporarily blinded the occupants. A set of German soldier's eyes peered inside the dark carriage and for a moment, the fumes that poured from out from the opened doors caused him to shake his head in disgust. Soon, he had gathered his composure enough to scream out a string of foreign words. It was not long before Leon realised their meaning. '*Raus, raus, schnell, schnell.* Out, out, quick, quick.'

Leon and Mikal were pleased to scramble off the train.

> The stink, everything was terrible.

They were happy to be outside in the fresh air. The guard indicated for the last few other boys and girls to stay. Worried looks must have passed between the children, who had bonded in a way that they would never forget.

Leon and Mikal stepped from the train and were ordered towards a nearby building. Meanwhile, the train lurched forward to continue south towards Munich. Zofia travelled on to the Pfarrkirchen labour camp, not far from the Austrian border. It was the last they would ever see or hear of each other.[58]

> Straight away, they took us inside. The women cut all of our hair off and showered us. [They had to shave] all our hair because we had lice. Then you put whatever you had, your clothes back on. All the clothes were sprayed with something [(to get rid of the lice], and then we had to put the old clothes back on. There was no washing [them] until I got to Haschaberg.
> They shaved, women everything and men, hair, and everything. Under the arms, our [pubic] hair, everywhere... very naked. Examine every one of them.

I asked Leon whether he found the ordeal embarrassing.

> No, not at that age. It wasn't embarrassing. If she was not embarrassed to do it to me, then why should I be embarrassed? What do you think? That it was her job to do it. She didn't do just one, she did everyone. There were stacks of them. She shaved us like shaving sheep, you know.

Having examined them all, the medical staff found them fit for work and sent them to their next destination. Unbeknown to Leon and the others, had they not been in good health, and therefore of no use to the German war effort, there was only one outcome – murder. There were no provisions made for the care of *Untermensch*. Legally, there was little difference between them and other conventional livestock.

> Then we went to a big [place], like a warehouse. They gave us something to eat and drink there.

It was such a relief for the children to feel relatively clean, fed and human again.

> It was pretty good there – we were all happy and talking.

They began to forget about their terrible ordeal and hoped that life in Germany might not be that bad.

Then, the next thing we were sitting down. I thought, 'What the hell's going to happen now?' Then we saw people coming in, walking around, looking, pointing, saying, 'That's the one.'

Then this man came. Then this big fellow came with a big rucksack on his back. '*Du!*' He pointed his finger at me. 'You are mine. I'm his,' he said, and another one, '*Du, auch Mein.* You're mine too.' His name was Papiransky, Nicholas Papiransky. He lives in Scotland now. Maybe he's still alive…and he took him and me. He was a little bit bigger than me, and very strong-looking too.

I wanted to go together with Mikal. I said, 'Brother, brother,' and this little fellow [pointing at Mikal] says, 'I'll take him, I'll look after him.'

They already spoke together. One lived in Geigant, and I went to Haschaberg. They knew one another. I knew more or less that they were friends.

I said, 'We're not splitting,' but the man answered, half in German half in sign language, 'Good, good, good, brother.'

I knew a bit of German then, you see, from the Germans [in Ukraine].

I wanted to go with Mikal together. I said, *'Bruder, bruder, brat, brat.'*[59]

Then this little fellow, the one who picked him [Mikal] up, said, *'Nicht weit, nicht weit!* Very close, very close. You don't live too far apart,' and with his hands, he indicated a close distance.

The boys understood and were appeased, at least for now.

Mikal, Leon and Nicolas walked with their owners back to the train station and realised that they were going on yet another train. '*Ni, ni, ni, bud laska. Nein, nein, bitte.* No, no, please,' they cried out in bits of Ukrainian and German. Not realising that the boys feared the prospect of another lengthy trip on a cattle truck, the men could not understand the boy's apprehension. However, when the train arrived, the boys calmed considerably.

Then we got back on a train from Cham. It was a proper train, with seats, not for cattle, and travelled north-east.

Such luxury!

The farmers allowed the boys to sit together in great comfort compared to the cattle carts. They could look out the windows and enjoy the beautiful countryside. Mikal and Leon began to feel optimistic about their future in Germany.

> I thought, 'Maybe it's not so bad here, after all.'

After about half an hour, they stopped at a small town called Geigant. It was there that Mikal's farmer indicated that it was time for them to get off the train. Once again, the boys feared separation.

> I wouldn't let him go. [They] said, 'Nächste station, nachste station. Next station, we get out.'

The boys could not understand, so he mimed, pointing to his watch and indicating that their destination, Zillendorf, was very close. Leon realised what he meant and explained to Mikal, 'He says this station, you get out, and we get off the next one.'

In time, Mikal found his farmer to be a kind and understanding man. He was extremely fortunate compared to most *Ostarbeiter*.

> It was a small farm. The owner was a nice man. It was nice there. They had only one cow. He had two girls [his daughters]. There was just an old man and an old lady. The girls managed the farm.

Leon, Nicholas and the farmer crossed the road and stopped at a restaurant near the station. They sat outside, where the farmer ordered the boys to sit on the ground near the big wooden table at which he sat. The farmer talked to the waiter, who brought him back a big glass of black beer and handed each boy a metal mug filled with water. For a treat, their first and only, the farmer gave each boy *ein bischen bier*, a little beer that the boys slurped thirstily. Even though they did not like the taste, it was wet, and it was cold; it was good.

> Then the farmer had a big rucksack, and he opened it up and gave me a big slice of beautiful white bread with salami or whatever it was, and gave one to Nicolas. Oh yeah, we ate that straight away, you know, no problem. Oh, it was beautiful. We didn't look at what was inside, we just ate it.

After they had eaten, the man indicated they should start walking. Leon noticed that the countryside was similar but somehow different from Ukraine, but could not grasp it. No more than ten minutes later, they arrived at a farmhouse, where the farmer indicated they could get out. They waited nervously while the farmer went inside.

A minute later, a group of younger people and an older woman came out to look at them. They talked, evaluating the boys as if evaluating cattle. They laughed and pointed at them from time to time but generally ignored them as far as welcomes go.

By that time, it was already late in the afternoon. The boys knew that they now belonged to the farmer. He now had total control over them. If he decided that their lives were not worth living, he could have them killed..

According to the Nazis, Leon Sokulsky was a subhuman, worthy only to serve.

> There was no paperwork to fill out, nothing at all. Maybe he did have to fill out something, some paperwork, sign some documents. I don't know, but it had nothing to do with me. I signed nothing.

The farmer communicated that his name was Leis, and then he showed the boys their room, an improvised outside shed, rather than a room. Mercifully, he ordered, *'Jetzt schlafen.* Now sleep.'

There would be many nights over the following years when Leon would see the glorious yellow wheat fields and rolling hills beneath the blue skies of Pidlyptsi in his dreams. Sometimes he dreamt of riding Shimmel, or of his mother or brother Mykhas, and always awoke disappointed. That first night, however, was not one of those nights. As soon as he placed his head on the raw mattress that lay on the floor, he was asleep.

27

The Tide is Turning – Maria, 1943

After Germany failed to take Russia before the winter, the death toll rose rapidly. Sometimes, the young men lasted a matter of weeks before they died. Before the end of 1942, there were five more confirmed deaths in the parish, with at least as many missing, never to be found.

On 12 February 1943, Maria celebrated her twenty-third birthday. A month later, she received news of the death of Johann Preiße. He was the first of her cousins to receive the call-up and was killed by a Soviet shell, on her birthday, as it happened. For the rest of her life, Maria remembered her beloved cousin on her special day.

Following enormous losses at Stalingrad, the German High Command amassed thousands of recruits to reinforce their next primary resistance line at Kursk. Most of the recruits, including Johann, went to an early death there. It was an increasingly unspeakable time for their families.

It was against this backdrop of despair that, in quick succession, the remaining young men in the parish, including Xaver, Wolfgang and Willi, received the letter they hoped would never come, ordering them to report for duty. Maria always believed that it was payback for their lack of support for Hitler that the Nazis sent the men of Döfering parish to the Russian front.

They all had to go. No one wanted to go! No one.

Xaver spent much of his leave with Maria. On their last day, they went out for a long walk, and after stopping at their favourite spot by the river, they sat down for a picnic lunch. Xaver had no idea where they would send him. Maria made him promise to write. After they ate, they sat for a long time, holding hands, with tears in their eyes. It was there that Xaver pledged that if he came back, he would marry Maria. The next morning, he, along with the conscripted others, headed out for a short and inadequate training period. Within a few weeks, they set off for the Russian front.

No wonder the boys had no passion for war. They had seen their peers leave and had attended their funerals. Now was it their turn to die?

Every day that passed with no bad news, Maria counted her blessings. Too often, though, and sometimes in multiples, she heard of the deaths of those she knew. Each time, she shuddered in anticipation that it might be Xaver whose name they delivered, praying in silent thanks that he was not among the dead.

It was a dreadful time for all families. Notwithstanding that, they rejoiced when news from their loved ones arrived. There were always funerals to attend. Rarely, though, did they have a body to bury.

Germany initially welcomed war with America, but in truth, Japan had awakened a giant.[60] Now the giant was on Europe's doorstep. The USA had far greater access to manpower and military resources than Germany. Together with the Soviets, who had access to over a hundred million soldiers and factories, out of harm's way, the Allies now turned defence into attack.

Catastrophic losses ensued on the eastern front. The subsequent surrender of the Sixth Army under General Paulus, with losses of over 200,000 men at Stalingrad, in the winter of 1943, heralded the unofficial turning point in the Second World War.

The North African campaign, after a promising beginning, was now in tatters. After nearly two years of bitter fighting, where both sides oscillated between victory and defeat, the brilliance of Field Marshal Rommel could not save the Wehrmacht from total collapse and the surrender of 800,000 soldiers after Hitler, in desperation, redirected essential resources to the Russian front. Consequently, the Nazis had to widen their recruitment circle, employing ever-younger boys and ever-older men, including Maria's Uncle Alois, into their ranks. They increasingly ignored disabilities; an arm or an eye missing no longer mattered, nor did flat feet. They also reduced the time for training recruits from years to a matter of weeks, as the tides of war swung further the way of the Allies.

> I always prayed for them. Nobody wanted to go. The next-door neighbour when he left, I went outside to give him my hand, and he said, 'Pray for me, Maree.' He was about five or six years older than me.

28

Verflucter Ausländer, Arbeit – Leon, 1942/43

The next morning, we were tired, you know. He already knocked on the door.
We were sleeping outside, not where the rest of them slept. We had a little, like a bungalow building, especially for us; two of us sleeping there.
And we were tired, and he came in, and he belt hell out of me, you know. *'Aufstehen…verflucter Ausländer, arbeit!* Get up, you damn foreigner, work!'
Straight away, we went. It was half-past four the next morning.

The first night at Leis's farm was typical. Every morning at four thirty a.m. on the dot, the boys had to be up and ready to work; otherwise, Leis would belt them. There was no idea of argument; the boys just had to do work; their lives depended on it. They worked all day, often as late as ten o'clock, when they would fall fast asleep for a few hours before doing it all over again.

We just had to get on with it.

Leis fed and housed the boys for one reason only – to work. Their first job was enormous. They had to supply water to the farm from the river, all of them digging a big trench, maybe four or five feet deep, from Leis's farm to the river – about 1.6 kilometres.[61] It took weeks of backbreaking work to complete the task, but it kept them healthy and fit.

That first week, Leon realised his place in the new Third Reich. He quickly learned words that defined his reality. Words like *schnell, schnell* (fast, fast), *Du Dreckige Schwein* (you dirty pig), and *Verflucter Ausländer* (damn foreigner) became indelibly imprinted into his everyday psyche. For Leon, who was dearly loved in Ukraine, it was a completely different reality. However, one thing that sustained him that he took with him from home was his pragmatism and adaptability.

> I didn't like him at all but what could I do. You keep going on.

Leon, moreover, soon knew he had to behave very differently in a Nazi household.

> With Leis, I'll never forget that day, one day when we just had our *Mittagessen* (lunch), at twelve o'clock or one o'clock or whatever it was, and this girl, Emily, she was a very strong Hitler girl. She shouted, '*Aufsteh*. Stand up. *Hitler spricht*. Hitler speaks.' So she lifted her hand like that [Hitler salute] and held her hand while he was talking for a long time, and we had to listen too. I couldn't understand everything he said, but you have to stand still. Otherwise, I was scared.

After that, Leon knew that he had to stand to attention and salute whenever Hitler spoke.

Ludwig Leis had sons who had recently enlisted, and three daughters. The family must have been incredibly proud of the boys, secure in the thought that, while their work was dangerous, they were a part of a historic mission. Leon and Nicholas were given to Leis to replace his sons. Perhaps that is why he detested them. 'How could two stupid boys replace his sons,' he likely thought. Leis's eldest and namesake was on short leave at the time of Leon's arrival.

> Two days later, his son came home from the front on holiday, you know. Ludwig, Ludwig Leis.

During his leave, there was a big family celebration to wish him well before his return to the front.

The next day, Leon was working in the field when Ludwig approached him with a thick stick in his hand. He said, 'Russian, Ruskie? Are you Russian?'

'*Nicht Ruskie, Ukrayina*. Not Russian, Ukrainian,' Leon replied, nervously as Ludwig pointed the stick an inch from Leon's face.

'Oh, Ukrayina… I shoot Ruskie, tuh, tuh, tuh, tuh; tuh. Oh, Ukrayina,' replied Ludwig as he swung the weapon from side to side, mimicking the actions of a machine gun. 'I shoot Ruskie, tuh, tuh, tuh, tuh…,' Ludwig repeated. To make sure Leon got the message, Ludwig pretended to fire his fake rifle straight at Leon's face. 'You, Ruskie, dead!'

Leon stared back, not knowing what to do or say and half-expecting Ludwig to strike him at any moment, which he could have done, had he wanted to. Instead, Ludwig stood there laughing, until finally, to Leon's great relief, he turned and walked away.

A few days later, Ludwig departed for the front, but not before leaving Leon a gift.

> He brought some clothes for me. He gave us clothes that he probably pinched from Ukraine or Russia.

Shortly thereafter, Leon was working outside when the mailman arrived. Before long, he heard a terrifying cry of grief coming from inside the house. He quickly entered the home to a perplexing sight. The whole family was weeping.

> He [Ludwig] went back again, and in about three weeks, four weeks later, Mam [Maria] will tell you, the postman came and said he was dead.

Yet another young man had died on the Russian front. Leon crept back to work. A few days later, he attended a typical wartime memorial.

> They had a funeral and his photograph, not a proper funeral, but just his photograph.

Leon's daily chores included ploughing, sowing, harvesting and chopping down trees for firewood and construction, and tending to many animals that produced farm products. The long hours kept him strong and healthy. The boys lived off the farm. They usually ate fruit or pickled vegetables, together with *Schinken* (ham) and water to drink.

Being growing boys, they were always hungry, so they pinched and consumed extra food when no one was looking, even at the risk of a beating.

That first winter was incredibly harsh. Leon had experienced freezing conditions in Ukraine but always had adequate winter clothing and housing to keep out the cold. The nights were bitterly cold in Leon's wooden room. He quickly learned that the most important thing was to have dry socks and shoes. After a long day of work, if his clothes were dry, he simply climbed into bed as he was. There was no suggestion of a shower or a bath in the winter. In the summer, he would have to jump into the river to wash.

The following February, Leon turned sixteen, his first birthday in Germany. Nobody cared to wish him a happy birthday.

29

Meeting Leon/The Doctor – Maria, 1942/43

One afternoon, Maria was at Brückl's farm, helping with the hay collection, when her eyes fixed upon a young man walking across the paddock.

> It was in June, I think. He was outside, and he came [over] with the next-door neighbour, [who lived] just another acre from where we were working. He, too, had been working in the fields, replacing another man who was sent to war. He was dressed in ragged work clothes and appeared very dirty.

As he came closer, the two, for a fleeting moment, made eye contact. Maria's first words to him were not 'Hello', but 'What religion are you?' Surprisingly, he understood and replied that he was Catholic.[62]

At first, Maria had little to do with Leon, except that they were co-workers at times. She laughed at the idea of any sort of relationship in those early days.

> Ha, ha. He couldn't talk. Sometimes I worked near him, but I never really spoke to him, and he never really spoke to me.

In the order of things, Maria did feel that Leon, being Ukrainian, suggested a higher status than other races. When I asked about this, she replied, 'Oh, I don't think so. He wasn't treated as badly as other people. He was an *Ostarbeiter*. Some Ukrainians fought in the German army.'

Fortunately for Maria and Leon, a romance did not immediately develop. Ukrainians may have been a step up from Russians and other Slavic races. However, according to the 1935 Nuremberg Race Laws, Ukrainians fell under the Slavic/*Untermensch* category. Undoubtedly, Leon would have been lucky to survive the minimum sentence of one year of hard labour in a concentration camp if he and Maria began an intimate relationship. Maria, on the other hand, might have been seen as his victim. If she played her cards right, she might have received a warning. Not that it mattered, because Leon was too scared to talk to her, and Maria was, for the moment, not interested.

> I got to know him. He said his name was Leon, but I didn't like him at all.

Was it because he was an *Untermensch*?

> It was not about that.

If first impressions were important, Leon's appearance would not have done him any favours.

> He had developed an infected mouth, and when the problem worsened, I had to go to the doctor with him to get some scabs fixed.

That day, the weather was miserable, so Brückl let Maria take his wagon. It was in the middle of winter, and deep snow covered the road. On the way, Maria visited Maree, who had become very ill with pneumonia. Maria ordered Leon to wait outside in the cold while she went in.

After a while, Maria mentioned that she was on her way to take Leon to the doctor.

'Where is he?' cried Maree, and mercifully insisted that he come in for a warm drink.

Afterwards, Leon and Maria continued on their journey to Waldmünchen. Waldmünchen, located close to the Czech border, was a beautiful, vibrant town that had become a hub for the movement of Wehrmacht troops.

The doctor examined Leon before prescribing medication for the scabs.

Next, they walked to a nearby shoe shop.

> There, I got into conflict with the big Nazis.

Maria had vowed never to use the Eisfeld shop in Cham now that Nazis owned it, and instead chose the shoe shop in Waldmunchen. Maria brought along her ration card to get herself some winter shoes, and Brückl provided her with a card for Leon, who had worn out and grown out of his old shoes.

Inside the shop, they hung up their coats and, Maria, with Leon in tow, began to browse for shoes. The store manager, a middle-aged fat man who wore a Nazi party badge, approached. Maria provided him with a certificate for two pairs of shoes, one pair of second-hand work boots for Leon, and one for herself.

The manager became annoyed when he asked Leon a question. 'What's wrong with him? Why doesn't he talk?'

'He's Ukrainian,' replied Maria.

'An *Untermensch?*'

Maria tried the silent treatment.

Leon got the message and left the store.

The manager was suddenly terse. 'We have no shoes for you. Look, you have shoes on your feet. You want to have winter shoes while our boys freeze to death?'

> I told him off a few times. I said, 'My shoes wouldn't fit a soldier, but yours would!'

He was so annoyed; he did not know what to say, but Maria continued,

> You've got a nice place here. It's warm here. Come on, change with me. Give me your job, and you take mine, and then you'll see how much shoes you need outside in the woods, in the fields, in the wintertime in the snow.

Maria passed over the coupon which, legally, he had to accept.

Reluctantly, he handed over the shoes, but not without a parting shot. 'I will have you arrested for insulting a Nazi party member.'

Maria went home frightened, but with two pairs of shoes. For the next few weeks, however, she expected that at any moment the Gestapo would come and take her away.

The store manager disappeared soon after that, and the shop had new owners again. Maria heard that he was in Dachau. That is how it was in those days. Nobody was safe.

30

Georg Brückl – Leon, Mid-1943

July 1943 saw yet another central turning point for Hitler's Germany. After taking control of the Mediterranean, Allied forces landed on mainland Italy and began bombing Rome. Italy, Germany's closest ally, then sacked and imprisoned its bull-headed leader, Benito Mussolini. The new Italian government supported Germany, but by September, after the Allies had overrun southern Italy, the new government surrendered. Hitler reacted by sanctioning his daring and successful rescue from his prison in the mountains of northern Italy. Next, he placed Mussolini at the head of Italy's resistance in northern Italy, where his forces prepared their winter defensive line at Monte Cassino.

At that time, just when it seemed that Leon would spend the war with the tyrannical Leis, his life was about to change again.

> Then, a year afterward, the next-door neighbour had a young boy working for him, and he had to go to the army. He was a German, so they took me into Brückl. I had to go there, so they left Nicholas with Leis.
>
> He had to go straight away to the army. I don't know what happened to him. He was about seventeen or eighteen. He had to go.

After a year of backbreaking work and many floggings,[63] Leon left with only the clothes he wore and not even a thank you. He was pleased to go but sorry to leave behind his friend Nicholas. He held no grudge.

> I owed them nothing, and they owed me nothing.

It was in the summer of 1943 when Leis transferred his ownership of Leon to Brückl. There was no changeover ceremony and not even a

Brückl's house, the second building in the foreground, as it was in the 1940s. The shabbier wooden structure in the foreground is the stable where Leon slept for two years during the war. It had two levels; the upper level is where he lived while horses and cows lived below, keeping him warm in the winter. None of the original buildings still stand. Nearly eighty years later, Georg's grandson, Oliver, used some of the original timbers in the building of his own home.

document to sign. Leis did not bother walking Leon over to his new home; he left that to Emily, who never spoke to him. Leon noticed, however, a difference in her since the death of her brother. No longer was she the confident, self-assured, opinionated and fanatical young woman he knew.

After handing Leon over to Brückl, Emily looked at him with sad eyes and murmured, '*Auf wiedersehen*, Leon.' It was the first time she had spoken to him cordially. Thenceforth, he became the property of the farmer, Georg Brückl.

Brückl was the quintessential Bavarian if ever there was one. Unlike the wiry, stubble-faced Leis, Brückl was dark-haired, broad-shouldered, stocky and clean-shaven; a formidable and powerful man, who, it seemed, could crush a person in a second if he wanted to. Leon nervously waited for his new master's orders and was surprised when instead of shouting at him or even belting him, he smiled and asked if he was hungry before passing him a piece of wurst (sausage). Leon devoured the gift at once. *'Danke viermals,* Herr Brückl. Thank you very much, Mr Brückl.'

'Now, to work.'

Unlike the Leis family, the Brückls were different. Leon still worked for nothing, but they treated him better. There was a sense of caring and kindness about them from the outset. As Christians, they believed that all people were created equal. Leon joined the family for daily prayer and weekly mass.

Despite Brückl's compassion, Leon still slept on a bed of straw in an outside stable. Below him, horses and cows shared his living quarters. The smell and heat in the summer were unwelcome, but the livestock's rising body heat kept him warm during the freezing winters.

Leon, nevertheless, kept his head down.

> I was too scared to say anything because maybe it would make things worse. Maybe he would give me a belting like Leis did.

But that never happened.

> You see, he never belted me. Brückl never belted me.

The Brückl family had five young children. Ludwig, the eldest, had just reached his teens, and Sepp, the youngest, was only two at the time. Leon had a natural affinity with children, and his master did not seem to mind when he played hide 'n' seek with the children even though he should have been working.

One rule did favour Ukrainians over the other *Ostarbeiters* because they did not have to wear identification to mark them as inferior.

> The Polish had to carry a P, the Russians an OST. The Ukrainians didn't have to carry anything. We could go to a restaurant. They treated us better.

Regardless, when Leon met Maria, he knew her to be in a different class and at the threat of cutting his life short, he could not risk any form of intimacy.

> I could never give her a thought as far as that goes. It wasn't allowed. I was too busy working.

Had things been different, he might have developed feelings for the beautiful farm girl, seven years his senior, who treated him with ambivalence. Leon was unaware that she had a boyfriend who was on the Front.

31

For Whom the Bell Tolls – Maria, Winter 1944

> No man is an island, Entire of itself.
> Each is a piece of the continent, a part of the main.
> If a clod be washed away by the sea, Europe is the less.
> As well as if a promontory were.
> As well as is a manor of thine own or of thine friends were.
> Each man's death diminishes me, for I am involved in mankind.
> Therefore, send not to know for whom the bell tolls; it tolls for thee.
> John Donne

Although it started well, 1944 was the worst year of the war. Initially, Maria had heard of no deaths amongst her closest friends on the Front. Every day, she breathed a sigh of relief when the mail carrier arrived empty-handed. He or she was always the first to know who had died and passed the bad news on to other households. On the upside, when a parent or loved one received word that their son was alive and well, the mail carrier passed on the good news.

From the summer of 1944, a terrible series of events began. First came word that Maria's childhood friend, Wolfgang, had died, along with thousands more in the siege of Sevastopol. The area was pivotal because it housed much of the Russian fleet and allowed Germany access to her ally Romania and her essential oilfields at Baku. Shortly after that, the death of Maria's favourite cousin, Willi, also on the Russian front, dealt her another savage blow. Albert was the only one of the three Preiße brothers who remained alive. He was the youngest, and, having just received orders, arrived at the front, knowing that he was the last.[64] His family no doubt wished that the war would end before he had to fight. They were to wish in vain. All three of her cousins, those she spent so much of her childhood with, died before the war's end.

Maria held onto the hope that Xaver would stay alive.

On 6 June 1944, after months of comprehensive planning, the Allies unleashed Operation Overlord, or D-Day, the largest and best-equipped invasion force thus far in history. Over three hundred thousand Allied troops successfully breached the German defences at Normandy in France. Ironically, it was a similar number to that which retreated from Dunkirk four years earlier. Within days, the number had swelled to over a million. Despite fierce opposition, and heavy losses in places, the Allies were too strong and continued to press inland, establishing a solid bridgehead. The Nazis were never to recover.

Most Germans barely heard about the invasion. As far as the news went, a small, insignificant landing had occurred, and the Wehrmacht and the Luftwaffe had the situation under control.

On the farm, the work continued, and while Maria saw Leon only as a labourer, she got to see and work with him for long hours, almost every day. Eventually, his face cleared up from his infection, and Maria could not help but notice that underneath the scabs lay a strong and handsome young man. Despite being seven years younger, Leon could not help but see the beautiful German girl who worked long hours by his side.

Brückl occasionally allowed Leon inside to eat with Maria and the family. In time, Maria's terse task-oriented comments became friendlier, and, as Leon learned the language, the two were able to converse. Maria never made Leon feel as though he was inferior and, as time passed, her kindness shone through.

One day she walked home to find a letter waiting at the front door. It had her address on the front and Xaver's name written neatly on the back. She opened the letter with a mixture of fear and excitement that turned to great relief and joy when she saw the handwriting belonged to Xaver, and he had written exclusively to her. In it, he expressed to Maria how much he missed her and the precious times they had together. He said that he longed for the war to end, to come home to marry her.

> At the end, he said, and I will always remember his last words to me. He said, '*Mary, bitte vergiss mir nicht, eurer Xaver*. Maria, please do not forget me, your Xaver.'

By the time Maria received it, he was already dead.

> Then he died; straight away. He died at the Black Sea, [at] Sevastopol, like Wolfgang.
> It broke my heart; so many times. We heard that our boys were dead – always in Russia.

Although the Cham region had hitherto been spared, word began to spread about the bombing and decimation of great German cities, like Hamburg and Cologne, resulting in massive civilian casualties. Initially, in the early stages of the war, no one compared the conflict to the Great War of 1914–18. However, as time passed and the death count rose exponentially, people realised that this war was already as awful as the last one.

But the worst was yet to come.

German radio and newspapers remained defiant, claiming that Germany was about to record a massive victory. Were that true, one might wonder why Joseph Goebbels, the minister for propaganda, saw fit to coin the phrases 'total war' and *'Rolle für den Seig'*.[65] Under that premise, he demanded that Germany sacrifice everything, committing all available resources and priorities to the war effort, to ensure victory.

The German High Command, however, had not reckoned on a long, drawn-out winter war in Russia and thus sent its troops into sub-zero conditions, unprepared. Most Germans gave warm blankets and so forth to the winter appeal, not for the sake of victory but for the unfortunate soldiers dying on the Russian Front. If Russian bullets did not kill them, the Russian winter surely would.

Hitler's policy of not retreating was to have devastating effects on the war. Had he adopted a pragmatic approach and strategically withdrawn armies from Stalingrad, Sevastopol and North Africa, for example, he might have saved many hundreds of thousands of lives. On the other hand, his stupidity shortened the war considerably.

While many forfeited their lives for the sake of one lunatic's ego, others, except if the Russians captured them, enjoyed an early end to the war in an allied prison camp. Word soon spread that you were far better off being captured by the Americans or British. Another of Maria's close cousins, Alois Junglas, disappeared at the front. Either the Russians killed him outright, or he, like a million others, perished in a Soviet gulag.

By 1944, nearly all of Germany's major cities were the victims of frequent bombing raids, usually the Americans by day and the British during the night. Cham, being smaller and of less military significance, was spared. Consequently, many evacuees, deserters, and bona fide Nazis began to flood into town, seeking refuge. In his fanaticism, Hitler refused to allow for surrender or retreat and labelled his cities and towns, including Cham, 'fortresses'. This meant that each person had orders to fight to the death.

32

Soviets Regain Ukraine – Leon, 1944

> Uki boys work our farms while our boys are away. There's work to do, more than enough for you.
> Don't worry. It'll be all right. You'll see your family soon when all is done, and the war is won. It'll be all right. You'll be home soon.[66]

Nazis promised Leon that Germany would win the war, and he would be home within a year. After that first year had passed, instead of organising a trip back home, Leon found himself at another German farm, albeit with a better family. Brückl never made any such promise.

Brückl knew that some thirteen-year-olds were already fighting with the *Volkssturm* and was scared that Ludwig would, like so many others, have to sacrifice his life needlessly. Brückl had experienced the horrors of the First World War. Now he longed for the arrival of the approaching American troops.

Often, whether he was working or resting, Leon's mind found itself back in Ukraine. He would see his parents or his little brother, who was now seven. They would be on the farm, and everything would be as it was. Then something would go wrong; someone would come, perhaps the SS officer who murdered Julik. Sometimes he would be there when the bomb went off, and he would see his friend's beanie in the tree, dripping with blood. At other times, his thoughts would often be about his family and what they were doing. It was harvest time. Was Stephan still collecting the cherries? Would Mykhas be helping now? How was the wheat this year?

Unbeknown to him, Leon had good cause to be concerned about his family. Two years had passed since his departure in 1942, and so much had happened in that time. By April 1944, the Russian front had moved to within sight of Pidlyptsi, to the nearby city of Ternopil, where weeks of Soviet bombardment with heavy artillery culminated in savage fighting, street by street and house to house. The Germans had no respect for the Russians, and the Russians had no respect for the Germans. Archival footage of the battle reveals German soldiers surrendering, broken, and at their wits' end. By the time it was over, nearly fourteen thousand Germans had lain dead there, and a further two thousand surrendered. These were the pitiful remnants of the once-almighty Wehrmacht. All this occurred less than thirty kilometres away from Leon's farm in Pidlyptsi, where Stephan, Marika and Mykhas waited glumly for the Russians to arrive.

Having captured Ternopil, the Soviets, now in pre-war Polish territory, halted their advance while other sectors, particularly those in the south, caught up. The front line had moved to Pidlyptsi's doorstep. In early July, the Soviets advanced. Fortunately, for the Mykulyshyn family, the Germans had retreated beyond Pidlyptsi to Zolochiv. The Soviets simply poured their army through the farmlands unopposed. By Christmas, they had advanced as far as the German border, awaiting the final push to Berlin.

If Leon's family sensed some relief that the war had passed them by, it was to be short-lived. A few days later, Stephan was outside tending to the yard when a Soviet truck arrived. Armed soldiers stepped out and ordered him, at gunpoint, to get in the back with the others. Markia and Mykhas barely had time to kiss him goodbye, and off he went without even packing a bag. Following the liberation, if you could call it that, the Soviets scoured the Ukrainian countryside, picking up every able-bodied male. The vehicles then went to Zolochiv station, where, like his stepson two years earlier, he too had to endure a cattle cart journey. At least in 1942, Leon knew roughly where he was going; Stephan had no idea where they were taking him.

33

To Help a Friend – Maria, 1944

Japan's superiority in the Pacific was short-lived. As with the English, the American codebreakers also succeeded in determining in advance their enemy's military operations. Consequently, a series of massive defeats of the Japanese imperial forces ensured that the Americans had the upper hand. They now controlled the sea as well as the air and land. One by one, Japanese controlled islands in the Pacific region fell to the US forces until Tokyo herself was within range. By the end of 1944, the Americans dominated the skies in both the Pacific and the Atlantic.

As the war in Europe looked lost, there was a handful of serious attempts to assassinate Hitler. The most noteworthy occurred in July 1944, when at a war conference, Count Von Stauffenberg managed to place a bomb inside a briefcase at Hitler's feet. The weapon should have killed him instantly, but Hitler survived because, at the last minute, an attendant noticed that the case was in Hitler's way and moved it to the other side of a thick table leg. Hitler survived the ensuing explosion literally by a table leg! The coup failed. Hundreds of arrests followed and those even remotely involved were brought to what the Nazis called justice.

Trials were short; summary executions occurred; reprisals were swift and gruesome. Stauffenberg and hundreds of his co-conspirators, including two field marshals, were executed. Some suffered a slow death by hanging with piano wire, their deaths recorded for Hitler's pleasure. The guilty included General Stülpnagel, who supported the Einsatzgruppen in the mass murder of hundreds of thousands of Jews, including those at

Zolochiv Castle, and those whose deaths Leon witnessed near Pluhiv. Stülpnagel, perhaps feeling guilty of his crimes, became increasingly disillusioned with the Nazis and arranged to assist in forming a government after Hitler's death. During his interrogation, he mentioned Hitler's favourite Field Marshal Rommel. Reluctantly, Hitler ordered Rommel's execution, after which, for the sake of propaganda, he received a Third Reich hero's funeral. Security all over the country increased, and a zero-tolerance approach to resistance emerged.

Concurrently, back in Döfering, Father Rockermann heard that Father Eigat was alive, hiding and in desperate need of help. As the war progressed, people began to hear about the underground, a resistance movement that fought a secret war with the Nazis, and the black market where you could buy food and goods illegally (usually at vastly inflated prices). It was there that Father Rockermann, through a connection, heard the excellent news that Eigat was, for the moment, safe and well in the historic town of Altötting. The resistance group that had helped him to flee the Nazis had been busy throughout 1944, creating havoc. Increasingly, acts of sabotage hampered German attempts to regain control. From the clandestine blowing up of bridges and vital transport and communication networks to brazen daylight attacks on German officers, the underground became stronger and the Nazis weaker. Still, there was much to do.

Following his escape, Father Eigat managed to contact the underground, who found him a suitable safe house in Altötting, a town well away from where the Gestapo was likely to be looking for him. Without papers, he had to rely solely on his host to provide all he needed. For over a year, the arrangement worked; however, food was scarce everywhere in the winter of 1944–45. Formerly available black market goods dried up or had become too expensive, and the harsh weather had made it impossible for his host, an old woman named Gerti, to get out to the stores.

Fortunately, amid despair, an unlikely source was working behind the scenes. Knowing Father Eigat's destination and knowing that he and his host would need help to get through the winter, Eigat's friend, now interned at Dachau, risked what remained of his life.

> Somebody, through the underground, yeah, it's gone all underground, like undercover.

Gerti's contact proved to be a good one. Father Eigat's plea for help, together with his address in Altötting, found its way to St Adagio's parish in Döfering.

> More people go to pray, and that's how they could sort it out.

It was there that Father Rockermann received word from Father Eigat that he was alive but needed help; he needed food and especially ration cards. The letter included his whereabouts in Altötting. Many more lives now hung in the balance should that information fall into the wrong hands.

> They brought already from out of the concentration camp letter from this friend [about] this house in Altötting. They brought the address to...the priest's house.

The next morning, when Aunty Resel arrived to help prepare for mass, Father Rockermann was there waiting.

> My Aunty Resel was working there, and then the priest told her that very quietly, 'I don't know what to do. A friend of mine is in a concentration camp; we know that. I'm so worried about the other one. He has run away in hiding. He can't get anything to eat, he has no ration cards. He can't go anywhere, he can't buy anything because it's very expensive, and you have to buy everything with ration cards.'

The two agreed that they should meet together after Mass to formulate a plan. The church was too open, so they chose the Keil House. It's uncertain who attended the meeting, but it would have been a small group. Very likely, Grandma and Grandfather Keil were there, as of course was Aunty Resel, who, for one reason or another, invited Maria to join.

About an hour or so after Mass ended, Father Rockermann surreptitiously made the short walk across the road and around to the back door of the Keil House. Everyone was there waiting, and the clandestine meeting began as soon as he arrived. They probably gathered in the lounge room. Father Rockermann reiterated the excellent news that Father Eigat was alive. However, he was in desperate need of food and resources to survive the winter.

'What can we do to help?' he cried. Father Rockermann pressed the need for urgency; otherwise, Eigat and his host literally would either starve or freeze to death before winter's end. Father Rockermann stressed that he had access to food and proceeded to lay out on the table a pile of ration cards, some full and some cut into smaller squares.

The Keils looked at the collection with wide eyes; these cards were in demand. Only with these coupons could you legally purchase goods. You could, of course, if you had the right connections, purchase goods illegally on the black market, but that was expensive and very risky; the penalty for procuring such goods ranged from imprisonment to execution. It amazed Maria how many ration cards Father Rockermann produced, and to those at the meeting, it must have looked like gold. There were enough to last several months for most items and, for others, even longer.

Like those in many other countries, the German government introduced ration cards to ensure fairness in distributing resources. Pregnant women, for example, had access to extra milk coupons without paying. The system worked well for everyone except Jews and other minorities, who had to make do with much smaller allocations than the regular population.[67]

By 1944, the broader community had become rife with corruption. The black market provided a steady supply of scarcely available goods to those who had enough money. But the system had its loopholes. The farmers in Döfering received food cards just as all citizens did, yet they had the advantage of producing their food; thus, they could accrue a surplus of cards and then trade them for other goods. Father Rockermann knew this and had already sought help from a few that he knew he could trust. Not only did they hand over their additional coupons, but they also provided surplus food.

A typical German ration card circa 1944. 'You don't need to take the whole card. You just take some scissors and cut out the pieces you need.'

He said that the farmers, they have their own food, and he had some special farmers. They gave him their ration cards and all sorts of smoked meat and all sorts of butter and things like that, you know.

The main point is ration cards. It was like that. You don't need to give a name, you get one ration card a month, and everyone has the same name on the ration cards.

You don't need to have the [whole] ration card at the shop. You just take some scissors and cut the ration squares up – this is a pound of butter, this is a pound of sugar, you have to pay for it, but you can give it to someone else. I can cut my ration card up and give it to someone else, and they can live from it. They go into the shop and give the square up. They have to take every square, and that was a good thing, and the priest had a lot of ration cards.

Thus, a farmer might typically swap a food coupon for some paraffin for lighting or a clothing card. It was a bartering system as such.

The real problem the group faced was, 'How do we get the cards to Altötting?' Methodically and logically, they assessed their options. One obvious way they discussed was by post, which had the advantage that they did not have to actually deliver the goods in person.

On reflection, however, for a good reason, that idea was dangerous. Post office workers were obliged to examine the package and alert the Gestapo of any suspicious contents. A scrupulous Nazi would then investigate who sent so many cards to a single address. The Gestapo in Altötting would be alerted. They would go to the address and arrest and ultimately execute the occupants, especially when one was a wanted criminal and the other was hiding him. First, however, they would need to discover, using torture, if necessary, who sent the goods in the first place. The Gestapo would then trace the package to Father Rockermann and his clandestine group of helpers. In turn, they would suffer the same fate as those in Altötting, but not before they revealed by torture, if necessary, where they got the cards. Mail was not a good idea. The only viable means was to deliver the ration cards personally.

Everyone was quiet. For the first time, the whole group must have realised the high stakes involved here. Even for holding this meeting, they were conducting illegal and potentially life-ending business. It was suggested that the underground could help, but the only contact that Father Rockermann had, had disappeared. Nobody even knew the man who delivered the letter at mass.

Maria suddenly knew what she had to do.

I said, 'I'm going!' What a stupid thing to do! In those days, I was not thinking about how dangerous that was. I could lose my life straight away. I would be straight away, shot, not just arrested, straight away, shot! To have so many ration cards is death straight away.

Despite Maria's certainty regarding execution, the Gestapo would have been unlikely to carry it out immediately – not before they forced her to reveal her contacts and her destination. The moment Maria mentioned her idea, the whole group simultaneously opposed it as far too risky and agreed that they should abort the mission altogether, even though it meant leaving Father Eigat and his host to their fate.

Eventually, however, Maria repeated her offer as the only viable suggestion. But how could she get through, and should she be the one to go? Despite Grandma's objections to Maria going, they began to discuss the possibilities.

It was clear from the start that Maria was the best person to accomplish the mission. Father Rockermann would immediately arouse suspicion by leaving his parish, Grandma was bedridden, and Grandfather was already in his seventies and too frail. Neither Aunty Resel nor her brother, Uncle Michel, who lived in the house were in good enough health and both were in their fifties. Maria, at twenty-four, on the other hand, was young, fit and healthy. She had to be the one. Now, how to get there?

They began to look at their other options and immediately eliminated walking or riding. If it was spring, summer or even autumn, it might have been possible to ride or even walk, but that would take at least a week and be fraught with danger. Maria would have to move from town to town finding accommodation, avoiding checkpoints and Nazi searches. Of course, all of that was insignificant because now they were in the middle of the winter. Either way, Maria would most likely freeze to death before even leaving the district.

The best viable option appeared to be by train, but you could not buy tickets for long journeys for civilian use without police or military permission. The group then discussed road transport but soon realised that that was out of the question. No buses ran, and no one had a car. Even if they did, petrol for civilian use was unobtainable.[68] The Keil family had a wagon, but the snow-covered roads were simply untenable at this time of year. The discussion went back to rail. It was the only way.

There were two big problems with train travel in Germany at that time. The first was the fact that rail transport was hazardous. Despite lame attempts by the Nazis to paint red crosses on some of their trains to make the Allies think they were legitimate Red Cross trains, everyone knew that the Wehrmacht used rail transport almost exclusively for military operations. Hence, the bright Red Cross that was supposed to dupe the Allied forces had the opposite effect and the trains became preferred targets for their now daily bombing raids.

Additionally, the total war mandate meant that civilian travel was heavily restricted.

> Altötting is about 200 kilometres from Döfering. Think about this. How would I get to Altötting? There were already no buses in those days; it was already '44. It was really [strict]. Everybody was on *'Reden, reden, Rollen fur das Zieg*. Alert, alert, roll for victory.' Nobody could [travel], not by car or something and not by train.

Such was the Third Reich crisis that they implemented a rule that civilians could travel by train no more than five kilometres.[69] Nobody could go further without a special exemption.

> You have to have, from the police, a new certificate to allow you to go further.

There were exceptional circumstances but none of them applied to Maria.

> When you go to the hospital or visit a soldier or something like that, you have to have a new certificate from the police. I didn't have that. I couldn't get that.

Despite the risk, Maria saw no other way.

Naturally, the group members had concerns about Maria's plan. She had no idea other than to travel nearly two hundred kilometres on a restricted ticket. If caught, the penalty for extending one's journey to upwards of one hundred and fifty kilometres would be severe, especially when they found her contraband. Perhaps she could have held out under torture, or would she break and reveal all of her contacts in Altötting as well as Döfering? The fact that Maria intended to supply goods to a fugitive would have made her demise more horrible than one cares to imagine.

Finally, with the lack of a better plan, and even though they knew the consequences of her risk, they decided to let her go. In the end, it was not a rational decision by any means, but one of faith. God would look after her.

The conspirators knew that Maria had to leave as soon as possible because the longer they waited, the higher the risk of starvation for Father Eigat and his host. Additionally, pneumonia was a considerable killer every winter, particularly for the frail; the cards and money could buy much-needed fuel for heating. Besides, it was December, and with the heavy snows continuing to fall, it would only get more challenging to travel.

The night before she left, Maria stayed at her grandmother's house. That evening she and Aunty Resel went over to St Adagios, where they met up with Father Rockermann. He handed over a basket of goods, mainly fresh meat and vegetables, together with the precious stack of ration cards and enough money to buy most of the products on the cards. If worse came to worst, they could even trade the tickets for goods or money on the black market.

That night, Father Rockermann joined the family at the Keil house for a final meal and prayers for Maria. Before she left, he passed Maria a piece of paper with a map of directions to the safe house. Then, he handed Maria a prepaid two-way restricted ticket before tracing the sign of the cross on her forehead and issuing her with a final blessing. Finally, he warned, 'Maria, if they catch you, you must destroy everything. Throw everything out of the window.'

That would be easier said than done.

After bidding farewell to her family the following morning, grandfather, Josef, Maria and Aunty Resel made the four-kilometre journey by wagon to Geigant station. Maria carried her basket to the waiting horse and cart, surprised by the weight and wondering how she would bring this to Altötting. The journey to Geigant in the blizzard-cold morning reinforced the impossible odds of making it safely to her destination.

At the station, Maria waited anxiously in the cold for her train to arrive. Before long, a group of soldiers joined her there, along with a few civilians. Mercifully, the train to Altötting finally arrived. Resel and

Josef kissed her goodbye, with a final warning that if things went wrong, to leave the basket, together with the cards, and run. Maria boarded, knowing that this was the point of no return. It was too late to change her mind. As the train lurched and crunched to a start, Maria looked back, and wondered whether she would ever see her hometown again.

34

Work and Leisure – Leon, Late 1944

From his childhood in Ukraine, Leon learned valuable lessons that helped him throughout his life. He knew how to plow, sow and harvest, milk cows, pickle and preserve foods. He could mend and build, ride horses, slaughter animals and babysit.

Tree chopping was probably one of the few jobs doable all year round, but most of Brückl's farm work occurred in the summer. So when the early snows fell early in the winter of 1944–45, they already had sufficient wood, stockpiled, dried out and ready to provide enough fuel for winter heating. Soon, a heavy shroud of snow covered the countryside in Haschaberg. Leon, confined mainly to working indoors, completed repair work in the house and stables. In doing so, he worked closely with Georg, and in a short space of time, Leon became competent enough to make and repair furniture.

Even though he still slept upstairs above the animals, their relationship became less slave and master and more apprentice and tradesman. Sometimes, Brückl and Leon would head out to a neighbour's property to help them work on projects at their homes and farms. While Brückl was no replacement for Stephan, working with him reminded Leon of how much he missed his stepfather.

Whereas Mrs Brückl was abrupt and aloof at first, Leon soon found her to be a kind and compassionate family woman who reminded him of his dear mother. Initially, Leon rarely spoke with her and rarely went into the house, but things had changed. Sometimes, when it became too cold, Mrs Brückl allowed him to sit by the fire, along with the children, with whom Leon had a natural gift. They loved to be with him, to play games, tell stories or read their colourful storybooks. This helped Leon with his written and spoken German.

When there was no work to do in the winter, Mrs Brückl allowed Leon and sometimes Maria to take the children outside to ride their sleds down the hills. It was an activity they all loved, especially Leon, because it reminded him of home. After that, they might build a snowman or enjoy a snow fight. Leon's favourite was young Sepp, who reminded him of his brother, Mykhas, at just three years of age.

Leon and Maria sometimes took the children ice-skating, and the best place for that happened to be directly outside the Keil house in Döfering. During the autumn, members of the community, including Georg and Leon, dug a rectangular strip, parallel to the roadway, about ten metres wide, thirty metres in length, and approximately a hundred millimetres deep. Then they added water, a small amount each time. They let it freeze, often overnight, before gradually adding more and more water into the trench until they had a beautiful, flat skating rink. With a little maintenance, it would last for the rest of the winter.[70]

It is unlikely, however, that the locals would have allowed a young slave labourer to enjoy himself on the ice while their boys were freezing and dying in the Russian snow.

When Leon went to Mass with Maria and the Brückl family, he always sat at the back.[71] If anyone objected to him being there, they never let on. After all, he was Catholic (albeit Greek Catholic, but they were not to know that). Mass was almost always a miserable affair. There was always news of someone dead or missing. Given his nascent comprehension of German, if Leon missed something in the translation, he could tell by their mourning whose family had suffered the most recent fatality on the Russian front.

One day, Maria never arrived for work. That was quite unusual, but Leon shrugged it off. However, when that day became two and three days, and when she failed to show for Mass that Sunday, Leon knew something must be wrong.

35

To Altötting – Maria, Late 1944

How would she get through? How would she get back? The more she thought about it, the more it looked like a suicide mission. Maria always had great faith in God, and now, she needed it more than ever. Before she left, Aunty Resel urged Maria to change her mind and abort the mission. Maria knew that her decision was an irrational choice, with only a small chance of success, but had made up her mind. A few days later, as she stepped onto the train, she also knew it was too late to go back.

> So I've [left] with this five-kilometre certificate on the train to go about two hundred kilometres. Is that not very… it's a death sentence. Still, now, it is really scary.

Maria's biggest concern was not the Allied bombing, but the consequences of her imminent arrest.

> Then you've got to know, on such a long trip, there comes a controller.

She made her way down the aisle and took a seat by herself.

> There was so much snow. I was sitting at the window of the train. There was a place, underneath the seat, where I could put the basket. I put my coat over the basket and sat against the window.

Soon, the train rattled and groaned as it painstakingly made its way southwards, towards Altötting. Without explanation, the train then made a series of nerve-racking, lengthy stops, seemingly in the middle of nowhere. Whether to clear the tracks or to let the prioritised troop trains through, Maria never knew. However, it gave her plenty of time

Maria required a long distance rail ticket, similar to this one, used by the military, along with personal identification documents, to travel legally from Cham to Altötting.

to think about the consequences of her actions and the substantial risk she was taking. Not only had she placed her own life in imminent danger, but also those of so many others dependent on her successfully carrying out her mission. It was for good reason the clandestine group of conspirators was small. Each member risked torture, imprisonment and execution if the Gestapo caught them supplying goods to a wanted criminal. Under duress, the group might have revealed from whom they received so many ration cards. Hence, the farmers, the co-conspirators who helped to provide the ration cards for the mission, would also be in the firing line.

Eventually, the train stopped at the town of Straubing, where Maria had to change trains. After lugging her heavily laden basket off the train, she faced another lengthy wait at a freezing station, surrounded by soldiers and guards. Carrying the contraband goods jangled her nerves on a knife-edge. She considered leaving them on the train and returning home. At any moment, she knew Gestapo agents could come and check her basket and her ticket, putting an abrupt end to her mission.

She could have brought another ticket at Straubing, but there was no point. Even then, she would be only halfway to her destination, and it would have made no difference to her journey's illegality.

On the certificate [ticket], it has which police amp [jurisdiction], which place I go, which Landkreis [district]. Everything is on [so] there is not a mistake.

When the connecting train to Altötting arrived, Maria and most of the soldiers stepped inside, much relieved to get out of the cold. As she began to board the train, her heart sank when a soldier stopped her dead in her tracks.

With his outstretched hand, he took hold of Maria's basket, and before she could react, he held it in his hand. *'Darf ich bitte?* May I help you?'

'Ja, danke,' replied Maria, forcing a smile as the soldier carried her basket onto the train. Maria nervously approached a vacant seat in the half-empty train. She turned to thank the soldier again before he passed the basket back.

With a deep breath of relief, she once again placed her lethal freight by her feet and covered it with her coat. The last passenger to step onto the train was a civilian, perhaps in his mid-forties, who looked very calm as he walked towards Maria, whose seat faced towards him. As he got closer, he nodded towards her and, with a half-smile, hung up his coat and took up a place just a few seats behind her. Maria looked at him and wondered whether he was a Gestapo agent; who was to say that he was not a wolf dressed up as a sheep? She knew that he would have seen the bulk by her feet and that that might be enough to arouse his suspicions. She hated that he sat where he could readily observe her. Maria looked away, too scared to look in his direction. She wanted to get up and move elsewhere, but that would only make matters worse, particularly if one of the soldiers sitting behind her reminded her that she had left her basket behind.

Along the way, the sound of planes overhead captured Maria's attention as she waited for a bomb to strike the train. She resigned herself to the thought that if that happened, at least her worries would be over. That would be preferable to capture by the Nazis.

Fortunately for Maria, the journey from Straubing to Altötting proceeded with no further unscheduled stops or delays. Praying helped to pass the time, giving Maria strength in her convictions in what she was doing. Under normal circumstances, with snowflakes falling outside and the warmth of the carriage within, it might have been a pleasant journey. Maria knew that she had pressed her luck, and as the train neared Altötting, her confidence began to rise. Perhaps Germany had more significant concerns than pursuing illegal rail travellers.

It was with great relief when Maria finally wiped the frost from her window.

Now I could see Altötting, the town, the churches and all the houses.

She started to focus on her next plan. Get off the train, find the safe house, and drop off the goods. She planned to stay with them overnight and, all being well, head back to Cham in the morning.

Finally, the train stopped at Altötting station. Maria prayed a silent thanks to God as she bent down to retrieve her goods.

Now came the controllers.

'*Bleiben Sie sitzen!* Stay seated!'

Maria turned as two well-dressed men in black coats entered the carriage. Her heart sank – she felt sure that these men were from the Gestapo.

'*Soldaten zuerst, durch kommen!* Soldiers come through first!'

One by one, the soldiers came through, showed their passes, and disembarked the train. Perhaps they were going home on leave or, more likely, changing trains on their way south, to where the battles raged, in northern Italy.

After the soldiers left, only a handful of civilians remained in the carriage. Slowly, methodically, the controllers went from passenger to passenger checking tickets. As they moved closer, Maria searched for a plan. She had a strong desire to leave the basket and head for the exit at the other end of the carriage. However, that would arouse suspicion, and even if she ran, they would catch her. Maria tried to push the basket further beneath the seat, but it was too big. She wondered if she could throw away the ration cards, but where? They would see her and search her and find the map and the money. As the two men moved ever closer, Maria's hopes sank. She feared for herself and those she loved who would suffer because of her. If Maria could have ended her life at that point, she would have done it.

The controllers paused to check the ticket of the man behind her and suddenly began yelling abuse at him. He had travelled too far! Maria saw the guards forcibly remove him from his place and towards the exit. The man pleaded with them, but they were not listening.

> They arrested someone from my wagon, just about two or three seats from me. He had travelled eight kilometres – just a few kilometres more than he was allowed.

Maria was sure that they were Gestapo. She peered nervously through the frosted window. As one of the men escorted his prisoner to the station room, the other man returned to the train to continue where they left off.

Maria could not believe it! The man had gone just a few kilometres further than his permit allowed. What would they do to her when they found out she had travelled nearly two hundred kilometres more than hers permitted? Maria knew then it was all over; she was about to be arrested, and there was absolutely nothing she could do about it. She had frozen with fear when the controller arrived at her seat.

> I did not know. You know when I think about it, I just think if somebody shot me, anyway, I couldn't give a *blöd* [care less]. I was really stiff, you know. I was really, really stiff.
> They came to me. One came to me. The other one was still behind somewhere. He took the other one out first. Now he came to me.

'*Ihr Ausweis bitte*. Confirmation of travel document please.'
What could she do?

> I was automatically, like automatically stiff, stiff like ice, and I gave him this five-kilometre certificate.

Only Maria's mind was active as she repeated a prayer that she made up herself. '*Maria Siege über alle Dämonen beten für uns*. Maria victorious over all the demons pray for us.'[72]

She remembered that she carried the map with Father Eigat's host's address on it and wished she could somehow destroy it. They would die too.

The controller scrutinised Maria's pass.

> He looked. He knows. He must know. He knows where I came from.
> He looked so long. He looked at me. He looked at me. Oh, I was so shocked. Then the other one came back, and he looked too, then they both looked at it. It must be God, really God, that they said nothing. Then they gave it [her ticket] back. Must be definitely God.

'*Guten tag*. Have a nice day.'

Suddenly it was all over – she was free! Maria was in shock. How could it be that they let her go? For all they knew, Maria herself could have been a Gestapo agent, there to check on the efficiency of the controllers.

> Then, both had to be trusting. In those days, you trust nobody.

Why then, did they, at personal risk, let her go? Perhaps it was because she was an attractive young woman, and they could not bring themselves to arrest her. However, she did not stick around to test him further.

> It was definitely God.
> I tell you, I was quickly out of the station.

Having made it to Altötting, Maria's ordeal was still far from over. She got off the train and carried her overloaded basket, ration cards and cash down the snow-covered street and well away from the station before surreptitiously unfolding and examining the handwritten map given to her by Father Rockermann.

Altötting had escaped the bombing that devastated Germany's largest cities and towns. Maria dutifully followed the directions on the map, trudging through the falling snow towards her destination. Maria knew Altötting because it was a pilgrimage town. Each year, thousands travelled there, by foot, from all over the country to pay homage to the famous Black Madonna, an exquisite fourteenth-century statue of Mary and Jesus. Maria and her family had made the journey on many occasions. Hence, despite the worsening weather, she roughly knew her way.

> I found the house, the little house.

She knocked tentatively on the front door and waited. Maria shivered in the cold and damp and rapped once more upon the door, louder this time. Eventually, a muffled voice from beyond the door confirmed that someone was home.

'*Wer sind Sie.* Who is it?'

'*Ich bin Maria, Maria Keil, aus Döfering. Pater Rockermann hat mir hier geschickt.* I am Maria Keil, from Döfering. Father Rockermann has sent me here.'

Thank goodness. eventually, the door creaked open to reveal the wizened face of a woman, perhaps in her eighties, peering tentatively at the young woman before her.

'*Liebe God!* Thank God,' the woman cried, with tears streaming down her face. She looked out furtively to see that no one else was around while simultaneously bringing Maria inside and locking the door behind her.

Inside, the house was dull and dark. The room was austere; a kitchen table with three chairs stood in the middle of the room, an old lounge rested against one of the walls, and a cast-iron stove stood in the corner.

Two old ladies and then the priest was there.

Maria, exhausted but relieved, put down her basket as the small group embraced her and showered her with blessings. The woman who opened the door introduced herself as Gerti and the other woman as Avia. They were extremely relieved to see that Maria arrived safely along with food and ration cards.

Maria noticed that the room was freezing. They had long since used up their last reserves of fuel for heating and cooking. Regardless, the group sat talking for a while and shared some food from the basket. Before long, Maria, exhausted from her journey, lay down on the lounge and, despite the cold, soon fell fast asleep.

36

Where Is She? – Late 1944

As 1944 drew to a close, in the Ardennes in Belgium, Hitler's Wehrmacht launched its last full-scale attack, throwing all available military hardware into the fruitless battle that became known as the Battle of the Bulge. The campaign aimed to push the enemy back into the sea, but as soon as the weather cleared, with the Allied forces in complete control of the air, and having superior ground forces, the attack failed abysmally. With little more to offer, Germany's industrial heartland, the Ruhr, lay exposed and ready for the taking.

In the east, Russia had consolidated its forces. With hundreds of armies, comprising millions of men, they amassed on the Prussian border and waited for the winter weather to subside. Whereas Germany's factories suffered from constant aerial bombardment and subsequent production delays, the Soviet factories continued unprecedented mass production unabated. Artillery, planes and tanks, in numbers that soon dwarfed even those of the German invasion two years earlier, rolled unceasingly towards the eastern front. Now, they held the upper hand. The forces that amassed along the entire Prussian border towards winter's end in January 1945 were fully armed and ready against a severely battered and critically under-strength German army. As soon as the winter weather abated, they would meet their fate. Germany continued to fight ferociously, especially in the east, for fear of communist reprisals, but the outcome was inevitable.

Although he would not admit it, Leon's worries mounted when Maria remained absent for an entire week. Eventually, he plucked up the courage to ask Brückl. Whereas Leis would have belted him for being impudent, Brückl explained, as Maria had told him, that she was visiting her friend in hospital in Munich. He said that he too was apprehensive, mainly since Munich and her railways had long been the target of Allied bombing raids, and that many civilians had died thus far as a result. The news that week confirmed that another massive attack on Munich occurred just a few nights before, just when Maria was visiting her friend..

Leon did not understand why he felt so upset at the thought that she might be dead.

37

In Hiding – Maria, Winter 1944

By the time Maria awoke, Avia and Gerti had already made a large pot of soup while simultaneously warming up the house with their little stove. Hot, nutritious food meant the difference between life and death for them. If they adequately rationed their resources, even with Avia being an extra mouth to feed, they still ought to have enough to last for several months and the worst winter weather.

For the next few days, the weather remained terrible and the group remained mostly indoors. Their days passed quietly in conversation, reading and prayer. Bible studies became a mainstay of their daily life. Together, they spent hours studying scripture, deriving comfort and hope in their dilemma.[73] Maria discovered Avia's crime for which she was in hiding from the Nazis. She was Jewish. She was a fugitive solely because of her religion. However, there was no disrespect for each other's beliefs, and Maria became very fond of her Jewish friend. To the group, everyone was equal. Eventually, the focus of the discussion turned to how Maria could get home. She was terrified to travel, thinking this time, her luck would run out.

> Every day, I prayed and prayed [at] the church, chapels and things like that. I was so scared to come back that I was nearly gone for a whole week.

Over the next few days, despite the cold, Maria and Gerti ventured out, taking turns and shopped at different stores. Maria also spent much of her time foraging outside in the snow for wood. Within several days, she had collected enough to last for the coldest months of January and February.

Maria enjoyed her time there; the food and the company were good, and with adequate fuel, the place warmed up. Other than the constant threat of discovery, Maria loved her time in Altötting. She could happily have stayed there, except she knew that while she was there she was using up precious resources. Besides, she missed her family and knew they would be worried.

Finally, among many tears, Maria left for Altötting station. They were sorry to see her go and promised their prayers for her safe return to Döfering.

That day, as she boarded the train back to Cham, the sun finally shone – a good omen, perhaps. The whole journey back was far less stressful, given that she no longer carried contraband goods, and the incriminating map that Father Rockermann had given her had long since provided a mere fraction of warmth on the stove. However, there was still a grave concern because she travelled back with the same illegal rail pass she used to get to Altötting.

On several occasions, Maria heard the sound of planes overhead, but they passed by passively, most likely on another way to decimate cities like Munich and Nuremberg.

At one point, the train had to divert via Regensburg, where Maria witnessed the damage caused by Allied bombers.

> In the time I saw it, I was shocked. When I came back from Altötting, oh, every station was bombed already. Every station! I thought the war must be finished.

Maria did not expect to be so lucky the second time the controllers inspected her ticket. However, this time she only risked her own life. Finally, to her great relief, as she stepped from the train at Geigant station, nobody stopped her for the whole way home and she began her journey home back to Döfering, alone, cold and in the dark.

When she arrived home and knocked on the door of the Keil House, everyone was in shock. It was as though she had risen from the grave.

They thought I was a ghost.

They had all but given up hope of ever seeing her again.

As Maria settled down, she saw the sadness in everyone's eyes and knew that something was wrong. 'Who is it?' she asked.

Grandma answered first. 'Othelia,' she said, 'has joined Maree. She died of TB this morning.'

Tuberculosis had killed two dearest friends.

38

The War Is Nearly Over – 1944–45

Increasingly often in defiance of Hitler's orders, the winter and spring of 1944–45 saw the Wehrmacht's continual retreat. When they could not retreat fast enough, they simply surrendered, hundreds of thousands of them. Paradoxically, when the Wehrmacht strategically withdrew, the people were supposed to stay and fight to the death.

Whereas in Western Europe, the public welcomed the Allies as heroes and liberators, in Eastern Europe, hundreds of thousands of refugees, fearing stories of Soviet revenge, fled to the west. A young Sudeten German woman, Rosa Swatosch, knew that the Russians were coming. News of Russian rape and murder preceded the Soviet advance, and Rosa knew that the window of opportunity to get out was rapidly closing. One night, after listening to the oncoming sound of missiles firing in the distance, she decided that it was time to leave.[74] Despite Nazi orders to remain indoors, Rosa packed for herself and her children, Steffi, Rosi and Marille and, with nothing more than a suitcase, headed west, on foot, from her hometown of Sofienthal.

What they all remembered the most about that night was the bitter cold that nearly froze them to death as they sought refuge. Within a few hours, they had crossed the border into Germany, and soon after, she could see the lights of a tiny village. There she knocked on the first house she saw. It belonged to a kindly older couple who gave them lodgings for the night. With not enough room to keep them, they suggested she move into a shelter they knew of at the charity house, set up for refugees in Döfering. She took the advice and went there the next day, temporarily, at least, safe from the war. That is where Maria and Rosa met.

Like Maria, Frau Brückl took a liking to Rosa and the children, and because there was always lots to do on the farm, she offered her some work. Hence, their respective children, Sepp and Marille, toddlers at the time, met for the first time. It was the beginning of a lifelong relationship. Seventy-five years later, the Pilgrims arrived and were welcomed into their home.

39

Stephan Mykulyshyn – Leon, c. Late 1944–Early 1945

For all that struck the earth, no matter if not bruised or spiked with stubble, went surely to the cider-apple heap as of no worth.
   One can see what will trouble this sleep of mine, whatever sleep it is.

After 'Apple-Picking' by Robert Frost

While Leon was welcoming Maria's return, the train carrying his stepfather, Stephan Mykulyshyn, together with every able person in Ukraine that the Soviets could muster, rattled on towards an unknown destination. They had no opportunity to take anything with them, so when their train reached its destination on the outskirts of Bratislava, and the passengers disembarked, they were starving. That was the least of their worries.

They alighted from the train to the distinctive sound of cannon fire nearby and immediately assembled while a Soviet officer addressed the group. He informed them that they collaborated with the enemy when they allowed the Germans to take over Soviet territory; hence, they were traitors to the Motherland. He went on to say that now was their time for redemption. Henceforth, they were proud members of the Soviet Army. Their immediate order, 'Charge over the hill, and you will find Germans on the other side. Kill them all. Anyone who turns back will be shot!' he warned, indicating the machine gunners placed intermittently along the line at the rear. 'Do not come back until they are all dead.' They had to share guns between every three or four soldiers.

The officer explained that those without rifles must follow those with rifles; and that if anyone carrying a rifle died, the next person had to pick up his weapon and use it to kill Germans. With no delay came the order to begin their advance. Tentatively, Stephan and the others moved forward, and then the officer screamed, 'Charge, or die!' Their walk turned to a run, and before long, they were within range and mown down mercilessly by German guns. The Soviets, knowing that the traitors would soon be dead, did not even bother to provide them with a uniform.[75]

Stephan and the others who charged headlong into the enemy died that day. Perhaps they even managed to kill a few Germans in the process, but generally, they never stood a chance; they just ran into a bloody massacre. In one fell swoop, the Soviet plan to dispose of their so-called traitors worked, along with the bonus of using up a large quantity of the limited German bullets. It must have been an unimaginably awful situation for the poor souls.

Leon's stepfather, the husband of his beloved mother, the man he loved like a father, who taught him so much and gave him his first horse, was just another piece of fodder for the Soviet Union, cast aside, 'as if of no worth'.

Back in Haschaberg, Leon, unaware that his stepfather was dead, anticipated the end of hostilities.

Even Brückl could not hide his feelings about Hitler. While he acknowledged that Hitler built the autobahns and gave everybody work, his response to Hitler's prospects in the war was one of fatalistic resignation. 'Leon, Hitler is kaput,' he said – words that could well have seen him imprisoned.

Brückl did not believe Nazi propaganda; otherwise, he might have expected, at any time, a massive turnaround due to a mystery weapon, Hitler's sheer genius, or the superior willpower of the German people. However, illegal foreign radio revealed the truth. Germany was in ruins; the Third Reich, on all fronts, had shrunk to a fraction of its former size. Surrenders numbered in their hundreds of thousands; the end was nigh. Bombed day and night for nearly two years now, the capital, Berlin, was in tatters, and by the end of January, the Russians readied themselves for their final onslaught to take the city. By March, the Ruhr, the industrial heartland of Germany, had fallen, and American and British troops had forced their way across the Rhine River. On 20 April, the US 6th Army group achieved a substantial strategic victory when they captured Nuremberg, the last major city, along with Berlin, between the Americans in the west and Russians in the east. Nuremberg's taking had a tremendous psychological consequence because it was the place of the infamous Nazi rallies and a significant source of Nazi propaganda.

Following the Battle of the Ardennes, counterattacks increasingly occurred only in the mind of the lunatic in charge. Hitler routinely moved around armies that no longer existed. Even his generals ignored his progressively irrational instructions in the final days. By 20 April, with Berlin surrounded by Soviet forces, he ordered General Wenck to liberate the city and counter-attack the Russian advance. The order was impossible given that Wenck's army was not even strong enough to hold their ground. Instead, the general chose to get as many civilians and soldiers away from Berlin as possible. The goal was to get across the Elbe, where surrender to the Americans was by far the preferable outcome.

In a desperate struggle under Russian fire, General Wenck made it across the Elbe and surrendered to the Americans, whereafter he served just two years of internment.[76] Many others, including SS murderers, got off even lighter or with no sentence at all. As soon as the fighting stopped, the Americans turned their attention to the new-found Soviet threat of communism. In contrast, those captured by the Soviets who survived served on average five to eleven years in prison. Over a million, or one-third of all German POWs, died in captivity of the Soviet Union.[77]

There was still plenty for the Allies to do. In the short term, resistance in parts of northern Germany, Italy and Austria still needed to be overcome, and a large corridor between Nuremberg and Prague was still in enemy hands. Unbeknown to Maria and her family, the American army, under the command of Generals Patton and Devers, was about to strike for the Czech border. From there, they planned to meet up with the Russians, who were approaching from the east, somewhere in Czechoslovakia. Across the Czech border, the fanatical Nazi Field Marshal Schörner had built a stable defensive position and was preparing for his last stand in the mountains. There was even talk of Hitler himself leaving Berlin to consolidate his position with Schörner amongst Czechoslovakia's forests.

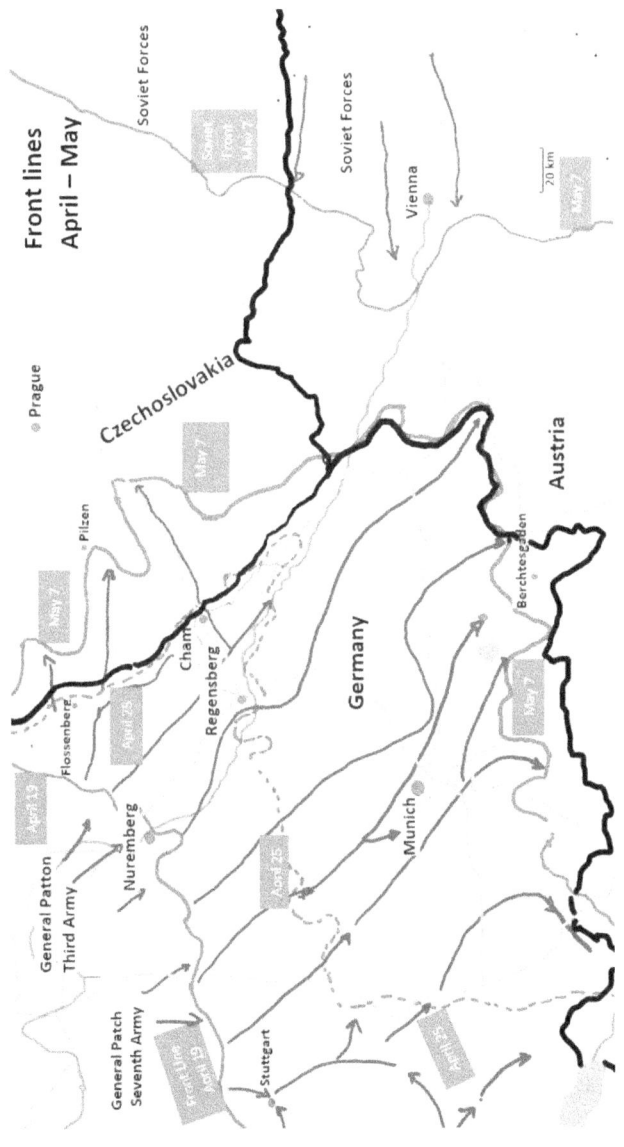

40

Death March – Maria, April 1945

There are numerous accounts of death marches that took place throughout Germany and the Nazi-conquered territories in the final stages of the war. They occurred because of Himmler's directive that no prisoners were to fall into enemy hands.[78] In response to the rapidly advancing Allied forces, and unable to murder all the prisoners, the Nazis chose to relocate concentration camp inmates by marching them to other camps within the Reich. As far as their captors were concerned, and given the resources available to them, it was the best way to dispose of as many prisoners as possible: natural attrition, through malnutrition, fatigue and deprivation, would kill them, thus saving bullets. To the Nazis, the more that died along the way, the better. Nevertheless, a decent supply of ammunition allowed for the *coup de grâce*, hence murdering those who fell behind.

As the Russian army continued advancing westward, Dachau, one of the last camps liberated in Germany, became the typical death march destination. However, orders to clear the camps, issued when communications systems were in disarray, may not have reached all of the intended destinations. Himmler might have planned this to mitigate his punishment if he were captured at the end of the war. He would not have wanted the fact that his last order as Reichsführer involved the mass murder of tens of thousands of innocent victims.[79]

Most of the camps' inmates had already survived unspeakable hardships and some had travelled from as far away as Auschwitz beginning in mid-January. They moved from place to place, just ahead of the Soviet forces. That any had survived is incredible in itself. Others came from places like Buchenwald, Sobibor, Berga, a camp for Jewish American POWs, and Terezin, a Czech centre, set up to show the 'favourable' treatment of inmates before the Nazis stopped worrying about propaganda. Many of the inmates travelled south via the Flossenbürg camp. From there, a large group continued towards Cham,[80] passing alongside the village of Haschaberg.

> I saw a lot.
> The next day, I don't know how I came through. You might think I made it up. I make up nothing. The day before, they bombed Cham. The planes, the station and the farmhouses that were close to the station, they bombed these too.

The English bombers that raided Cham that night had neither the time nor the inclination to be concerned about civilian casualties when targeting military establishments. They were after the munitions.

> They had guns and all these things in the station and the American air force bombed that.

Thus, for the Allied war effort, the sixty-three civilians who died on the night of 18 April 1945, were collateral damage.[81] For Maria and her community, the war had finally reached their doorstep.

The sixty-three deaths, while substantial, were relatively low in terms of other raids on cities such as Dresden and Hamburg, where the deceased numbered in their tens of thousands. Due to the recent influx of refugees, Cham's population, however, had doubled to over ten thousand in recent months; it could have been much worse had a full-scale, indiscriminate raid on the town occurred.

The bombing of Cham was part of the start of a much broader major offensive. At the time of the attack, the Allied front line was still a hundred and fifty kilometres away on a front that extended for over five hundred kilometres from the Swiss border through to Stuttgart and Nuremberg. The next day, the US Third Army, under the command of their most famous wartime general, George S. Patton, set out for their designated destination, Czechoslovakia. Patton's enthusiasm was understandable. No lover of communism, he was determined to prevent the Russian army, who might well have claimed Bavaria as part of the Soviet Union, from crossing the Czech border into Germany first. All being well, he hoped to meet up with the Soviet advance somewhere deep within Czechoslovakia. With the Wehrmacht in full retreat, Patton's advance proceeded virtually unhindered. On or about 19 April, one of his advance tank units arrived at the outskirts of Cham. There, they waited for the rest of the front line to catch up.

The village of Haschaberg is about fifteen kilometres north of Cham, but also a hundred metres above sea level higher than Cham. On the night of the raid, Maria saw the bombers as they made their way to the overcrowded town. She prayed that they were on their way elsewhere, but soon the sounds of bombing and the glow from fire and flames emanated through the night confirmed that it was Cham's turn. Maria, who had no idea that the attack centred upon Cham station, was gravely concerned about her mother and her family.

> In the morning, I didn't know if my mam was in Cham, are they dead or whatever.

Maria decided that the only way to be sure was to go and find out for herself. Nazi radio, while conceding the whole of Bavaria was under siege, implored its citizens everywhere to resist until death if need be. However, most people, knowing that their best option was to wait for the American forces to arrive, took little notice of the directive, hoping instead that the Nazis would capitulate without a significant battle on their doorstep.

Concurrently, American planes passed over the local villages' farms, frightening everyone that the battle had begun. Instead of dropping bombs, however, they showered the locals with leaflets, warning them that they were to remain indoors for the next few days.

With the whole area locked down, and the advice from both sides to stay indoors, Maria decided to ignore the warnings. Despite boggy conditions, she rightly knew that if she did not leave, then she might not be able to get there at all.

> Now, nobody could get out a day later, nobody. It had rained quite a bit, so I got up, I took my bicycle and went.

Soon after she embarked on her journey, Maria caught her first sight of some of the most decimated victims of Hitler's evil masterplan.

> From the village [of Haschaberg, down past the] Bleschenburg and [across to Döfering, to a rough, gravelled road]. I saw them walking *früher* [earlier] from Haschaberg out, still. On the *Rad* [bicycle], I saw them. I didn't know what these people are; they were all concentration camp people, and there were so many. He had marched them for about fifty kilometres, or longer. From this side, this place out of Nuremberg, there came a lot of concentration camp people.[82]

Maria was stunned by what she saw as she followed the road on her bicycle towards the village of Fleishbach. Along the way, what looked like piles of rags were scattered intermittently down the road. She soon realised, however, that they were the emaciated dead bodies of concentration camp prisoners. Maria, who had never seen anything even remotely like it, could not understand what she was seeing. Filthy rags covered their bodies. Most of them wore the infamous blue and white striped clothes synonymous with concentration camp victims. Tragically, after enduring unspeakable hardships and surviving the camps, so many had succumbed so close to freedom.

> One young German officer; he was in charge of them and he drove them along the road for so long. They were so hungry, and many really fell down and died. They had been for so long in a concentration camp they had no food for a long time, and now they were walking for so long. They could go nowhere because he would shoot them down.

Maria could see the people were in terrible condition. They passed by, ambling with grey, gaunt faces, so thin, with nothing in their eyes, just dark, sunken holes. She wanted to help, but she had nothing to give them. When one of them fell by the roadside about fifty yards further up the road, Maria instinctively ran over to see if she could help. She arrived to find that it was an older woman who had fallen. In hindsight, most likely, the woman was far younger. With an agonised face, the distressed woman tried forlornly to get up as Maria moved in to assist. Suddenly, before Maria could reach her, the German officer appeared and fired a single shot into the woman's stomach. The officer did not flinch or show the slightest emotion. He looked at Maria and, with his rifle waving, ordered her to move along.

Another woman then arrived from further up the road and accosted the officer. 'Why do you do this?'

To her horror, Maria noticed that the dead woman was pregnant. The bullet to her belly would have killed both mother and child instantly. The officer threatened to shoot her as well.

Maria was powerless.

> How could you help? We are civilians, we have no guns, they chased us all away. They had machine guns.

Maria could do nothing other than to get back on her bicycle and continue her journey. After her traumatic experience, she decided, rather than take the main road, to go cross-country. It must have been a surreal and depressing ride to Cham. The trip across the ranges was initially downhill and easy going. Then the hills gave way to relatively flat terrain, as she travelled off-road.

As she reached the outskirts of town, Maria's eyes beheld a grim sight.

> Now, I came to Cham, through the bush. When I reached the top of Cham, I could go no further. Everything on the roadside, everywhere, all too much army there, watching and everything, with tanks and everything. This way, I couldn't get through.

The American military had beaten her to Cham and had blocked all access in or out of the town.

> They wouldn't let me go this way and this way any more.

Cham, as with every other city and town in the rapidly shrinking German empire at the time, was designated by Adolf Hitler a fortress.

Everybody, therefore, had to hold out indefinitely, or until death, against the Allied advance. Cautious about the level of resistance they might encounter, the Americans, rather than enter the town and risk immediate conflict, chose to isolate Cham before making their next move. However, they did not know that whereas some cities and towns like Breslau followed the directive, Cham's leaders looked forward to surrendering peacefully to the Americans. It was a life-saving decision. Thankfully, most partisan Nazis had already left for the Czech mountains to join in the last stand with Field Marshal Schörner.

Fortunately, it was to the Americans, and not the Soviets, that the city was to surrender to on 23 April.

Maria, cautious about how the Americans would react to her presence, decided to take evasive action. To the west of town lay a large forested area. She knew that by skirting around the roadblocks, she could reach Cham via the Cham Cemetery.

> All the ranges here; fifty miles of it, from Kreuzberg [Cross Mountain] down, straight away, [to] a cemetery.

She alighted from her bike, wheeled it up and back into the woods, circling the US Army cordon. Maria prayed she never ran into any soldiers patrolling the area as she instinctively tramped upwards through the forest before looping back towards Cham. Finally, she found what she was looking for:

> There was one little path from the Klosterkirche [Monastery Church] out and higher up the Kreuzberg, [where] I came out. I went through the little door of the cemetery, and there was no watch in the cemetery. I came through.

It was there and then that she once more came across Holocaust victims.

> Through the cemetery next to the Klosterkirche is just the one road and then into town, and when I came through, I'll never forget that – there were so many concentration camp people. They all were dying, or they were dead already.

These were part of the same group that Maria came across on her way to Cham.

> They [concentration camp victims] came to Cham, and then I came, in the cemetery.

Sadly, many of the victims died on the brink of freedom through acts of kindness.

> Then people ran straight away, and they told me. I didn't see that, but they said to me that the people gave them straight away water to drink, and they were eating straight away. A lot of them died while they had it too quick, and they died.

Their emaciated bodies were so feeble that they could not tolerate solid food, and their organs shut down. At first, Maria could not understand why.

> That's when I saw the dead ones in the cemetery. That's when I said, 'What's that! They're not shot!' They were dead just like that.
> That's when they said, 'Get out of here. Get out of here.'

Maria then made her way across town towards her mother's house. Along the way, she noticed that some of the buildings had suffered from the bombing raid. Maria prayed that her family was not amongst them. She also saw that groups of refugees, gaunt and depressed, huddled along the streets and riverbank. Soon, Maria arrived at her mother's house and, to her surprise, found the front door ajar. She stepped inside and noticed that the first floor was empty. The SS had cleared out. She quickly climbed the steps to the second floor, where, to her great relief, she found her mother, stepfather and brothers, badly shaken from the air raid and apprehensive about what might await them.

Barbara was pleased to see Maria but angry that she had taken such a dangerous risk in coming to see her. Meanwhile, her stepfather sat fixed in his chair, irritated that, on his wife's insistence, he could not send his six-year-old Adolf out to get his beer.

For a while, Maria sat with her mother, and each recalled events of

This building, simply known as the Großtturm (Big Tower), was the place of residence of the Kolnhoffer family during the Second World War. At one point, SS officers occupied the first and top floors, and the family the second. It was said to be always cold and damp, and perhaps for that reason it became a place of cheap rent, for poor people. Built c. 1438 as a defence tower, part of the old city walls, its unique design has made it a town icon. Ironically, the SS may have intended to use it for its original purpose, to help defend the town. They would have seen its potential as a lookout and stronghold in street to street fighting in the battle for Cham. I knocked on the door but, from what I could tell, no one seemed to live there any more.

the past few days. It seemed inevitable that the battle for Cham should begin at any moment. Barbara urged Maria to leave while she still could. It was pointless to try to get Johann off his seat and the rest of the family to join her, so she bade farewell and headed back to Döfering.

Maria retraced her steps back through the cemetery, where the number of bodies had grown since her arrival. Hundreds of victims now lay in piles awaiting the completion of work on one large improvised grave, about twenty metres square. More bodies were arriving in trucks from the direction of the train station. Directly adjacent to the pit, workers were beginning to lay a series of graves that extended almost the whole cemetery's width. These graves were to be for the sixty-three victims of the air raid on Cham station the day before. Whereas the mass grave for the Jewish concentration camp victims had to be dug deep enough for over four hundred victims buried in layers, on top of each other, the adjacent graves for the air-raid victims had the bodies laid side by side.

Maria, shaken by the sight of so many dead, made her way back through the cemetery and back through the forest and around the American cordon to where she could see the tanks still waiting outside the town. After reuniting herself with her bicycle, she began her journey home back through the woods.

Before long, from out of nowhere, stepped a dishevelled German soldier, who grabbed her handlebars, blocking her path. For a moment they stood, face to face, with no more than a few inches separating them. Startled at first, Maria realised that his eyes and gaunt, dirt-black countenance revealed the man's fear.

'*Bitte konnen Sie uns helfen?* Please, can you help us?.'

Before she had time to process his plea, another two of his comrades stood beside him.

'*Wir wollen uns ergeben.* We want to surrender,' they expressed but were scared that the Americans would shoot them on sight.

Maria hesitated. Perhaps the Americans would shoot them all.

I helped them to surrender. I showed them where to go.

Maria led them through the woods and walked with them towards the American roadblock. *'Hände hoch.* Hands up,' she ordered, and they approached with their hands held high.

The American soldiers raised their rifles but did not fire. Maria gently pushed them forward. For them, the war was over. Maria made eye contact with one of the lead American soldiers and backed off towards the woods whence she came. They let her go.

Soon after, Maria linked up with the autobahn. Built in 1938 as part of Hitler's grand construction scheme, the highway was now littered with the randomly scattered, hopelessly emaciated bodies of deceased concentration camp victims. Some bore gunshot wounds, while others had simply collapsed and died from exhaustion and malnutrition. Maria rode as far as the village of Birkmühle. She peered right along the road to Döfering that she usually took to get home. However, boggy from the recent rains, it now additionally carried the deep scars of the American tank tracks that recently claimed this part of the country. Reluctantly, for she knew it added about ten kilometres to her journey, she chose to go a long way home via the highway.

To her great dismay, as Maria continued her journey up the highway, she continued to pass dead bodies. Eventually, she reached the intersection near her friend Annie's house, where once more, she came across the American army. Army trucks had taken control of what was a critical intersection. The northbound and southbound highways were the main thoroughfares to Berlin and Munich, respectively, while the road west went to Nuremberg and east to the Czech border. Maria was perplexed because a group of locals had gathered amid quite a commotion outside Annie's house.

Maria arrived as the crowd dragged a man towards Annie's front yard. As he passed, Maria recognised him as the German officer who murdered the concentration camp victims and threatened to shoot her. For him, it was the end of the road.

> The young officer brought them [the concentration camp victims] here to Fleishbach, a little village next to the road, not far, just about

ten minutes from Döfering or a bit before. There, the main road passes through, and there they brought them to Fleishbach where my friend [Annie] was. There was still a lot of concentration camp [people] everywhere.

Maria anxiously ran to the house. There, she met Annie, who explained what had happened.

Now, from the other side, there came some others, like Americans. They wanted that German officer, [because]) he had all over the road, about fifty kilometres out from Nuremberg's direction [left the trail of the dead].

The American army unit literally had been following the trail of dead for fifty kilometres!

On 19 April, some sixteen thousand prisoners evacuated the Flossenbürg concentration camp to march to Dachau. By 22 April, the first of the groups had reached the Cham district, a third of the distance to their destination. While the Nazi leaders hoped that forcing the critically emaciated prisoners to walk south for over two hundred kilometres in the open with no food or water would be an efficient way of murdering them, they did not succeed completely.[83]

For many victims, their passage began at the end of the German winter. When it rained, their wet clothes turned to ice. If not for the generosity of onlookers who, despite warnings from the Nazi guards, managed, on occasion, to throw them some food, barely anyone could have survived to be liberated. Nevertheless, Heinrich Himmler's directive that no inmate was to fall into enemy hands meant that only about 1,600 ultimately survived.[84]

The Americans who followed the 'line of death' had reason to be infuriated when they finally caught up with the main perpetrator.

So many on the roadside, left or shot, and there at my friend's house, they got him – the young German officer who killed them all there on the roadside.

Faced with immutable odds, the officer had lowered his rifle and surrendered to the US army.

Then there were hundreds and hundreds lying dead on the road.

The Fleishbach residents, enraged by what they had witnessed, demanded the officer pay for his crimes.

Maybe he had some others with him, but he did it.

At least some of the Americans agreed, but while they too were furious and hungered for retribution, especially since some of the victims were American POWs who had travelled from Berga concentration camp. They had been warned by higher authorities, however, not to take matters into their own hands. Not to be thwarted, therefore, they allowed justice to take its course.

Then, the Americans did nothing – the army – but the others, the civilians, wanted something.

They allowed the locals to take him.

This one, they took him, and they hung him in my friend's yard on the *Birnenbaum* [pear tree].

His execution was a gruesome sight.

And he was screaming the whole time. Then he was scared about death too.

*

Of immediate concern was the removal and burial of hundreds of the dead.

Then all the concentration camp people, who were dead to here, they took them for a quick burial by the roadside for fifty kilometre. So many, hundreds and hundreds of them.

It was a short-term solution. A week or so later, American soldiers gathered groups of civilians who they believed had contributed to the Nazi cause and forced them to work. Maria thought that they had got the right people.

> Later on, there were Nazis who really were Nazis. They came, and they had to take them [the corpses], all out, and they had to bury them in cemeteries...

Ultimately, they could not leave the SS officer hanging from Annie's pear tree. It would be inappropriate to bury him alongside his victims in the cemetery at Cham.

> This other one, this officer, they buried him outside the village not far from Döfering. [At] the other village, Fleischbach, they buried him. For a few years, the grave was there until one day, some of his family found out what happened to him, and took him, took the bones, and took him home to Radebe. I think he came from Anaheim, in this district [destination undecipherable].[85]

One of the few survivors that day was a Polish Jew named Raimi Rejngewirtz. He was among thousands of inmates forced to leave Flossenbürg camp in the face of the impending arrival of liberation forces. His horrific journey began in Auschwitz and ended on the outskirts of Cham.[86]

> Raimi lost his sense of time and direction due to starvation and illness but was liberated by US forces near Cham, Bavaria. He recalls the SS shooting most of the marchers just prior to liberation... Some liberated prisoners died due to excessive food intake after liberation.[87]

*

> Later, I found out that they had buried them all in the mass graves. It was the end of the war. There is a *Denkmal* [memorial] there, for remembering.

Naturally, I wanted to find the *Denkmal* of which Maria spoke. On our first night in Cham, Steffany, Milla and I visited the cemetery, mobile phone torches alight, to attempt to find it. Alas, after nearly an hour of fruitless searching amongst the gravestones, we came up empty-handed. While Milla suggested that our mother was mistaken (it happened almost fifty years before the interview, after all), I went back on my own early the following morning, convinced to try again.

With the sun rising on a clear and cloudless morning, it was shaping to be a glorious day. I came across an older woman with a bunch of freshly cut flowers tending to a grave and asked her if she knew anything about a Jewish memorial. She did not but, pointing in the direction of a building within the cemetery, suggested I ask the groundsman. There, I waited for several minutes and knocked on the door, but no one answered. With nothing to do, I continued my search amongst the graves. The cemetery was extensive. Eventually, I returned to the building. This time I spotted, through the glass door, a man inside sipping coffee. I knocked, and he opened the door. I repeated my quest to find the Jewish *Denkmal*, and this time, after a moment's hesitation, he nodded.

'Can you take me there?' I urged, my excitement building

The man then walked me up the cemetery until, eventually, he stopped and pointed me in the direction of another man, about fifty metres away. 'Ask him,' he said. 'He knows.'

Within minutes, I stood there, at the very place that Maria had stood some seventy-four years earlier as she witnessed the reality of Hitler's Holocaust. Surrounded by hedges and nestled amongst pretty flowers stood the memorial of which Maria spoke. The inscription confirmed the extent of the tragedy that had unfolded before Maria's eyes:

> To commemorate the 446 K-Z [concentration camp] prisoners from the camp Flossenbürg buried here on 23 April, 1945 reburied in August 1957 to the K-Z cemetery Flossenbürg.

The elderly gentleman who showed me to the grave explained that rather than leave the bodies stacked in a mass grave, they reburied the

The memorial to the victims of the Holocaust at Cham Cemetery.

The graves of the sixty-three residents killed in the raid at the Cham station on 18 April 1945.

bodies that had lain there for over twelve years at Flossenbürg in a dedicated cemetery along with thousands of other concentration camp victims. Despite all of the evil that preceded, the quote at the top of the memorial called for healing.

> If the new generation knows for what the old one is in debt. Do not call for reassurance, and do not call for revenge this time.

To my right, as I stood in front of the memorial, lay a long row of graves that, initially, I believed might belong to the holocaust victims. My guide explained that they were victims, but of a different kind. There lay sixty-three graves, side by side, each inscribed with the name of one of the residents killed in the raid at Cham station on 18 April 1945.

41

The Last Battle – Leon, 1945

On the days before, the sky rained paper, falling in fluttering waves across the countryside. Leon and Maria were outside to witness the strange event. Leon picked up one of the sheets and, unable to read it, looked inquisitively at Maria in the hope that she could decipher its meaning.

'*Wir müssen ins Haus bleiben. Die Amerikaner Kommt.* We have to stay in the house. The Americans are coming.'

Whereas Maria was worried, Leon had a different approach. He welcomed the Americans.

> I was not scared. I've already seen too much to be scared. I knew they would bomb the cities, Hamburg and Munich, and not the villages.

For the next two days, everyone remained housebound.

The clock ticked slowly.

Unlike Leis, Brückl invited Leon to the house to share meals with Maria and his family; otherwise, he worked in the barn. They prayed regularly to let the war end soon.

Nothing happened.

Little by little, complacency set in, and they began to venture outside. There was work to do, and staying inside, especially in the middle of summer, was not at all practical on the farm.

All around them, Nazi resistance crumbled as the Allies advanced deep into the heart of Germany, closer and closer to Haschaberg. As a last, desperate response, the Nazis threw into the front line, and almost certain death, boys and girls as young as twelve and men and women of all ages. They were not only expected to halt the Allied advance, but somehow, they had to turn the war around, or at least die trying.

A person's nationality had ceased to matter. Poles, French, Greek, Ukrainian, Romanian: everyone was welcome to sacrifice their lives for the lost cause. The fact that most had neither the stomach for a fight nor the belief in the Nazi cause meant that with most of the elite Wehrmacht forces long dead, the walls crumbled all the more quickly.

In the end, it was up to the *Volkssturm* (home guard) to repel the might of the combined Allied armies. At that point, even Leon, the *Untermensch*, and Maria, the woman, were not exempt from the fight. Had they been in town rather than on the farm, they would likely have had to attend training on the *Panzerfaust*, an anti-tank missile that fired from close range from the shoulder. Ultimately it was a suicide mission.

The American army was ready to drive through Bavaria towards Czechoslovakia. Understandably, they proceeded cautiously, anticipating a possible counter-attack. However, in reality, the only thing standing in the way of the US Sixth Army was a handful of *Volkssturm* guarding the main routes through villages like Haschaberg and Döfering.

Leon was outside when British planes passed over the farm. Brückl called him to shelter, and they watched together as the aircraft headed off in the distance. A few minutes later, they heard the sound of a distant bombing. Cham was under attack.

After close to three years in Germany, Leon, now seventeen, yearned ever more for his homeland. He had written to his parents but had not heard from anyone since leaving Ukraine, not that the Germans would or could have delivered domestic mail to the USSR at any time, let alone during the winter of 1944–45. Moreover, concurrently, Soviet forces had overrun Ukraine.

Ironically, Leon could soon return home, not because Germany had won, as they promised, but because they had lost. Leon had long since realised that even had Germany emerged victoriously, they would never have allowed him to return home. He would have remained a slave in Germany.

On the morning that the war came to Haschaberg, Brückl woke Leon before dawn and told him to come with him. Together, they untethered two horses and from the stable, and having gathered some long ropes, the two rode out in a northerly direction. Before long, and just as the first rays of light began to emerge from the darkness, they arrived at a crudely constructed anti-tank defence that extended across the road. Erected a couple of days before by the *Volkssturm*,[88] they consisted of crossed timbers logs bound and fixed together. In theory, they would halt the American tanks so that the *Volksturrm* could finish them off with *Panzerfausts*. However, a collection of antique rifles and pitchforks was all that they had to repel the American army. It was a ludicrous proposition.

Having surveyed the barriers, Brückl instructed Leon to tie one end of each rope around the posts. They then tethered the other end to their horses and, simultaneously, they remounted and proceeded to pull the posts apart. Brückl did not want to delay the American advance. Had they been caught by the Nazis, their treasonous action undoubtedly would have meant their summary execution. Instead, they had cleared a path through to Cham.

On the way back, when they reached the top of a hill just a few kilometres away from home, they had a fantastic view as hundreds of American planes flew overhead. On the other side of the hill, they could see row upon row of tanks spread out along the horizon.[89]

By the time Leon and Brückl arrived back at the farm, Maria happened to be outside. At once, Leon ran to Maria to warn her, but she could not hear him; it was too late. The tanks were coming straight towards them. From there, everything happened so quickly. Leon was a hundred or so metres away from Maria when the tanks passed between them. The last he saw of Maria was her running back towards the farmhouse.

Leon had no choice but to run in the opposite direction and hide in some nearby bushes at the base of Bleschenburg. There he found some cover, catching his breath and amongst a group of startled cows. He waited in awe as the massive tanks passed by unchecked by any form of opposition. Leon had seen tanks before, but never anything like this. Hundreds of them, in rows that stretched for miles heading from west to east, their motors revving loudly in a chaotic symphony. The ground, wet from recent rains and recently sown for the summer crop, instantly became a quagmire as the tanks passed, but that was the least of Leon's concerns as bullets fired around him, and nearby explosions made his heart pound.

Then came the infantry, amidst trucks filled with soldiers that tried in vain to dodge the bog. Leon stayed hiding where he was until they passed before squelching his way back through the churned-up field to the farmhouse. It was empty.

Leon, in his short life, had already experienced several invasions. The Russian attack on Polish-controlled Ukraine was the first. They were not too bad, but they were not too good, either. Then came the Germans, who seemed decent, but ended up being far crueller than the Russians. This time, it was the Americans. Leon had no idea what to expect.

Regardless of the risk, Leon decided to go and look for Maria. Staying within the trees to avoid the open spaces, Leon continued in an easterly direction towards Döfering. Further along, he came across a group of American soldiers checking the forest nearby. Luckily, Leon saw them first and went the other way. He was fortunate indeed, but it meant a significant detour. Undoubtedly, the soldiers would have shot first and asked questions later had they seen a young man lurking through the woods.

42

Trapped in Battle – Maria, April 1945

The American army entered Cham on 23 April. Other than minimal resistance from a zealous group of Hitler Youth at the Regan River bridge, the Allied forces captured the town with ease. Still, the liberating troops had to guard against possible resistance and closed off the town as a precaution to isolate any rebel Schutzstaffel (SS) troops. Perhaps, groups of fanatics were hiding in the area planning for a counter-attack. Moreover, with the Russians and Americans closing in from both sides, it made sense for fugitives to hide in the swollen overpopulated town.

By now, as word of their heinous acts from witnesses at liberated camps, like Auschwitz, Sobibor and Treblinka, spread among the Allied forces, the SS had become wanted criminals.

In mid-April 1945, the Germans set up their defences along the Czechoslovakia border in a final futile effort, just a few kilometres from Brückl's farm in Haschaberg. From all directions, retreating fragments of once-mighty armies, including many SS, who wanted to fight on, had accumulated in a contracting corridor between American and Russian forces in the west and east, respectively. These desperate men were attempting to link up with the fanatical Nazi Field Marshal Schoerner, who remained in control of a sizeable but heavily depleted army in Czechoslovakia.

Many delusional Nazis considered Bohemia's mountainous areas and the Sudetenland virtually impregnable to the Allies and planned to hold out there indefinitely, perhaps forcing a stalemate. They did have the advantage of the naturally elevated defensive position of the mountains and forests and the former Czech fortifications, where they waited forlornly in the hope that Hitler would join them.

Delusional, they were. Complete Allied aerial and ground force superiority made a defence in the mountains impossible to maintain and destined to fail. Now that Cham had fallen, only small villages and towns, like Döfering, Hasherberg, Geigant and Waldmunchen, stood between them through to the Czech border. The autobahn provided a good resting point, and along that line, the Americans gathered, waiting for the order to push on.

> That was the terriblest thing that happened to me in the war.[90] Did you know that? We were outside still, [at] the border, and in the mountain, there was a German base up there; that the Germans took from the Czechoslovakians in [1938]…and they knew that a lot of German armies were up there. The Russians were coming from this [other] side already. The Germans were squashed in.

The Allied plan allowed Wehrmacht troops to gather from all directions in the strip between the autobahn (B22) and Czechoslovakia. It was a grim picture for those trapped in the middle.

> This was an ambush that they had. This was not just a coming through, it was a real ambush.
> It was so quiet, and in Döfering, there is a hillside, bushes and things like that. We heard for days, shelling and bombing and things like that, but we didn't know it was so close because the Germans would be bombing from the mountain out too. We would be all killed because we were right in the firing line. Where we were, the houses and all, we were right in the firing line, between the mountains [on one side] and from this side the Americans coming.

As the Americans waited for the order to make their move, compassionately they warned the residents.

> It was for days; we were watching, [we] couldn't go out. They [the Americans] said everywhere with a *Flugletter* [airdrop], 'Don't go out any more. [You] will get shot if you come out because [we] don't know who it is.'

In other words, 'If you go outside, we will not know if you are friend or foe, be warned! We will target anything that moves. The only way to be safe is to remain indoors. Brückl ordered everyone to heed the warning but as time passed and nothing happened, their anxiety gave way to boredom.

The Americans meant well by warning the locals. Still, anyone living on a farm, including Maria, who loved the outdoors, could not stay inside for long, especially with cattle to feed and crops to tend. Hence, in the morning, when the American army advanced, she was outside in the fields.

> All of a sudden came a plane down from high up to us down to the road. They were shooting and [strafing]…and the tanks. They shot our neighbour next to us. They shot her dead [because] she was outside. She was outside and wanted to run inside the house. She didn't know. We were outside too. A tank [bullet killed her].

'How, exactly?' I asked.

> The tanks. They come with this, like a snake.

Now, I was confused.

> The tanks have cannons too, but they were shooting over us at the base. You know, the tanks they come with, like snakes, I hate snakes,[91] and they *schießen*, fire, all the time.

I could not understand at the time of recording what she meant. Twenty years later, when reviewing the tape, I realised that Maria was referring to a machine gun. The snake-like thing was the ammunition belt.

Maria saw her neighbour, who had six children and was pregnant with her seventh, fall. Her children came rushing out from the house, crying out at their mother's death. Maria ran to where she lay. At the same time, a group of American soldiers arrived with their rifles raised. One soldier ran up to the deceased mother. She was dead straight away.

Maria was angry. 'Why would they kill an innocent woman?' she wondered. However, when she looked closer at the eyes of the soldier who was standing over her dead neighbour, Maria saw that he was crying. She looked to the other soldiers, and they too were distraught by her death, as they tried in vain to console the inconsolable children. They did not mean for her to die like that.

*

In 2019, I asked Sepp Brückl if he knew about the incident, thinking that it was unlikely but worth asking. Surprisingly, he recalled the experience and her name, Barbara Wagner, the place she died, and the number of children she had. He said she died because she defied the order to remain indoors. The Americans had orders to shoot to kill. They could not be sure that she was not a Nazi who was about to warn the enemy of the attack. In fact, she was running to get the white flag to surrender.

The heatwaves that overwhelmed Germany during the summer of 2019 abated enough to allow for delightful conditions on the morning that Sepp and his good friend, historian Henryk Gierlik took the Pilgrimage to the top of Bleschenburg. There we stood together, admiring the spectacular views of the district through which the American army passed seventy-four years before.

Two significant buildings adorn the top of the mountain. First, we visited a recently and beautifully rebuilt tiny chapel which, we learnt, replaced the one that Maria regularly used for prayer and reflection in her youth. The other, in contrast, consisted of an imposing wooden observation tower. Onsite workmen confirmed that it was not yet open for general admission to the public. Unperturbed, Henryk, who held some noticeable sway amongst the respectful tradesmen, invited us on an impromptu climb up over a hundred and sixty steps to the top of the tower. We felt priviieged to be probably the first tourists to scale the tower.

The breathtaking views at the top made it worth the while. To our right, to the east, the Czech mountains loomed largely, and almost directly below us, with it rolling green fields of farmlands, lay the sleepy village of Haschaberg. From that place, we could better appreciate, and to an extent, recreate in our minds how it looked that day when the tanks rolled in supported by the infantry and air support. I could picture Maria closest to us in the first field and Barbara Wagner in the next field as the tanks and planes passed by with the infantry following.

*

> Until we looked, I was surrounded by tanks.
> I ran in the field between the tanks. The tanks were before me, and hinter [behind] me and on the side and everywhere, and they shot and shelled everywhere. When I think about it, I was scared. I was very scared. They ambushed us. We were in the middle. They couldn't stop. They passed us one after another.

The war had come to Haschaberg. Within minutes, hundreds of American planes, tanks, and vehicles, along with thousands of infantry, dominated the landscape. Maria, perhaps in shock, ran away from the soldiers directly across the field to where she found cover in some bushes. She arrived to find herself confronted by the sound of bullets firing close by. Maria waited a few moments while more tanks passed, and, after a few deep breaths, sprinted back for the house.

> They were shooting before us, tanks shooting, shooting over us, everywhere I looked. They went past us. Then I ran into the house. There were tanks everywhere.

Out of the corner of her eye, Maria could see an army jeep bearing down upon her. Desperate to beat the vehicle, she ran ever faster and made it to the house just as the jeep pulled up about twenty metres behind her. She slammed the door shut and peered out through the curtains. To her great dismay, two men, an officer and a soldier, jumped from the vehicle and headed to the door. They entered the back door into the kitchen, where they found Maria had pressed up against the wall as if hoping it would swallow her whole. They must have seen her running towards the house and decided to follow. Unlike the American soldiers who were so humane when her neighbour died, these two were very angry. Moreover, knowing that she had ignored the warning to stay indoors made her fearful that they would shoot on the spot.

> Then an officer came to me and put a gun in my back, you know that? Then he took me away [in his jeep], for questioning.

Maria had no idea where they were taking her. Soon, they drove up a hill to arrive at a well-constructed three-storey house that the Americans had requisitioned due to its high vantage point.

It was very frightening. The officer ordered Maria out of the jeep and into the house. There, on the ground floor, she observed groups of American soldiers busily going about their jobs, studying maps on tables, reading documents, talking on wireless receivers, smoking, and so on. A few of them stared at Maria as she entered but said nothing.

The officer nudged his rifle further into her back, indicating for her to go upstairs, and up they went.

> Steps and steps and steps, right up to the attic. When [we] arrived in the attic, he still had the gun in my back, and he said [half in English, half in German], 'Where are the SS?'

Maria stood mute. Perhaps she thought she could try the silent method that had worked so well with her teacher. This time, it did not work. The officer, instead, pressed his face so close to Maria's ear that she could feel the bristles of his unshaven beard.

'I know you know,' he insisted. 'I saw you running away from the bushes.'

Maria could not deny it. His next comment left her utterly confused.

'You were running from the bushes where we found your SS friend. You were trying to warn him, but you were too late. We have killed him already.'

When Maria expressed her confusion, he went on with his interrogation. 'Why were you outside?'

It was so dangerous in the bush where we wanted to run, you know, with the cows. That's where they shot an SS, just before us. I don't know where the SS came from. They came from the bases or whatever.

Maria, of course, knew nothing but she realised that she had to think quickly.

So I said, 'No SS here.'
No? He didn't believe me.

The officer spun Maria to face him. 'Tell the truth,' he demanded.

Now I was really [firm]. 'No, SS. No! No shoot! They're all gone, gone, gone! No shoot any more.'[92]

Maria, at that point, knew that she was fighting for her life.

I don't know how this came out of me. [I said], 'No shoot, they [the SS] are all gone, gone! Not shoot any more.'
He must have really really believed me it was true!
Then he put the gun away from my back, and he said to me, 'I understand that. I'll stop firing. Now, I'll stop firing. Until tomorrow morning, I'll stop firing. You have to get away [from here]. Until tomorrow, then you can come back.'
Then he [said] something on his radio.
The next minute, everything, the whole range, the whole of what you could hear and see, everything stopped. The firing stopped, the tanks, the planes, everything; everything! He said it to me in the attic up there: he stopped firing. I convinced him so much, not to shoot any more. I don't know how I convinced him of that, but I must have convinced him. Then, the next minute, exactly in the next minute, the battle stopped.

Maria sensed his authority.

He was in command. He was the *Oberst* [colonel]. I think he was the *Oberst*. He was in command.

The commander clearly had considerable influence in the battle and orders to clear the corridor between American and Czech-German border lines.

Having assessed the situation, the colonel communicated with his units that the area was now clear. He then explained to Maria that they had evidence that deserters had been in the same building and the same room they were now standing in.

> He said, 'There were a few *Vermisters*, deserters, up there, you know, in the attic. They were lying up in the attic. They came out from Czechoslovakia, and the boys, they ran away, and they left their rucksacks. They searched through the backpacks and found that one had an SS picture in a photo. They knew there were SS [there because of the one they shot earlier]. That's why they thought the SS were [still] here.

But Maria had talked him out of the idea.

Having assessed Maria as a reliable witness and not any sort of threat, the colonel allowed her to leave. Beforehand, however, he warned her that if the Germans fired first, the battle would start straight away. He stressed that if the enemy even fired 'one shot from the mountain to their base, then it's finished, they would wipe everything out. One shot!'

> But I had him so convinced that he stopped the fire, and he stopped it, [called a ceasefire] until the next morning, [provided] they stop, and they don't start it in the morning. Then we can get out, otherwise [the war would begin again, and there would be no holding back]. We'd get killed.

The colonel was grateful.

Having heard her recount story many years before, I thought Maria had intimated that the colonel had then made a pass at her. 'Did he try to kiss you?' I asked.

> No. Then he put his hand on my shoulder, and that's all.

He then had his driver drop off Maria back at the farm. The journey back was bumpy, going over holes from tank tracks and shell blasts, so at the top of the hill, about half a kilometre to her back door, he indicated for Maria to get out. She walked to the farmhouse with her back to the driver and wondered if it was a trick. For a second or two, Maria half-expected a bullet in her back. Instead, she heard the roar of the motor as it accelerated away.

43

The Volkssturm – Leon, April 1945

Leon passed amongst the bushes and trees until he reached the outskirts of Zillendorf. From there, Leon intended to loop back and head south towards Döfering. There, he found several rows of roadblocks that the *Volkssturm* had erected along the road, similar to those he and Brückl had destroyed the previous day.

> With the *Volkssturm*, there was a lot of fighting going on. They used to get old people and young people to cut down trees and block the roads.

Wisely, Leon decided to stay off the road and go around the barricades and keep to the bushes to avoid detection. After a while, he once more heard the roar of American tanks. From where he was, he could see through the trees as a Sherman tank appeared from around the corner and headed straight for the barricades. Behind it came infantry, and then came another tank with more infantry. Several more followed. Further back were open fields, but now the road passed through the woods; it was the perfect place for an ambush.

Then, from behind the barricade, a group of *Volkssturm* appeared and began to fire at the advancing Sherman tanks. It was like trying to stop a man with a feather. The tank fired back, mowing down everything in its path, and continued into the forest.

Leon moved deeper into the woods and found a place to hide. Soon, the gunfire ceased, but he still waited another hour or so before cautiously returning to the scene of the battle. The roadblocks and the soldiers behind them proved highly ineffective.

I've seen Americans, killed some German soldiers. The tanks just rolled over them. What could they say? They were scared. They accepted it.

Leon stuck to the roadside and headed back to Haschaberg, but as he got closer, he found that the tanks and infantry had arrived ahead of him and had blocked the road to Brückl's farm. Again, he had to go around via the back way, where he eventually passed by a very familiar farm. It belonged to Leis, and there, outside in the shadows, stood Emily.

'Quick, get inside,' she ordered. Leon knew better than to refuse an instruction from Emily, so he skulked inside.

The front room was in relative darkness with all the curtains drawn, save for a single candle that burned in the middle of the kitchen table. Leon saw that the family had gathered there, occasionally peering out from various windows, looking to see where the Americans were. Leon expected at any moment that Emily or Leis would order him to do this or that, or even to belt him for whatever reason, but instead, Emily turned and said, '*Bitte*. Please,' as she offered him some *Schinken mit Brot*, ham and bread.

Leon sat and ate and waited.

Emily spoke first. '*Es tut mir leid.* I am sorry,' she said, with tears in her eyes.

Leon nodded; it was the first time anyone had said those words to him. He stayed with the family for two or three hours, during which he realised that the Leis family no longer supported Hitler. Sadly, it took the needless death of their sons to understand that. They were just one family of millions who lived to carry with them for the rest of their lives the heavy burden of loss caused by the war.

There were three girls, Emily, Rosa and Maria – they all survived, married and moved away.

Eventually, Leon bid farewell to the family and carefully made his way, sticking to the shadows, back to the Brückls. As he neared his destination, there were still plenty of tanks about, so Leon had to wait until dark before creeping the final bit of his way across to the farmhouse. When he arrived, he was surprised to find the place empty.

Finally, Leon found everyone at the neighbour's house. There, before he learned of Mrs Wagner's death, he was much relieved to see that Maria had made it back alive.

That night, nobody slept. They prayed for those who had died that day, including the *Volkssturm* in their senseless effort to save the already doomed Third Reich.

44

The Ceasefire – Maria, 1945

Maria returned to find that everyone was at the Bösl farm. Given that the last time they had seen her was in the thick of the battle driving off in an American jeep, they were immensely relieved that she had made it back. Maria stayed there a while but soon became restless and, albeit relieved to be home, considered other options.

> Now, what I did is, I went out of the house. People went inside and prayed, I went out from the house from Bösl, out the door, and down to a little road.

I asked, 'Why couldn't you all just run away?'

Maria answered, just a little annoyed that I had broken her train of thought.

> They can't. It's too late, they couldn't go away. We'd have to go down the hillside; they [wouldn't know who we were]. We would be shot. Where would we go? From the [German] base at the mountain, here. The Germans and the Russians were fighting over there.

During the ceasefire, the communities of Haschaberg and Döfering remained trapped in between the American and German forces, knowing and at any moment, the battle might resume.

> We were in the middle of a battle; in the middle of the ambush, I ran in the middle of the ambush of hundreds and thousands of tanks. You couldn't see them for hours.

Maria, realising how volatile the situation was, threw herself at God's mercy.

I gone outside and got down on my knees and prayed to God. 'Please, don't let there be shooting any more.' We were all waiting for the next shot, then it's finished, they would start straight away. One shot from the mountain, from the base, then it's finished, they would wipe everything out. And for this, they were waiting. They came so fast to the ambush here.

All of a sudden, in this house where I was with him in the attic, they stopped the fire. Must [be] something. God helped them, otherwise, we would all be dead. Must be something. They would all be gone.

I tell you that, they don't know how lucky they were, Waldmunchen and Haschaberg and all, they don't know how lucky they were that the man [the colonel] stopped the fire up with me. I've got to say that – because nobody knows, just I know because he told me that. He told me we could go back in the morning if they don't shoot.

And at night, I really asked God to help us. 'Don't let shoot.' They were waiting for every shot.

Paradoxically, after having played a significant role in obtaining the ceasefire, Maria now endangered it.

There were tanks everywhere next to me. They had no lights. They sat there so quiet, like ghosts, like ghosts, they were.

Maria realised that in the darkness, she had inadvertently walked into where many of the tanks had gathered.

After standing in the middle of the battlefield waiting for the next shot to take my life, I asked God to take my life if he wanted to. This is true: take my life wherever you want to in the world, but please don't let there be shooting any more. From then on, my life was never my own.

On a warm spring, moonless night, not far from Döfering, in the open, her eyes fixed towards the heavens, Maria prayed in the darkness and waited for the morning.

Up to Cham, everywhere, there were all sorts of tanks and arms. I stayed out [all night] and prayed.

The Americans waited in the darkness, too, their tanks on the roadside everywhere. Maria was close by and felt that they must have seen her. She felt their presence and didn't dare move. She knew that with so many tanks around and so many soldiers, somebody must be able to see her.

> They must know somebody was [outside]. The tanks on the roadside everywhere. They were very quiet, they were watching every little thing, then any little thing, BANG, and they would start it, wiping everything out, you know.

Maria understood the fragility of her situation.

> I don't know if they saw me there on the road, kneeling. It was dangerous. They could shoot me straight away.

It was the longest night of her life.

Finally, after not a minute of sleep, the sun ascended, lighting up the horizon along the countryside on what promised to be a glorious day. Maria trusted that the colonel was true to his word; she was now safe and could walk around freely.

> The morning came, and everything was quiet. When I went home, they were at home in the Bösl house.

They had wisely stayed there together throughout the night. The more people out, the higher the risk. Maria was relieved to find everyone, including Leon, there. They were upset that Maria had gone off into the night but pleased to see her alive and well. Maria, and perhaps the entire community, was fortunate that no one saw her.

> That's why the next-door neighbour was shot. They (said) nobody could be outside…they have the order to shoot them; (because) they don't know if she is a spy.
>
> That's another stupid thing I did. I could have been shot two times, shot ten times, if God had not protected me. I know he (the colonel) told me they'd stop the fire until morning… If they don't shoot first, if they [the Germans] don't start it again, in the morning, then we can get out.

While Leon was thrilled by the manner of Maria's survival, she thought otherwise of Leon.

> He was stupid! Ha. I said, 'Where have you been?'
> He wouldn't say. When the Americans came, he was hiding just outside Haschaberg. He was just a coward! Ha, ha, he ran away![93]

The comment was typical of Maria, especially in later life. She regularly tried to get one up on her husband. Her criticism, some fifty years afterwards, was somewhat unfair.

45

Freedom – Maria and Leon, May 1945

The next morning, Maria, who knew almost all of the local *Volksturm*, asked Leon to take her to where they had died. They walked to the location and arrived to find a group of civilians, under the supervision of a small group of American soldiers, clearing the flattened barricades that the *Volkssturm* had erected to halt the advance.

'Come on then,' said Maria. 'It's about time we surrendered.'

When the American soldiers saw them arriving with arms aloft, one of them stepped forward, with his rifle at the ready and questioned them, especially Leon, in German. When he realised Leon was a slave, he told him, *'Du brauchts nichts mehr helfen. Du bist jetzt frei.* You do not need to help. You are free.'

Leon stood there for a moment, taking it all in. He glanced at Maria. Soon, they were helping to clear the debris.

Amongst the foliage lay the dead remnants of Hitler's last throw of the dice. They were either overwhelmed by machine-gun fire or crushed beneath the tracks of the mighty Sherman tanks.

They removed a piece of foliage to find the lifeless body of a *Volkssturm*. Maria and Leon helped drag his body out into the open, after which an American soldier walked casually to the body carrying a pick. In stupefaction, they watched. For young Leon, it was another sight he would never forget.

> I've seen an American soldier with a pick, drive it into his mouth, and drag him along.

As they worked, Leon could not help but stare at Maria, who

worked beside him, with tears in her eyes. She knew some of the dead. He did not quite understand his feelings but liked being around her.

Before leaving, Maria walked over to the line of dead *Volksturm* and, oblivious to the risk of upsetting the Americans, crouched down to where the first one lay. Gently, she traced the sign of the cross on his forehead, saying, *'Gott segne dich, im Namen des Vaters, des Sohnes und des Heiligen Geistes.* God bless you, in the name of the Father, the Son, and Holy Ghost.' Then she moved on to the next and blessed him, and eventually blessed them all.

One by one, they loaded the dead on the back of a truck. Afterwards, an American threw Leon two packets of cigarettes. Leon's confidence grew. These people might be all right, after all.

46

Aftermath – Maria and Leon, Autumn 1945

On 25 April, US and Soviet forces met for the first time at the River Elbe. Political ideology meant nothing as they celebrated the defeat of their arch-enemy. This followed a massive rush of civilians and soldiers from the east to reach the American-held west bank ahead of the Russian army. Such was their reputation for cruelty that people left their homes, often permanently, rather than surrender to the Soviets. Now, only isolated pockets of resistance remained dotted throughout the once-mighty Third Reich.

On 26 April, the US army halted Just a few kilometres past Haschaberg, near the Czech border, where they set up their artillery. The heavily wooded forest there provided well-camouflaged hiding places for the Wehrmacht to hold back the advancing forces. Walking blindly into the woods was suicide, so the Americans set up their artillery a safe distance away from the foot of the mountain. From there, they pounded the forest for several days with explosions that set the whole area ablaze. In the end, the few Germans who were there had no chance of holding out.

*

All that remains of the one-sided battle today is a small memorial cross with the names of a handful of German soldiers who died there inscribed upon it. Located on the walkway through the picturesque forest at the Czech/German border, the place is now a popular cultural recreational site. There we pilgrims stopped to enjoy a celebratory evening with the locals, who had levelled out a section of the mountain to create a beautiful picnic area. They make a massive pile of wood at the celebration and set fire to it internally to smoke rather than burn it. It takes weeks to scorch through the entire firewood collection. Somehow, the process creates high-density charcoal that they can sell for their fires for the winter. We were more interested in the schnapps, the great food, excellent company and beautiful surroundings, to be fair.

Just before dark, I decided to go for a walk through the forest. For about twenty minutes wandering through the scrub and remembering the way back, I could not help but wonder what secrets these woods held. How terrible it must have been for the soldiers here as the bombs crashed, lighting the forest like a torch. I wondered how many bullets, and even bodies, still lay here somewhere, lost. Bodies are still found regularly in the forests between Berlin and the Elbe River.[94] Somewhat edified, I snapped out of my reverie and rejoined the celebrations.

*

With all effective resistance gone, the Americans advanced deep into Czechoslovakia. Within another week, they had progressed almost to Prague to where the Russians were coming from the east.

On 30 April, Hitler and his new wife of a matter of hours, Eva Braun, committed suicide. His propaganda minister, Joseph Goebbels and his wife, Magda, having murdered their six children the following day, followed suit. Before he died, Hitler, having fallen out with the obvious candidates, Himmler and Goering, appointed Grand Admiral Karl Dönitz as his successor. Two days later, Berlin fell to the Soviets. Unlike the First World War, this time, nobody could argue the outcome.

Despite some obsessive Nazi hopes that Schörner's army would hold out indefinitely in Czechoslovakia's mountains, their cause had no long-term chance of success. On 7 May, a week later, Dönitz met with Allied representatives at Reims in France to sign the unconditional surrender of all German armed forces in all combat areas. The directive, effective from 8 May, allowed twenty-four hours for word to reach the various commanders and combatants. While people still needed to remain vigilant, the remnants of the once-mightiest nation on earth laid down their arms. The war in Europe was finally over.[95]

Following a prearranged agreement with the Soviets, the Americans withdrew from Czechoslovakia, allowing the communists to control the country. They stayed for another forty-eight years.

> When we knew the war ended, everyone was happy. Even those who previously supported Hitler, I suppose they were happy too.

Resistance, however, continued in some areas.

> Some of the Nazis used to sit in the church and kept shooting; machine guns tried to kill the Americans, [but] where I was, nobody was trying to kill Americans.

Leon may have been referring to resistance by the notorious Werewolf group, who vowed to continue to fight for Nazism against Jews and Communists. They believed the war should continue just as the Resistance did against the Nazis in countries throughout the war.

Leon settled quickly into life in Germany after the war. Almost as soon as they arrived, the Americans offered him and other foreigners employment, helping build a new army base outside Cham. For the first time in his life, Leon received a wage for his work.

> Oh, when they came, I was eighteen or nineteen. It was great. They gave me cigarettes, chocolate and gave me a pair of shoes, clothes...

Leon was proud to be a free Ukrainian and pleased that the Americans recognised him as Ukrainian, not Russian. However, any international recognition of Ukrainian sovereignty was short-lived. From the start, the Soviet Union refused to grant Ukraine independence, resulting in a civil war that was to last for several years. Other than some, like General Patton, who wanted to continue to fight the Soviets, most had no appetite for another war. Without Allied support, the Soviets annexed Ukraine and the other Eastern European countries, including Poland, ironically over whose independence the war had started.

Ukraine stood no chance. Stalin argued that the Soviet Union lost twenty million citizens in the war, and were therefore entitled to an increased buffer zone for their defences. Of course, this meant subjugating the Eastern European lands along with their people and resources.

All of this was at that time unknown to Leon. All he cared about was that the end of hostilities meant that he could go home before 1945 was out. Thus, he wrote hopefully to his mother. In his letter, he said that he was alive and had survived and expressed how much he longed to be back with his family on the farm, riding Shimmel. The letter never arrived. In the meantime, Leon, while a free man, still had to remain in a defeated, occupied country. He was adaptable and resourceful and knew how to survive. His first decision was to leave Brückl's farm.

With the war over, many Nazis, particularly those of the SS, had to face the executioner. At the time of Cham's liberation, Heinrich Himmler, the most wanted of the many Nazi war criminals, was on the run. It was to be another month before his capture. Many of the Nazi hierarchy, including Hans Frank and Julius Streicher, were among the criminals who met their fate with the hangman following the famous Nuremberg war trials. However, Hitler's chief henchmen, Goering and Himmler, controlled their destiny by committing suicide before their imminent execution.

Other notorious Nazis, including Joseph Mengele, the Doctor of Death at Auschwitz; Adolf Eichmann, one of the leading Nazis prosecutors of the Holocaust; and Klaus Barbie, the Butcher of Lyon, managed to flee the country, and hence justice. The Nazi fugitives, like many others, escaped via Italy by the infamous Rat Line, with the assistance of groups sympathetic to the Nazi cause, including from within the Vatican. South America was their favourite destination.[96]

While almost everyone was incredibly relieved when Germany surrendered, the terrible reality of another defeat and another lost generation took its toll on all of the survivors. This time, four million young men, along with hundreds of thousands of civilians, lost their lives in Germany alone. The Döfering parish lost more than its fair share.

> A lot of school friends went, and they didn't come back. Look, from a little town where we lived, there were [about] fifty houses. Not many came back. Oh yeah, my boyfriend was killed, Xaver. There was more. My school friends and those who were a bit older, I knew them all. There were four cousins from me from the same village [who] died. A few of the houses had three or four boys, all killed – the people I grew up with were all gone.

It is unimaginable the extent to which people across the country felt that loss. Everybody lost someone. Sometimes, whole families, who would otherwise have gone on to lead full and productive lives, disappeared forever.

On the day Leon gave notice to Brückl of his imminent departure, he managed to steal a moment with Maria, and he implored her to leave the farm. Maria decided to take his advice. There were other reasons to go. While she received a meagre wage and could have stayed on, she felt the need to exercise her freedom now that she had a choice. Helped by Leon's reassurance that all would be well, she told Brückl that she was leaving and moved back with her grandmother in Döfering.

Maria never had romantic feelings for Leon during the war. But he was no longer a scab-faced *Ostarbeiter*; but a handsome, eligible and independent young man. Maria still mourned Xaver, as she would for all of her life, but she knew that the vast majority of would-be available German men lay dead on faraway battlefields. Even for the few who came home, their suffering continued.

> From all those who left to go and fight, my Uncle Alois, he was the only one. He came back a few years later.

*

Alois returned a broken man. My sister, Maria, and I met with him at his house in Burglengenfeld in 1985, a few years before he died. We found him to be a man of few words. Rather than converse, he habitually muttered something unintelligible under his breath. It was as if his experiences caused him to suffer in perpetual torment.

In his house, I noticed, hanging on the wall down the corridor, a close-up photo of Great-Uncle Alois, looking proud and smart in his German Wehrmacht uniform.

Before leaving, our lovely cousin Ziglinde presented me with Grandfather Keil's original Liberation from Nazism document from 1946.

This photo, taken from a unique position under construction observation tower at Bleschenberg, shows the sleepy village of Haschaberg today. Maria stood near the dark patch in the foreground, as the American tanks rolled across the fields on their way to the Czech border. Bleschenberg was a favourite praying spot for Maria. Having passed the village, the Americans then set up their artillery at the foot of the mountain, where, for the next few days, they constantly shelled where they believed the German positions to be in the mountains.

47

Revenge – Leon, Autumn 1945

After hostilities ended, Ukrainians found themselves spread all over Europe. Unlike elsewhere, some Wehrmacht leaders saw the value of harnessing their collective potential as Ukrainian soldiers by allowing them to fight cohesively in one army rather than split them as they had done in Russia. Along with Schörner's command, they were some of the last Wehrmacht to surrender. However, unlike those who succumbed to the Soviets, these did far better.

> After the war, they had about 12,500 [Ukrainian] prisoners of war in Italy. They gave themselves up to the English, a place called Rimini. Then from Rimini in 1947, '48, '49, England took them over [allowed them to emigrate]. They were completely free – everyone had a bicycle. They could go to different farms, work on the farms, and do what they wanted. After they finished, they released them all, gave everybody civilian clothes, said go where you like. That's why there's so many of them in places like Bradford and Leicester.

No sooner had the fighting ceased, however, than the Soviets demanded the return of all of its citizens, significantly more than three million, including Leon, who worked for the Germans. Initially, the Allies were fully compliant, as were the majority of displaced Soviet inhabitants. They all wanted to go home. It all seemed simple enough and, initially, hundreds of thousands of *Ostarbeiters* crammed onto trains from all over Europe and headed back to the homeland, with joy in their hearts. However, it was not to be a fairy tale return.

Ivan, a member of the Ukrainian community in Newcastle, described what typically happened next. The trains, destined for Kyiv,

Leon with friends at Windischbergerdorf refugee camp, c. 1946.

continued to travel east. After some time, the people started to realise that they had passed Kyiv an hour ago, yet they still headed east – to Siberia. They were in transit to the Gulags. People panicked and started to jump off the trains, do anything, to stop going to the camps.

After helping build the American base, Leon gained employment in the construction of new refugee camp at Windischbergerdorf, just outside Cham. His work included felling trees and preparing the timber for building and construction. After the completion of the buildings, Leon moved into the camp, enjoying free food and accommodation.

In Cham and its outlying regions, the American army maintained a robust military presence until around 1949. American tanks, now fearful of Soviet Union aggression, were continually patrolling up and down the Czech border outside Brückl's farm in Haschaberg.

*

During the Pilgrimage, I asked Ungarn, the old man I met in Cham's town centre, about the Americans' arrival. He fondly remembered the soldiers as exceptionally generous. They provided him and his friends with luxuries like chocolate and large citrus fruits. A young boy at the time, Ungarn was thrilled by their magnanimous behaviour, particularly that of the group he called 'Niggers'. There was no ill intent in the phraseology; it was merely the vernacular of the time.

*

Soon after fighting ceased, Leon learned that many of the newly liberated refugees, mainly those poorly treated by their overlords, wanted revenge.

> Some of the people like myself, the ones who had terrible jobs or terrible farmers or terrible people, they used to do some harm to them, you know. Like they used to go stealing things, taking things away from them. Robbing them, they were scared.

The tables had turned. Former slaves like Leon were now free to do as they pleased. One of the first steps they took was to arm themselves. It was a free-for-all.

> I mean, there were guns. You could have guns. There were guns everywhere, you know. The Germans left them. The Americans would give you them if you asked them. You go to the farm, you take whatever you want. Go to the shops, take as much material, or a suit, whatever you want.

Initially, the Americans turned a blind eye to many acts of reprisal. However, Leon's family taught him to treat all people respectfully, and he knew that retaliatory actions and crime would lead to ruin.

> Why should I [steal]? I thought to myself, well, I'll buy it myself. If I go stealing, eventually, I'll get killed. I wasn't badly treated either.

While others were violent towards their former masters, who were very scared, Leon saw no reason to be vengeful.

> Brückl treated me well during the time. Why should I wish him harm? If I had stayed with Leis, then things might have been different. He never hit me like Leis did in the morning when he shouted out, 'Verflucter Ausländer, Aufsteh.' Mind you, he never gave me anything extra except for one time when I was seventeen or eighteen. He said,

> 'Leon, come here,' and he gave me a cigarette. 'You're old enough to have a cigarette.'
> I know Brückl used me as free labour, but he gave me what I needed: food, clothes, a place to live. I was grateful.

It was strange at first, being able to walk around town a free man. People looked at him differently now. Perhaps it was due to the tailored suit he wore, now that he was earning a wage, or maybe they no longer saw him as *Untermensch*. Photos of Leon shortly after the war showed him to be a handsome, well dressed and charismatic young man with evident pride in his appearance. Once more, he adapted to external change and, ostensibly at least, was able to put the horrors of war behind him to move on with his new life.

> I used to go to the Gasthaus, where they sell beers. They didn't mind me. Everyone used to like me. I spoke good German then too. I was the first one who could really speak German properly. Everybody understood me. I was interested to learn. The Polish took three or four years to learn.

At the American base outside Döfering, Leon had no trouble convincing the authorities of his refugee status. After his clearance, Leon had two choices: stay in Germany or get back to Ukraine. The Americans liked him for his ability to speak so many languages, Polish, Ukrainian, Russian, German, and even a smattering of English, and invited him to work for them. While others rushed to go home, that short period of grace probably saved his life.

Social life became necessary at the war's end. Leon liked to get together with his fellow Ukrainians, including Joe Sherbiac, who also came to Germany on the cattle carts in 1942, and the two became best friends. Along with other fellow refugees, Americans, and even Germans, they regularly met and played card games, a staple leisure activity throughout post-war Europe. The beauty was that you just needed a deck of cards. It was a great way to pass the time while enjoying drinks and cigarettes with friends and strangers alike. While there were many games playable without gambling, more often than not, they played for

Leon, centre, with a group of well-dressed, successful young former Ostarbeiter, including Joe Sherbiac, far left, c. 1946. Leon said, 'If you wanted a suit, you just took it.'

money. Leon became an excellent card player with an extraordinary ability to count cards and intuitively know how to play his hand.

> Mind you, we used to win a lot, the Ukrainians in the private houses; we used to play Twenty-One.[97]

The impact of war on individuals continued long after the fighting stopped, as Leon recalled.

> One morning, under the roof, we were playing [cards], and this bloke went to the toilet. He shouted, 'Come here!' so we came down.
> Here a German bloke had hung himself. Nanna [Maria] knows who it was.

He was one of the prominent Nazi supporters in Waldmünchen. Leon and a few others went to take him down.

> We weren't allowed to touch him. Some of the older blokes said, 'Don't touch him. It's a police job. You have nothing to do with it. Let's clear off and go home.'

One might ask if the Nazi sympathiser did kill himself, or was it an act of revenge? Regardless, suicide, murder and death had been a part of daily life for so long.

Leon somehow understood that hard work and intelligence were the keys to success. He liked working for the friendly Americans, who admired foreign workers like Leon, who made an effort to assimilate.

> They gave me a pair of boots, and in the wintertime, I used to go through the snow, through the forest and even Frenchmen used to work there, prisoners of war, all the Ukrainians, Polish, Russian all young people. We used to cut the trees and pack them for the army.

Just as Leon decided that it was time to go home, rumours circulated that the Soviet Union never intended to grant independence to the Ukrainian people. They heard that groups like the Ukrainian Insurgent Army had combined to fight a full-scale war for their freedom back in the homeland. However, compared to the Soviets, they were poorly equipped, relying mainly on discarded or stolen weapons acquired during the war. They desperately hoped that the Americans and perhaps the English would come to their rescue. However, they were disappointed.

Stalin, rather than open his borders, closed them to the west and satellite nations like Poland, Bulgaria, Romania and Czechoslovakia became puppet states behind what Churchill would call the Iron Curtain. Paradoxically Poland, the country most directly involved in Hitler's prewar demands and whose fight for freedom was the fundamental concept behind the outbreak of war, ended up controlled by the Soviet Union. The Stalinist regime remained conspicuous by its people's subjugation. While the outside world was generally sympathetic, nobody stepped forward to help. Nevertheless, many Ukrainians, despite overwhelming odds, continued to fight for freedom.

Whenever Leon and his fellow Ukrainians met, the question of returning home was usually a high priority. The stories of the battle for Ukrainian independence, no doubt, challenged their desire to join in the struggle. However, the risks and uncertainty caused them to hesitate.

> We heard that it was very dangerous to leave Germany. We knew what was going on over there. People came and told us people were still fighting there. Partisans were fighting the Russians. They were still fighting until 1947. They said, 'You go home, they'll take you to the partisans – you'll be dead. The war is finished here, but it's still happening over there.'

Leon also became aware at the time of another major obstacle to going home.

> As far as the Russians were concerned, we were all traitors because we worked for the Germans. [They told us], you go home, they will kill you, you will be dead if you go back. After that, we stayed in Germany. Nobody wanted to go home.

Leon began to appreciate that he was stuck, potentially for the rest of his life, in a foreign land. The upside was that he began seeing Maria regularly. Even though there were plenty of refugees around, including Ukrainians, Leon decided on Maria.

> We went out, and eventually, I asked her to marry me.

48

Engaged and Married – Maria, 1946

The first thing the victors had to do was to determine who was still a Nazi. Hence, every adult had to confirm his or her identity as a citizen no longer associated with Nazism. After that, the occupying Allied forces demanded that all Germans henceforth must carry his or her Liberation from Nazism identification card. Those not complying risked arrest and internment.

Having established their freedom from Nazism, what began very tentatively began to blossom. In those days, strange was normal. Leon and Maria came from very different circumstances: one, a defeated Aryan, the other a victorious *Ostarbeiter*, yet when Leon asked her out, Maria accepted his invitation. No doubt, they began to sow the seeds

'Liberated from Nazism' ID, issued 2 September 1946 at Waldmunchen. It belonged to Maria's grandfather, Josef Keil.

earlier but never considered a formal relationship, given that a romantic association in Nazi Germany would probably have resulted in imprisonment for her and execution for him. The tables had turned. Together, they went out and enjoyed the nightlife of post-war Germany. Soon afterwards, Maria announced that she was pregnant. Both Leon and Maria knew the importance of having a father around; the couple decided to marry.

The wedding took place at St Jacob's church in Cham on 23 January 1946, less than nine months after the war ended. Attendees probably included the Keils and Brückls, Schwatos and her family, Joe Sherbiac and Mikal. Of Maria's close childhood friends, only Annie was alive to attend. Johann Kolnhoffer gave Maria away – perhaps their relationship had improved. On 22 June the following year, they welcomed their first child, Maryl, into the world.[98]

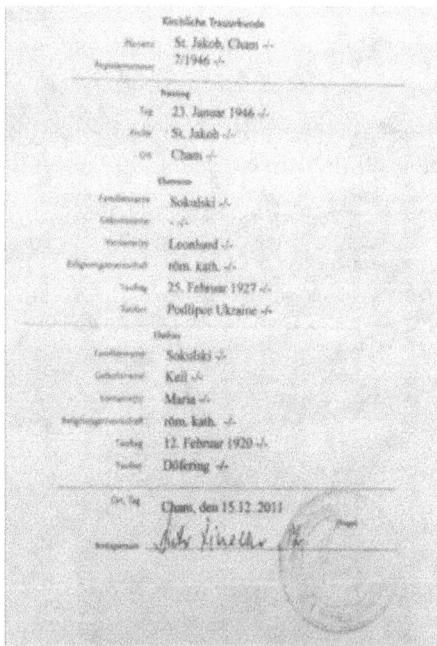

The wedding certificate of Maria and Leon. For some reason, they have his name as Leonard and surname ending in an 'i'. They were married just eight months after hostilities ended.

49

Stolen – Leon, 1946

Word soon spread that to go back home was a potential death sentence. Voluntary repatriation to the Soviet Union, after that, came to an abrupt halt. Unsatisfied, Soviet agents went to great lengths to bring their traitors to justice.

> Oh, yeah, we knew that we couldn't go home. The Russians used to go around [across the border] and try to pinch people, young boys, Ukrainians. They asked you on the street. They would kill you if they had to or take you back.

It was a worrying time for displaced former slave labourers from the Soviet Union. Their greatest fear was being stolen and brought back for imprisonment or execution as traitors.

> People used to jump from anywhere, commit suicide, as long as they didn't have to go back home. Of course, I wanted to go and see the family, but I knew what was going to happen if I went there. They straight away would take me to Siberia. They say, 'You worked five years for the Germans, now you work five years for the Russians.'

Five years in a Russian gulag, that was akin to a death sentence.

It was a good reason to leave Europe forever, and many, including Leon, eventually did. Despite the lies, going back to the Soviet Union was not an option. Other communist-backed places were no better.

> They promised them, 'You go on a train, and you will go straight home.' [Instead] people used to go on a train and go to Yugoslavia, and when they got off the train, they shot everyone. Thousands and thousands [died because] they said they were helping Hitler. The boys didn't want to go, they ran away, till everything settled down.[99]

*

Another Maria, now ninety and remarkably healthy, is an active member of Newcastle's Ukrainian community. She survived because she worked for a German woman who was pregnant at the time. The two had become best friends, and she begged Maria to stay in Germany until after her baby was born. By that time that happened, the knowledge was out, and she stayed in Germany. She knew that going home could well prove deadly.

Soviet agents inconspicuously continued to cross the border.

> They take anybody they wanted to take. They could take their people back home wherever they came from. They used to pinch all sorts of people.

*

US President Roosevelt died just before the war's end, leading the Nazis to harbour false hope that things would turn around for them. The new President, Harry S. Truman, wisely chose to appoint the late president's wife, Eleanor Roosevelt, as US delegate to the United Nations Assembly. She had heard the news of the Soviet Union's treatment of repatriated citizens and set out to save those still in Germany. In 1946, she visited the Windischbergerdorf refugee camp. Leon and Maria were there at the time.

> Mrs Roosevelt stopped it. I don't know why. She said, 'No more! Everybody can go wherever they want to go.'

The following year, the Declaration of Human Rights issued in 1948, Article 14 (1), stated, 'Everyone has the right to seek and enjoy in other countries asylum from persecution.' Article 13 (2) added that 'Everyone has the right to leave any country, including his own, and return to his country.'

> A moratorium between the Allied powers at that time meant that refugees had twenty-four hours where they were free to go to wherever they wanted.

Many of them went to the Ukrainian army or went to POW camps in Italy and afterward immigrated to England. Leon chose, for the moment, to remain in Germany.

Contrary to the mandate, Russian agents continued, albeit secretly, to cross the border to steal their former citizens.

Soon after he married, Leon was working, cutting trees, with another man in the drizzling rain, when another man appeared from out of the woods. He had a long coat with the collar curled up to keep himself dry. Before they could say 'Hello', the man revealed a pistol that he aimed straight at them. He spoke Russian and Ukrainian and ordered them to walk through the forest towards the Czech border. To where? Leon knew what this meant. His worst fear was about to come true. He had heard of Russians looking for so-called traitors, and now he was captured. Paradoxically, the Germans forced him to leave Ukraine in 1942; now, four years later, the Russians were forcing him to return for a lengthy stay and a miserable death in a Siberian gulag. With a gun aimed at his back, he could neither run nor fight.

They walked for about fifteen minutes to a clearing where an old German army truck waited. Someone had painted black over the German logo.

'Keep moving. Get in the back,' he ordered.

There was another man with the truck guarding two other men, both of whom Leon recognised. One of them was a man named Hryhoriy.

Leon and his companion sat with the other men in the back of the truck. It had a canvas roof and back flaps that their captor tied together when they were all inside. Their captor sat near the exit, pointing his gun at them while the driver moved into the forward compartment. Leon sat next to Hryhoriy in the left-hand corner, near the driver's compartment.

The guard waved his gun menacingly at the men and threatened to kill anyone who tried to escape.

'Why are we here?' one of them asked.

'You are traitors to the Soviet Union!' he replied, 'You worked for the Germans during the war and will face justice in the Motherland. From now on, if you speak, I will blow your brains out.'

The group was terrified as the truck drove off towards the border. They all knew what would happen to them in the gulags back in the Soviet Union.

Leon could never understand why the Jews passively accepted their fate and walked to their deaths without a fight. He decided that he would not die peacefully, and his mind worked overtime, devising a plan. Perhaps he could make a break for it when the truck slowed down, or maybe they could take out the guard before he could shoot them all.

As the truck rocked and rattled on the bumpy road, Leon felt a nudge. The man beside him, Hryhoriy, without speaking, revealed a pistol from inside his jacket. Leon was momentarily shocked but nodded his understanding. As the truck bounced along the potholed road, they waited for an opportunity, but the guard's rifle never wavered. Leon prayed for something to happen before they got too far away from Germany. If the truck stopped at a Russian garrison, they were as good as dead. If there was to be a fight, it had to be soon.

Leon kept glancing at Hryhoriy, expecting him to make his move, but while the guard pointed his gun at them, it looked impossible. Perhaps if someone decided to sacrifice themselves to distract the guard, the others might make it out alive? As the truck passed deeper into Soviet-held Czechoslovakia, it had to be now or never. Just then, the vehicle slowed and came to a stop. Had they arrived? Was it already too late?

Then the driver opened the hatch that divided his section from the rest of the truck and peered inside.

'What's wrong?' asked our guard.

'The road is flooded. I'll have to check the depth to see if we can get through,' replied the driver.

'Can't you go around?'

'It will take too long.'

Through the hatch, Leon could see that a vast body of water

stretched along the road, blocking it from west to east. They heard the door open and slam shut as the driver alighted from the vehicle. Leon saw him heading towards the water. He was looking for something. Before long, he had it, a tree branch, with which, as he steadily began to wade into the water, he intermittently checked the water's depth.

The guard was anxious to get a better look to see what was taking so long, but he was sitting at the back and his prisoners were in the way. With his rifle, he ordered the group to move to the side so he could get a better view. As he strained his eyes to look forward through the hatch, he took his eyes off Hryhoriy, who had sidled a fraction out of his peripheral vision. The mistake cost him his life.

It was all very easy for Hryhoriy, who was sitting only a yard or so away from the momentarily distracted guard. Hryhoriy silently removed the pistol from his jacket, and, without hesitation, aimed and fired. An ear-splitting sound filled the inside of the truck, temporarily deafening all occupants, except the guard, whose blood and brains splashed throughout the truck's interior and over Leon and the others inside. It must have been a horrible sight, but none of them minded. Knowing they could not afford to delay for a second, they opened the back canvas and, stepping around the corpse of their former captor, climbed down and out of the truck.

The driver, having heard the bang, came back to see what had happened. He already had his gun out as he reached the truck, but he was too late. Using the truck's bonnet as cover, Hryhoriy fired first, striking him in the shoulder, spinning him to the ground and dislodging the gun from his hand. The driver frantically tried to reach his weapon, but before he could get it, Hryhoriy finished him off with a bullet to his head.

It was all over. For a few seconds, nobody knew what to do. Then, in turn, they thanked Hryhoriy for saving their lives. Then they all simply got back into the truck, dumped their guard's body and drove back towards Germany. Leon had to endure the return trip amid the blood and gore in the back, but that did not bother him at all; he was alive.

Leon (right) and Hryhoriy. The photo sat tucked inside the frame of a much larger picture on one of the walls of the family home in Elermore Vale. Barely noticeable, I recall seeing it but never bothered to ask about it. After my brother-in-law, Peter, proofread a draft copy of this book, to my surprise, he told me about the time he asked Leon as to the identity of the person in the picture. Leon replied, 'That is the man who saved my life.' He then went on to recount the same story of abduction, escape and execution to Peter as he had to me. The huts to the left may be the accommodation at the Windischbergerdorf refugee camp.

Before they reached their destination, they dumped the vehicle and walked the rest of the way back to their camp. That night, they enjoyed the quiet celebration of their freedom.

Afterwards, they soon went their separate ways. Leon never knew what became of them, but at some point, he had a photo taken with Hryhoriy, determined never to forget the day that saved his life.

50

I Am Nothing – Maria, 1946

Economically, politically and socially, Germany was a devastated country. Yet refugees still poured into displaced person camps from all over Europe. More often than not, they arrived disappointed, with no work and no money. The camps were soon full.

After their wedding, Leon and Maria moved into the refugee camp. However, the place was soon overflowing with thousands of desperate and disparate people from all over Europe, many of whom were partakers of questionable activities for a young Christian mother. It was not a pleasant place.

On one occasion, an elegantly dressed VIP arrived at Windischbergerdorf. Maria and Leon were part of a small crowd that gathered to see what all of the fuss was about. They were even more perplexed when the VIP singled them out. She politely asked if she could ask a few questions about the camp. The VIP listened carefully as they explained that the situation was bearable, but that the conditions were overcrowded and generally unhygienic. She asked whether they were worried that Leon might have to return to the Soviet Union, to which they explained how terrified the Ukrainian and Polish boys were of abduction. When the woman left, she promised that things would improve. Throughout their life, Maria and Leon believed that the VIP was Eleanor Roosevelt, wife of the late US president, and that she helped Leon and others.[100]

Following her fact-finding mission, Mrs Roosevelt successfully lobbied other countries to accept nearly a million Europeans, most of whom lived in Germany. Further to that, she successfully implored the ruling powers, including France, the USA and England, to mandate that foreign countries, particularly the Soviet Union, could not force refugees to return to their country of origin.

The United Nation's Declaration of Human Rights, Article 15, states that 'everyone has the right to a nationality' and that 'no one shall deny'. Many refugees chose to stay in Germany, while others sought to see what other foreign lands could offer.

Maria hated it there. The camp was no place to raise a child, so she returned to Döfering to acquire free accommodation at the community-owned *Armenhaus*, poorhouse, for German women who had fallen on hard times.

The Döfering community, appreciating the need to care for its needy, established the poor house as a shelter for Germans left homeless by the war. Rosa Swatosch and her children found themselves living with Maria Keil.

> It was a difficult time. There was no work, people were burning everything, and the dollar was devalued. We had nothing.

Against this backdrop, the women formed a close bond of friendship and support for each other. Swatosch's daughters became a great help in raising Maryl, and Victor, who was born a year later.

There was little privacy living in a single room with up to six other families, with a shared toilet, bath and kitchen. Sometimes, an older woman named Myrel generously looked after the children, allowing Maria to work and the daughters to attend school.

Soon after registering the marriage certificate, Maria received a distressing letter from the government. Maria could not believe her eyes. How could her country disown her?

> I received a letter from the government telling me that I was no longer a German citizen but stateless. Somebody came along and took my nationality, and to this day, I don't know why. I have tried to get information on why they made such a decision, but nobody could give me an answer.[101]
>
> At the time, people wrote about the *verlust*, or lost nationality. I wrote back to the authorities. 'I have *verlust*. What did I do wrong?'

No one answered her letter, but the truth was that she had married a Ukrainian and the law stated that, upon marriage, the wife would adopt her husband's nationality. The fact that Leon also had no citizenship seemed to make no difference to Germany's bureaucratic bungling.

Leon contributed to the family's needs, but lived close to work at the refugee camp.

After Maria fell pregnant for the second time, she began to suspect that Leon might have been unfaithful. In the days before phones, communication was vastly different. One day, Maria decided to stop by unannounced at the camp. There, she found Leon's cabin door opened by an attractive young woman.

The woman looked horrified and explained that she was a refugee for whom Leon had provided accommodation.

Maria's world was falling apart. She was in danger of remaining homeless and destitute, with no nationality and two children. Despite the hardships, Maria had her pride. She gave him an ultimatum. Her or me! Perhaps the values instilled in him from his mother caused him to choose Maria and the children.

51

To England – Leon, 1948

While maintaining a presence until 1955, the American forces gradually withdrew with each passing year, thus paving the way to create a new and independent West German nation. Germany's rebuilding was a massive task. Often with upwards of over seventy-five per cent of their infrastructure destroyed, there was plenty of work for everyone. However, as time passed, there was less work and less opportunity, particularly if you were not a German citizen.

In this context, Leon heard the British government offered work and citizenship to thousands of displaced persons (DPs) from all over Europe. Given that Germany provided limited long-term support to refugees, the newly married couple decided to pursue the offer. Another great adventure was in the making.

However, the government only wanted displaced workers. Leon would have to go alone, leaving Maria with no income and two infant children.

> I talked with her about it and promised her that I would come back for her and the kids after I had earned enough to buy a house.

The process was relatively easy. Leon visited the British consul in Frankfurt, where, following an interview to ensure that he was not a Nazi, Leon signed travel documents for the United Kingdom. In mid-1948, Leon bade an emotional farewell to Maria and the children at Cham station. Nicolas Papiransky, Joe Sherbiac and Mikal Bunko, who also had just married, were among those leaving at the same time.

Leon could not help but wonder how this journey would compare to his cattle truck ride in 1942. There were similarities in distance and

Leon, centre, and two friends in Paris in 1948, looking like they would not be out of place in a 1950s Hollywood gangster film. The man on the left is an unknown Mickey Rooney lookalike, while the man on the right became a good family friend who we knew as the 'Uncle from Gloucester'.

time and the prospect of empty promises and even slavery; he had no guarantee the English were better than the Germans. However, some differences inspired confidence: no cattle trucks and proper seats for starters. There was lots of joking, smoking, food and relaxation. There were no armed guards to shoot you if you got off to get a drink of water. The train even had a toilet; you did not have to do your business on the floor. The signs were good.

The train stopped in Paris along the way, where they had the opportunity to spend a few days to see the great city. They had a fantastic time, seeing the sights and taking in the Parisian nightlife. Afterwards, their train brought them to the port of Calais, where they embarked on a short boat journey across the channel to England.

Leon remembered his awe at seeing Dover's magnificent white cliffs as his ship approached the English coast. Another long train journey followed, ending at an overcrowded immigration camp at Aberdeen in

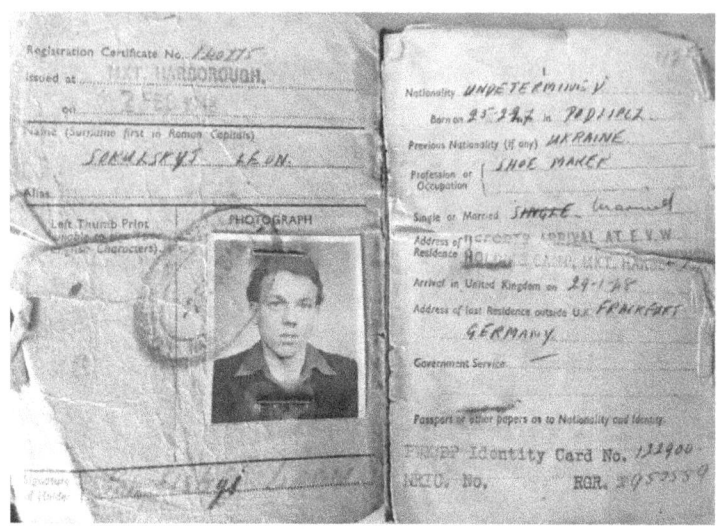

Leon's official identity card issued 3 February 1948. It yielded some interesting observations. He initially wrote 'single' before someone else seems to have crossed it out and written 'married'. Like Wasyl and many others, Leon added a 'J' to Sokulsky. For whatever reason, he later dropped the 'J'. Although he never mentioned it as a career, it appears that he may have written 'shoe maker' to suggest that he was a skilled worker. Leon's nationality is 'undetermined', indicating that he could not list Ukrainian as his nationality and that he never identified as a Soviet citizen.

Scotland. Together with thousands of other displaced persons from all over Germany and Europe, they eventually settled in various cities and towns throughout the United Kingdom.

Like many POWs and refugees, Mikal Bunko found work at King's Lynn, a seaport town north-east of London, and later moved to London. There, he met and married his second wife, another refugee whom we knew as Aunty Elizabeth. He and Leon remained close. For the next fifty years, a trip to the UK was never complete without visiting Uncle Mikal and Aunty Elizabeth.

> I saw my brother [cousin], Mikal, every weekend. Either he came to me, or I went to him.

Meanwhile, Leon and friends Joe Sherbiac and Walter Klempko were offered work at the newly constructed Drakelow power station just outside the towns of Burton-on-Trent and Derby, a city in the heart of England's midlands.

Leon, then twenty-seven, adapted quickly.

> It didn't take me long to speak English. I went to work. I went to an apprenticeship. It didn't matter [his age]. They took us because they knew what had happened [in the war]. There was a war in Korea, and I used to make the pins for the tanks. I didn't finish my apprenticeship with the company where I was working [because]) the company got bankrupt or something, so they shipped us over to International Combustion.

With so many Ukrainians around, it did not take Leon long to settle in Derby. After the war, England was a country of massive public works and rebuilding. International Combustion sent Leon to work at various construction projects, especially on the power stations that were popping up all over the country. Leon began to save for the house.

Leon quickly rose through the ranks.

> When I finished my apprenticeship, I went straight away to leading hand and then to foreman.

Leon was in demand because of his ability to solve complex construction problems and bring jobs in on time and within budget. He was a tough boss, though, as his son-in-law could attest when Leon fired him for bludging.

One of Leon's key attributes was his ability to work with the increasing numbers of foreigners in the English workforce. He was already fluent in Ukrainian, Polish, Russian and German; he quickly learned English and soon developed the ability to get by in most immigrant languages like Macedonian, Slovakian, Serbian, Croatian and Romanian. Of course, he knew all of the swear words.

Unlike the farmlands of Germany and Ukraine, Derby was a bustling city. He was thankful for the opportunities that life had presented.

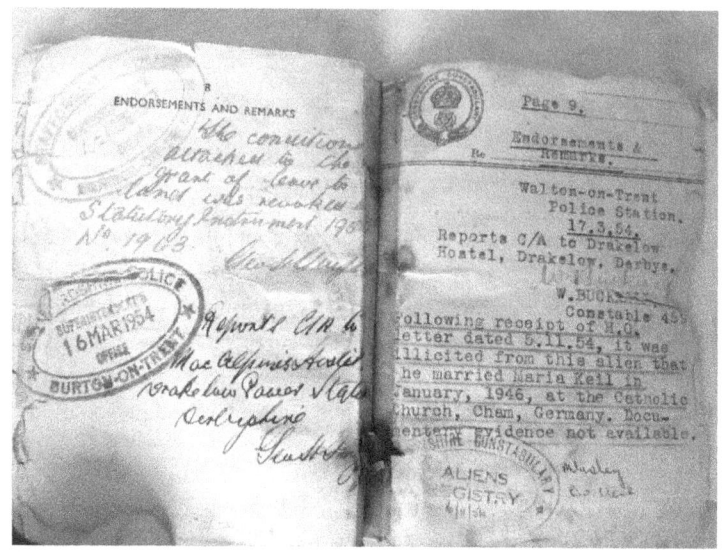

Leon's endorsement passbook, detailing his movements up to 1954. It includes stamps from, top left, Staffordshire, bottom left, Burton on Trent and bottom right Yorkshire. It also acknowledges Leon's marriage to Maria in January 1946 and identifies them under 'Aliens Registry'.

Nobody forced me to work for nothing. Nobody belted me. I could take a bath, sleep in a proper bed. I had money in my pockets. I was a free man.

Leon, along with other Ukrainian immigrants, contributed to building their own social club. Before long, a vibrant Ukrainian community had emerged in Derby, and Leon developed a strong network of friends. Most of them remained connected by their experiences of slavery, war and survival Sometimes, they reminisced about their families in Ukraine, to whom they could never return.

52

Poverty, Faith – Maria, 1948–53

One of Maria's favourite recollections was when she was out with Maryl and Victor, just three or four at the time, in the middle of winter. She had collected goods from Haschaberg and was driving them through the snow back to Döfering. About a kilometre from home, a wheel broke and her wagon toppled over into the snow. There was nobody within sight and it was freezing. Maria was tired, exhausted and miserable that she could lose both the wagon and her precious cargo. What could she do?

She decided that she had no choice but to leave the wagon where it was and take the children home before they literally froze to death. She knew that this would mean the cart would end up buried deep beneath the snow and be far harder to retrieve. She began to gather Victor and Maryl when an unknown man suddenly appeared, seemingly out of nowhere. He was middle-aged and wore a brown coat and cap, from which grey wisps of hair curled out from the edges. His kind eyes shone. He could see Maria was in trouble and asked if he could help. 'How could he help?' thought Maria. It needed three or four strong men to lift the wagon, let alone fix the wheel.

Maria thanked him but insisted that she abandon the wagon and get the children home. She would come back later, hopefully with some other helpers. The man nodded, standing beside the cart as Maria nervously took the children home, thinking that perhaps the man would steal from the cart. But she had no choice. After walking just a few hundred metres, and with the snow increasing, she decided to go back and get some essentials, just in case she couldn't return later that day. What

Maria with children, Victor and Maryl, circa 1950 in the beautiful Döfering countryside.

a shock! The man had disappeared, leaving the wagon mended and in the middle of the road. Somehow, he had fixed the wheel. Maria often spoke of the strange man who appeared out of nowhere.

> He must have been an angel. It says in the Bible, 'There are strangers who are angels in disguise.'[102]

Despite some money coming in, Maria struggled financially to support her children in the years after Leon left. A pauper's Christmas was the norm. Maria still did as best she could with what little she had.

One year, little Maryl opened her present to discover a colourful rag doll to her delight. She loved it, and it instantly became her most cherished possession. However, soon afterwards, it disappeared. Maryl was so scared to tell her mother because she knew how disappointed she would be if she lost her precious toy. She subsequently forgot about the doll until the following Christmas when she opened her mother's gift; inside was her prized possession, the rag doll. Once again, she played with it for a few weeks before it disappeared, only to reappear the following year when she opened her mother's gift.[103]

Except for a rare letter, as the days stretched to weeks and then to years, Maria seldom heard from Leon. She was a good-looking, ostensibly single mother. Inevitably, men called.

> They told me, 'He won't come back for you. He's gone. If you come with me, I'll look after you and the children. I'll give you a better life.'

Maria may have been interested, but her faith forbade relationships with other men. She felt bound to remain loyal to Leon and trust that he would return one day.

> I told them 'No' every time.

However, Maria must have worried about Leon's fidelity, and since

A studio photo of Barbara, Heinrich and Johann, c. 1952. They are well dressed and well off enough to take the time to procure the services of a professional photographer. There is a level of confidence in young Heinrich's eyes, which does not bespeak the political, social, emotional and economic circumstances of his time. He looks to be a boy protected from the horrors around him while his parents have taken that burden upon themselves.

she had not heard from him in years, perhaps he was already off with someone else. Many men left their wives and families after the war to start new lives. Even bigamy was common in those days.

A young Mykhas Mykulyshyn – Leon's brother.

53

Post-war – Leon, 1948–58

One day in 1953, a strange man, dressed in a suit and tie, came over the field to where Victor was working with his grandfather, herding geese. Suddenly the peculiar man ran over and grabbed Victor before throwing him into the air and catching him, and in the process, frightening the little boy. Then he said, 'Hello, Luckle, I'm your father.'[104]

It didn't cost much in those days to travel to Germany. However, it took time to get there and back, and it was over five years before Leon could get time off work to see Maria and the children.

Maria was naturally thrilled to see him, but Leon could not stay long. However, before leaving, he promised Maria that he would soon have enough money to buy a house and bring the family to England to live.

> I didn't want her to come over with nothing there, you see.

Due to increased energy demands, Leon, now a foreman, supervised contracts in power station construction throughout the UK.

> Well, I knew there was work there for people. You can learn something, do something about it. I knew my job. I was very good at drawings. You see, in construction work, you have to know your drawings. You had to be good at drawing. I had about 180 men working for me. You know, I put my mind to it and learned straight away.

By the beginning of 1954, Leon had earned enough money to purchase and fully furnish a house in the suburb of Clumber Terrace, Derby. He then sent Maria the fare for her and the children to travel from Germany to England.

Leon, on the right, with two friends. Walter Klempko is in the middle.

I worked day and night [and finally] bought a house, bought everything inside it, and then I went [back] to Germany [and asked] her to come over.

Despite writing home, none of Leon's letters found their way to the tiny village of Pidlyptsi. The turning point came when Mikal sent and received a letter from his mother. She said that she had suffered severely from an injured leg, which she had received in the crossfire of one of the battles fought in their area. With the help of her sister, Leon's mother, she gradually recovered, but now would forever walk with a limp. Leon's worst news was the loss, in late 1944, of his beloved stepfather, Stephan. The letter revealed that he had died fighting for the Soviet Union. It would take the family many years before they found out the actual circumstances of his death.

The good news, however, was that Leon's mother and brother had survived. In the interim, his mother had remarried a doctor, and Leon now had a nine-year-old sister, Anna.

Knowing that Mikal's letter got through, Leon decided to write to his mother via Mikal's mother.

In 1957, Leon received a letter from his brother, Mykhas, who described their mother, at fifty-seven, as 'old'. No doubt, the war and harsh living conditions had aged her prematurely. Leon immediately wrote back, and at the beginning of 1958, he received a reply from his mother in Ukraine.

His mother's joy in hearing that Leon had survived the war was impossible to put into words. She had not heard from him for sixteen years and naturally feared the worst. It is hard to fathom how difficult it was to endure so long without knowing whether he lived or died, nor her joy at learning that he not only survived but was married with children; and doing well in England.

> 12th January 1958
>
> Dearest son, in response to your letter – Glory Forever!
>
> Dearest son, I would like to inform you that I received your letter for which I am sincerely grateful. Since you wrote back to me, I could find out about your health and life. I am glad that now I can know a little about your life.
>
> Other people's children wrote, but there were not any words from you. I wondered if you were alive or not. There was no news about you. You say that you wrote to me in 1946 and 1948, but I never got any mail from you until now that you wrote to Mykhas. You found him and asked him to write to his parents' home.

His dad, Jasko, is old and cannot work any more. He is left alone with Parashka and a young daughter. Oleshka is married and lives elsewhere.

Dear son, all your friends have married and always talk about you.

Son, I wanted to tell you about our Wasyl.[105] He wrote from Germany last year and then stopped writing. That's all for now.

Keep well. Hope to see you soon.

Greetings to you and my daughter-in-law and grandchild.[106] The whole household sends you greetings also. Please write again soon.

Mum.

The letter served to make Leon want all the more to see his family in Ukraine. However, the border to the Soviet Union remained tightly closed, especially to traitors like him. The Iron Curtain that separated east and west would not fall for another thirty-three years. Merely writing to her son was a risky proposition. In Soviet parlance, she was collaborating with the enemy.

In 1960, Leon received a photo of his mother lying in her coffin, surrounded by flowers and many onlookers, many of whom he recognised as friends and family. Attached was a letter from his brother saying that she had died peacefully. Her passing was a terrible blow to Leon. He had last seen her through their tears at Zolochiv station in 1942. Mykhas went on to say that he remembered all through his childhood, every day, that his mother would pray for her lost son, that he was safe, and that she could one day see him again. Leon's devotion and love for her were unsurpassed by time and space, as was hers for him.

54

Leaving Germany – Maria, 1954–69

Maria was heartbroken when, in 1953, the most significant influence in her life, Grandma Keil, died after a long illness that had left her bedbound for several years. At the burial site, Maria recalled an extraordinary event that profoundly supported her faith.

> When my mother's mother died, there came a white bird flew in and sat on her coffin at the grave, and it sang so beautifully for a long, long time it sang, such a beautiful tune. It was a sign that she went straight to heaven.

One day in 1954, Maria experienced another central turning point in her life. It occurred when she received a surprise in the mail. The parcel came from Leon. It contained a one-way ticket and a five-week visa to England for both her and the children. As it was, there was little holding her back in the country that denied her citizenship. Those to whom she was closest had gone. Grandma, her best friends Othelia and Marie, and nearly every man she had grown up with were all dead. Annie, her dear friend, upon whose pear tree hung the German officer, married Heinz and moved to Heidelberg.

At the time, Maria worried that her mother had now become the victim of generational bullying at the hands of her son. She recalled that she visited her mother shortly before she was due to leave for England. Together, they were in church when young Adolf, barely fifteen at the time, burst in and accosted his mother, demanding money for alcohol. Barbara refused and, in front of Maria and the parishioners at the Klosterkirche, Adolf raised his fist to beat his own mother. Maria literally stepped in between the two, risking herself to protect her mother.

> I feel sorry for Heinrich and for Adolf, but I can never forget what happened that day at the *Klosterkirche*; forgive yes [but not forget]... If hadn't come in between them, he would have hit her in front of other people. I was so ashamed that I took out my own money from my purse and gave it to him.[107]

Maria would miss her mother, and perhaps Heinrich, whose condition had made him a placid boy, but not Adolf, nor her stepfather, who she blamed for Adolf's addiction.

> Kolnhoffer sat in the same chair, his chair, and never got up. He would send Adolf to the *Wirtshaus* [pub] to get the beer, but Adolf would drink half of it before coming home. When he got back, Kolnhoffer would see that half of the beer was missing and belt Adolf for drinking it. Then he would send him back to get more because he was too lazy to get it himself.[108]

Maria never really doubted her next move but turned to Father Rockermann for his blessing.

> He told me that I was standing between the nations with no place to go, not a stone to turn. I have to be with my husband.

Maria promised Father Rockermann that she would send Víctor back to Germany to study at the Monastery school in Cham.[109.]

Finally, it was time to leave. Maria remembered clearly her last day in Bavaria. It was 15 August 1954. It was very hard for her to go, as she loved her home and her family, but knew she must move to England to be with Leon. On the morning of her last day, she went to mass, and as she walked home, she turned to look at the beautiful hillside. The church bells began to ring at that moment as if they were saying goodbye to their Pachel Maree, and she began to cry.[110]

Difficult as it was to say goodbye to her friends and family, everybody seemed to agree that it was for the best.

It took several days to get from Cham to Derby. The journey involved a long train ride to Paris and Calais before catching the night ferry across to Dover. From there, they travelled by train to London.

There was no going back.

> None of us knew what to think. We could speak no English. We knew nobody. Even Leon, I didn't know if he would be there.

Maria fully understood the enormous risk that she and the children had taken. Even if he did show up, her visa was for five weeks only. If England changed her mind and rejected her, where would she go? She had a one-way ticket. Her statelessness meant that Germany had no obligation to take her back.

The children were cold, hungry and miserable, and for the hundredth time, Maria reread Leon's letter, in poorly worded German, asking her to meet him at Euston Station. He knew that she would arrive sometime on 17 August. Maria prayed as she huddled with the children that he would keep his word.

One can only imagine the relief and the joy when he arrived, suavely dressed and thrilled to embrace his wife and children. Leon brought food and something warm to drink with him, and that cheered everybody up. Soon, they were on another train to their new home in Derby, after which they caught a taxi to their address in Clumber Terrace. By all accounts, Leon had done an excellent job preparing for his family's arrival. That night, the three exhausted travellers slept soundly and peacefully. At last, they were home.

After five weeks passed, Maria received a call from the immigration office in Derby, ordering her to attend an immigration meeting. Upon arrival, a German-speaking official ushered Maria to a desk and quizzed her about her wartime activities, including her attitude to Hitler. She then asked about her family allegiance to Nazism, her friends in the Wehrmacht, her knowledge of concentration camps, the persecution of Jews and so on. Maria's responses were nervous and truthful, but the woman who interviewed her seemed cold and unimpressed. After some deliberation, she handed down her verdict.

> I will never forget what she said. She said, 'Maria, your visa is for five weeks only. No one in the world will take you.'

Maria was understandably shattered and in shock as the news began to sink in.

Then suddenly, the woman smiled warmly at her. 'No country in the world will take you, except if you take on British nationality.'

That was the most beautiful thing she had ever heard. Maria signed the necessary papers and, for the rest of her life, acknowledged her gratitude to England, her former enemy (if you believed the Nazis propaganda), who accepted her and gave her a home.

As one might expect, settling in was difficult. Maria found the language extremely challenging but found joy that this country acknowledged her as a person.

> Every six months, I had to report to the foreign office to show them that I was settling in. I remember I forgot to go one time, and I got a letter from the Derby police reminding me to go.

Maria and Leon soon had more children on the way. Milla and Elizabeth were born in 1957 and 1958, respectively, followed by Leon and Stefan in 1961 and 1962. Their growing family meant they needed a bigger house. In late 1961, Maria and Leon went house searching, but everything was too expensive for what they needed. They had all but given up when they stopped at 96 Chaddesden Park Road, Derby. It was perfect for what they wanted but far too expensive. However, the owner, Mrs Walker, who had recently lost her husband, took a liking to the family and offered them the house at a significantly reduced price. The family moved in and, within two years, the last of the seven children, Josephine, was born. During that time, Maria was able to establish some beautiful friendships. Her kind neighbours, the Wraggs and the Mounsys, provided selfless support for the family in adjusting to their new life.

In 1964, the family visited Germany. Leon and Maria packed the children and drove from Derby, via ferry, to Döfering. Grandma Barbara was there as well as their uncles, aunties, cousins and friends. It was a great homecoming. They stayed for a few weeks and had a wonderful time.

55

To Australia – Leon, 1968

The decision to immigrate to Australia in 1969 occurred because of a series of events. At that time, the Australian government required thousands upon thousands of workers to help their burgeoning economy. They advertised all over Europe, especially throughout England, for skilled and unskilled workers to start a new life.

The stars aligned at just the right moment.

> I was working with an Australian bloke from Melbourne. His name was Hoffman – bred and born Australian bloke. He was an engineer. He said, 'Why don't you go to live in Australia…we need people like you there.'
> I said, 'I'm all right. I've got a good job here.'
> He said, 'You will never be sorry.'
> I went home and discussed it with my family. The children said, 'Oh yes, Dad.'

At the time, Leon's health had been steadily deteriorating. Heavy smoking and working long hours in cold and damp conditions led him to the brink of emphysema and tuberculosis. His doctor had suggested he move to a warmer climate.

> We went to Manchester, on a minibus, all of you, and watched a video of how beautiful it is there. Even Newcastle [Australia], how beautiful, flowers, everything, you know! Amazingly, when Maria saw the video, she said, 'I know that place, I've seen it, as clear as day.'

I put my name to it.

International Combustion Limited

DERBY DE2 9GJ ENGLAND

Re: Reference.

To whom it may concern,
Dear Sir,

Leon Sokulsky, exept for a short break, has been employed by this company for the last eighteen years. For almost all this time, he has been solely employed on Steam Generating Plant at various Power Stations, maintaining and constructing boilers and milling plant and was for the past two years attached to our Central Erection Unit, which only the best of our site employees are allowed, by invitation only, to join. It would in fact be no exaggeration to state that he is considered by many here at I.E.D. offices, as our top Maintainance Foreman.

He has held the position of Maintainance Foreman for the past eight years and at Drakelow Power Sation were he has spent the last six years, we did not deem it nescessarry to put him under the supervision of a Site Engineer, and there, he has held the title of Senior Foreman-in-Char

As you can imagine, we are very sorry to lose him, but wish him every success.

On behalf of International Combustion Ltd., P.E.Dept.,

J. Mallender
(Personnel Admin Management.)

Leon's reference from International Combustion is testimony to the high regard in which his employer held him. In the space of ten years, Leon progressed from being an unskilled, non-English-speaking foreign worker to senior foreman in charge. Not bad for one of Hitler's 'Untermensch'.

56

Why Did We Go To Australia? – Maria, 1968–69

After learning the language and making some friends, Maria began to love England. In 1963, like Leon, she became a British citizen.

> Why [then] did we go to Australia? One day I had a dream where I saw the shape of a land. We had a world atlas at home, and so I went through the pages one by one until eventually, I found it. I knew straight away that the land I was looking at in the atlas was the same land I had seen in my dream. I recognised the very distinct shape of Australia. In particular, Cape York stood out, and the big bite at the bottom was very, very clear when I found it.[111] I had to look to see the name of the country and read out the word Australia. I knew then that this was where we must go.

Having decided, Leon inquired and found that International Combustion had a branch in Rydalmere in Sydney. They offered him a job, which Leon accepted. The decision to leave occurred on 26 January 1968; a day that the family had not yet learned was Australia Day. In June 1969, they boarded the *Fair Star* and sailed across the world to the 'land down under'. To give their children a better life and believing it was God's will, Maria and Leon relocated to a faraway country. Maria looked back and said that she didn't even know about Australia when she was a child and would never have dreamed that one day she would live there.[112]

It took six weeks to travel on board the *Fair Star* to Australia. They arrived on 20 July 1969. That same day, Neil Armstrong stepped onto the moon. One giant step for the family…

Epilogue

Settling in was difficult.

> In Australia, we were just too far away, I was very homesick, and I cried all the time. However, life so busy with six children and in starting a new entity that I had to keep going.[113]

My parents lived for the next forty-plus years together in Australia.

When Dad, forty-two, and Mum, forty-nine, arrived in Sydney with six kids in tow, they once again had to start more or less from scratch. However, things were quite different this time. Strange though the Australian accent sounded, they at least knew the language. Whereas before they travelled with virtually no possessions, they came to Australia with a dozen or so purple-painted wooden crates, packed with our family possessions.

At first, we stayed at the Villawood migrant hostel in Sydney before moving to another hostel in Mayfield, Newcastle, about a hundred and fifty kilometres north of Sydney. The hostels were rudimentary and overcrowded. A hodgepodge collection of mismatched cultures from all over the world gathered there in temporary accommodation in the hope of finding something unique in a new world. However, many brought with them a lot more than their physical baggage: their emotional scars came with them.

It was challenging to settle amid the dust, the flies and the heat, but eventually, we found a home at Elermore Vale in Newcastle. Over time, the family grew; rarely a year went by without a new birth or a wedding. Christmas and Easter were exceptional occasions. The meals were massive, with a great deal of preparation, days in the making. At Christmastime, Mum spent weeks creating the nativity scene and decorating the tree and every year, on Christmas Eve, as the family grew, the gatherings became larger.

New Year's Eve was always a subdued affair, with Mum insisting that the occasion was not one for celebration and parties, but one for quiet reflection and prayers of thanksgiving. As we got older and moved away from home, she expected a call before midnight. Woe betide anyone who failed to call.

Every new year, Mum sang the same song. Translated, it goes,

'Before I go to bed to sleep again, to thee my God, my heart I give.'

When asked, Mum would explain that it was the song they used to sing together every New Year's Eve in the church when they said 'goodbye'.

Maree, Othelia, Annie and all the boys used to sing it. Now she sang in their memory.

Over the years, 54 Jubilee Road became the regular meeting place for children, grandchildren, great-grandchildren, and countless friends and acquaintances. Five of the six children settled in Newcastle; three daughters within a kilometre of Mum and Dad's house. Everyone agreed that 'Nana and Pop's' house on Jubilee Road was a special place.[114]

Life was typically hard for a while, with Dad often working away for weeks at a time. Eventually, he secured permanent employment as a fitter and turner in Newcastle at Tubemakers Australia, until his retirement. Dad was regularly on strike for better wages and conditions. To make ends meet, Mum obtained employment there as a cleaner at Dad's work. For ten years, she started as early as four a.m. before completing her shift six to eight hours later. In the late 1970s, Dad lost an eye in an accident at work, causing him pain over many years and eventually leading to his early retirement in the mid-1980s.

Our property in the suburb of Elermore Vale was the equivalent size of two regular blocks of land, so we had enough room to grow fruit and vegetables and keep chickens, ducks, pigeons and other sorts of livestock and pets. As well as providing healthy food for the family, it gave Mum and Dad a little taste of home. As he did in Ukraine, Dad continued to pickle food.

In the mid-70s, Mum, once a daily churchgoer, became disillusioned with the Catholic Church and, after that, rarely attended. In many ways, she returned to the Waldensian ways of her grandmother. Her faith lay with scripture rather than with institutions. She showed us that you do not need to be a churchgoer to be a Christian. Mum prayed and studied the Bible daily and would sit contentedly and speak with anyone about religion; whether you wanted to listen or not made no difference. Mum did most of the talking while I often drifted in and out of sleep. I never minded. Time was precious, and Mum had earned the right to say what she wanted. I only wish I had listened more.

Never did a family member visit without receiving a blessing from Mum before leaving, nor did she ever turn away anyone with an interest in religion. Jehovah's Witnesses, Seventh-Day Adventists and Mormons were amongst our regular visitors. Dad, while sometimes an active participant, was more pragmatic. He would be the one to uninvite anyone who, in overzealously trying to convert us, had overstayed his or her welcome. Mum, nevertheless, remained faithful to her word when on the fields of Haschaberg and surrounded by tanks: she promised God that her life belonged to Him.

Mum's best friend in England was Laura Mather. A single parent with four young boys, she immigrated to Australia soon after us. She settled in the Central Coast area, about an hour's drive from our home, and they continued to see each other over the years.

For whatever reason – perhaps she wanted to leave the past behind – Mum lost contact with her family in Germany. If she knew that Heinrich died in the 1970s, Johann in 1973 and her mother in 1978, she never told me.

In 1985, Maryl and I visited Germany. Strange as it may seem, one of our goals was to find out whether our grandmother was still alive. In Burglengenfeld, we met up with Barbara's only living sibling, Alois, and his daughter, Ziglindy, who informed us of our grandmother's passing in 1978. She told us Grandma spoke fondly of her family in Australia and how she would love to see us all again.

On the same trip, we visited Uncle Adolf in Germany at his residence for alcoholics. Despite ongoing treatment for renal failure, he wanted us to take him for a beer. It was sad for me because it seemed he was not interested in what his long-lost nephew or niece had been doing, as long as he could get a drink. The alcohol had done too much damage to his liver, and he died not long afterwards. We also visited beautiful Döfering, with its houses decorated with pretty flowers at that time of the year. We asked the first woman we met on the street, with a nothing ventured, nothing gained attitude, whether she knew Maria Keil. The woman immediately showed recognition and broke into tears when we told her who we were. Emotionally she recalled *da Pachel Marie* (Maria), *und da Maryl und der Luckle* (Maryl and Victor).

We then travelled to Austria to visit Leon's Uncle Wasyl, his wife Maria, and his family. One of their children, Sepp Sokulskyj and his wife Christa,[115] came over several times to visit us in Australia in the ensuing years. They loved it so much; they once stayed for six months with the family at Elermore Vale.

In 1989, the world changed forever when Soviet leader, Mikhail Gorbachev, saw that communism had run its course and set in motion the break-up of the Soviet Union. Massive protests supporting the break-up ensued throughout Europe, leading to the destruction of the infamous Berlin Wall that separated East and West Germany. The physical and symbolic divide between the opposing ideologies of communism and capitalism came crashing down.

Ukraine naturally joined in the wave of nationalism that swept the continent and announced her independence on 24 August 1991. I recall Dad's great excitement when, after 1989, he could finally return to his Motherland. He had only just turned fifteen when he departed Ukraine in June 1942. The promise that he would return in one year was never to be. It was not one year, but forty-eight years before Leon finally made it home.

The following year, Mum and Dad visited England for the first time since 1969. They spent time with Mikal and his wife Elizabeth, in London, and Maryl and her children in Derby. They visited our family home in Chaddesden where, perchance, the occupants who had bought the house off them, still lived. They were shown into the backyard and Mum on a whim walked to a place heavily covered in foliage. There she uncovered a grotto, the same grotto that she had built over twenty years earlier. The centrepiece was a lovely picture of Our Lady that Maria had herself painted, still perfectly preserved behind a glass frame.

'We couldn't remove the grotto, we know how much it meant to you,' they said. They were a sentimental couple who then asked Mum, the rightful owner, to keep the painting, and it came back with her to Australia.

Afterwards, Mum built a replica grotto in our backyard, nestled beneath a large willow tree, at Elermore Vale. It became her favourite praying place for the rest of her life.

Subsequently, Dad visited Ukraine, while Maria travelled with her grandson Peter to Germany. Sadly, many loved ones and friends had died. Others were still alive; Dad saw his brother, Mykhas, and sister Anna, who was into her forties when he saw her for the first time. Mum, meanwhile, visited her cousins Ziglindy, Sepp and Alois, as well as her great friends Annie, Rosa Swatosch and the Brückls.

Dad's homecoming spread joy around his hometown and beyond, and soon after he arrived, a journalist contacted him to do a feature article for the local newspapers. His story about a boy forced to leave home at fifteen to return forty-eight years later made news both locally and nationally. 'Mykhas recognised me straight away,' Dad recalled.

> In Ukraine, we had a big reunion, a fantastic, big reunion. When I got out of the train, Mykhas, my brother, and his sons met me with a bunch of flowers. It was 'Uncle Leon, Uncle Leon,' you know.

Despite drinking more vodka than he cared to remember, Dad's family provided him with a most memorable experience. He recorded on VHS his proud return to his home in Pidlyptsi, where his sister Anna now lives with her family. Dad visited many places in that time, including his old church, where the Nazis hanged Helena Serben.

Like Dad, Mykhas was a survivor who had done well for himself both under communism and the birth of capitalism.

> He went and joined the Communist Party. He was all right then. First, he was checking the fields, the farms. Then he took over building fences, putting in gas pipes for the people, things like that he took over – like a foreman. He had about sixteen people working for him.

Unsere toten Helden

Döfering	gefallen	Döfering	gefallen
Ludwig Bösl	13. 1. 45	Michael Nagler	1. 5. 44
Michael Birzler	20. 7. 42	Alfred Hoffmann	10. 12. 43
Xaver Dirscherl	19. 4. 41	**Rhan**	
Peter Gschwendtner	10. 7. 45	Josef Brey	18. 7. 40
Wolfgang Gruber	7. 5. 44	Max Bruckmayer	23. 7. 42
Alois Heumann	8. 5. 45	Alois Leiß	28. 2. 44
Xaver Kärtner	12. 3. 45	Josef Maier	1. 2. 46
Michael Kärtner	Juli 46	Josef Stangl	11. 6. 40
Wolfgang Malterer	15. 1. 42	Max Stangl	12. 9. 44
Ludwig Malterer	24. 1. 45	**Lixendöfering**	
Xaver Malterer	6. 2. 43	Ludwig Dirnberger	19. 10. 44
Ludwig Preißer	27. 4. 44	Michael Zwicknagl	25. 1. 42
Josef Wagner	12. 10. 43	**Haschaberg**	
Jakob Wagner	7. 1. 44	Ludwig Leiß	18. 6. 42
Johann Preißer	12. 2. 43	Willibald Leiß	1. 11. 44
Willibald Preißer	24. 6. 44	**Almoosmühle**	
Albert Preißer	13. 3. 45	Xaver Rohrmüller	Ende 44

Vermißte

Döfering	Rhan	Josef Riedl
Alois Junglas	Michael Leiß	Franz Stauber
Johann Kärtner	Michael Malterer	**Flischberg**
Josef Nagler	Ludwig Riedl	Johann Dobmeier
Alois Schneider	Johann Riedl	Johann Dirnberger
Josef Wutz	**Lixendöfering**	**Haschaberg**
Ludwig Junglas	Xaver Ederer	Josef Leiß

Die dankbare Pfarrjugend

The photo, taken during the Pilgrimage in 2019, shows the names and date of death of 'Unsere toten Helden. Our dead Heroes.' In the close-knit community, many were related, including five from the Leiß family and Maria's three Preißer cousins, including Willi. Below the dated names is a list of those whose bodies were never found 'Vermißt. Missing'. The final inscription pays final homage to the 'Die dankbare Pfarrjugend'. The 'grateful' parish youth. Alois Keil was only one of two who ever returned home from the district. He survived having spent six years in a Russian camp.

When Mum visited Döfering in 1990, she stopped at her old church of St Adagio. Just outside as you enter the grounds is a memorial dedicated to those 'Heroes' who died in the Second World War. Mum's grandson, Peter, recalled that day and how she cried when she put her finger by the name of the first boy, Victor Bösl, and described him in detail: his appearance, his interests, and so forth. Then she moved her finger to the next boy, did likewise, describing his appearance and so forth, and continued to do that for each boy on the list. When she reached Xaver's name, she cried fresh tears. Wolfgang Gruber and cousins Willibald, Johann and Albert Preißer were also there among the names of those with whom she spent so much of her young life. The loss of almost the entire population of men in the district must have been indescribable for the local community.

Five years later, in the mid-90s, Mum's great best friend Anne and her husband Heinz visited us in Australia. They stayed for about a month and had a wonderful holiday with Mum, reminiscing about old times and enjoying the hot Australian summer. Around the same time, another visitor from Germany arrived with two of his friends. Dad recalled the conversation.

> We were talking, and I said I used to work in Germany at the address: Georg Brückl, Haschaberg Post Geigant Oberpfalz.
> One of the boys said, 'That is my grandfather. I used to live there!'

The boy was Olivier Brückl, the grandson of Georg.

In her later years, Mum suffered more and more from chronic arthritis, particularly in her right knee that she injured when coming over to Australia on the boat. Nevertheless, she loved to get out and go for long family drives or just sit on the back veranda surrounded by nature.

To acknowledge the injustices to Mum and Dad during the war, both received small monthly pensions from the German government in the latter years of their lives. With his command of six to eight languages, Leon sometimes helped as an interpreter for his son, Leon, who had established a legal firm in the city. Our neighbour, Peter Tarasenko, was a Russian deserter who could never return home. He left his wife and children in Russia for a new life in Australia, marrying again and raising a second family. In contrast to Leon, who spoke fluent English, Peter could barely say more than 'Daddy home?'

Our parents argued regularly, but their love grew more profound as they grew older. As Mum became frailer, Dad, with the support of his children and grandchildren, became her full-time carer. Each night, Mum and Dad sat together, sometimes until the early hours of the morning, talking, reminiscing, praying and just enjoying each other's company.

Mum's love of wildlife continued throughout her dotage, and she passed that on to her children. If ever we came across a sick or injured bird, we took it to Mum, who would somehow restore it to good health. Sometimes, the bird would become a family pet, as was the case of their beloved sparrow, Bibbi, who lived inside the house. One of Mum and Dad's less palatable tricks was when they trained Bibbi to eat directly from between their lips. Maria's health worsened in her last years, and knee and hip injuries confined her to bed and lounge most of the time.

Of Dad's later years, Milla wrote,

> Leon loved playing dominoes at Wallsend RSL, playing cards, and growing vegetables for his family. He was an active member of the Ukrainian community and, despite being tone-deaf, was in the Ukrainian choir. He was St Nicholas in the Christmas pageant and was very proud of watching his grandchildren participate in Ukrainian dancing and cultural activities. In later years, he was awarded the Premier's Award for services to the Ukrainian community.

I finished the 1998 interview by asking Dad whether he had any regrets.

> Why would I regret it? I have a house, I have kids, grandkids here. I've been back home to Ukraine, to England. I have no regrets whatsoever.

In 2010, Maria enjoyed her ninetieth birthday celebrations surrounded by loved ones, including her seven children and twenty-two grandchildren. Maryl and her four children flew out from England to pay homage to their amazing mother and grandmother. Granddaughter Rachael interviewed Maria for the occasion. She wrote,

> Grandchildren and great-grandchildren are one of Nanna's greatest joys in life. She always takes pride and interest in them and their achievements, no matter how big or small. She loves them all. Nanna has been the most selfless, loving Nanna ever. She is always happy when we are there, and nothing is too much for her. Nanna always puts her family first.
>
> Together, Nanna and her grandma would collect mushrooms and berries for their family. Nanna laughs as she tells the story of how she was sometimes naughty and stole strawberries from other people's gardens – even the priests! Nanna's love for wild birds came from her grandma. Birds would always fly to her, and (she) remembers thinking how beautiful that was. To this day, Nanna loves to feed her magpies, kookaburras, and all the wild birds that gather in her garden every afternoon. She often likes to sit, look out at the birds and garden, and it reminds her of her childhood in the woods with her grandma.
>
> Nanna said that she wouldn't change one minute of her life, good or bad, as this has made her the person she is today. Nan feels very blessed to reach ninety and has had a wonderful life. She has seen her children, her children's children, and even their children, and thanks God for all the love and blessings in her life. Nanna wanted to thank all of you, friends, and family for being with her today; she is very humbled and happy.

Maria Sokulsky died suddenly of a heart attack on 9 June 2010. Her passing broke our hearts. A few days before she died, I visited with my children. Mum asked me to go and get some chicken while I left her with the kids. As we waved her goodbye, Mum sat up and smiled. It was the last time we saw her alive.

Mum's passing broke Dad, and his health declined rapidly as a result. Despite his worsening dementia, the family tried the best it could to keep him at home. Maryl stayed with him for over six months, having flown out from England for Mum's funeral. We all chipped in to help. Dad developed a form of dementia called Sundowners, which meant that his condition worsened at night. I stopped over each weekend, usually staying Saturday night.

On several occasions, he would wake me at some ungodly hour with his shopping bags packed, saying, 'Steven, it's time to go home.'

'But we are home, Dad,' I'd say.

'Don't be stupid. Take me home,' he'd plead.

Eventually, I would yield, saying, 'OK, get in the car.'

After a trip around the block, we would arrive back at our starting point. Dad, placated that we were home, would then go to bed.

In the end, Dad needed full-time care, so we moved him to a nursing home at Cameron Park in Newcastle. He was the first patient to arrive at the brand-new facility. His survival capacity continued, and over the next three years, we saw one new patient come each week until the place was full with perhaps thirty patients. Dad outlived the entire first generation and almost all of the second generation of patients in his ward before passing away in 2014.

Despite his dementia, Dad never lost his sense of humour or his love of dance and song. At his door, a recent picture of Dad with a broad smile on his face, embracing a horse, was there to remind him of his beloved Shimmel.

My last memory of Dad was his smiling and waving goodbye as my family and I bade him farewell during what was to be our last visit. He may or may not have known who we were, but he appeared happy and lucid at the time. His passing, though distressing, fortunately, came before dementia had utterly taken his mind and his dignity. His brother Mykhas died within months of Dad and Mikal died of Covid 19 in 2020. It was the end of an era.

At Mum's funeral, when they were lowering her into the grave, Dad was heard to say, 'Don't worry, Mam. I'll be with you soon.' Once more, Dad was true to his word.

Appendices

Appendix 1

Communication in and out of the 'Iron Curtain' was challenging in the post-war era, especially during the 'Cold War' period, where the threat of nuclear war became a very possible reality.

In early 1958, Leon received a letter that his brother Mykhas had sent a few months earlier. They continued to keep in touch for the rest of their lives.

> 07.12.1957
> Glory to Jesus Christ!
> Dear Brother, I want to let you know that I got your letter and thank you very much for it. We probably thought of each other at the same time, as I have recently written my letter to you and you will get it soon. I found your address with our mother, and I was not sure if it is correct or not. I live well enough and work as a tractor driver. I got married on Mykhas's saint's day, on 21/11/57. My wife does not come from Pidlyptsi; she comes from the Brody district. If I get a response from you, we will send you our photo.
>
> We do not live with our mother but in Pidlyptsi. Dear brother, if you get this letter, I ask that you send me your photo with your family. Write to me more often as we now receive messages from England. Iva is in England, writes very regularly, sends parcels, and promises to come. Grits, Wasyl, and Mikal (Bunko) also send packages. Our mother is old and unwell for work, but father still works. Our grandmother still lives; Zoska still lives. Basil lives on the old place and has four children already. Hereon I finish my short letter.
>
> We greet you and your family. Sincerely.
> Goodbye.
> I am waiting for your answer.
> Mykhas

Appendix 2

The Sokulsky family in the early days in Derby. Leon and Maria are flanked by Maryl and Victor, with babies Elizabeth and Milla in front.

Appendix 3

Maria's baptismal certificate (Taufzeugnis), shows the occupation (Beruf) of the mother (Mutter) and father (Vater) is 'Cottager's' daughter and son respectively. This means that they were unemployed and living with their parents at the time of her birth.

Appendix 4 Notes on Ukraine

Dad would be deeply distraught following Vladimir Putin's Russian invasion of Ukraine on 24 February 2022.

Once more, Ukraine is fighting for its very existence. We have received messages of hope and defiance from our Ukrainian family who believe passionately in the defence of the Motherland, just as our ancestors have done for centuries.

At the time of writing, Andrii, Oksana and two daughters had moved to Poland to live in a church in Tarnobrzek. 'We are warm, we are taken care of, but we are very homesick,' she wrote. Their eldest daughter Olia, twenty-six, is a lawyer and currently in Australia on a humanitarian visa. She is loving the country and her Australian family. She is taking English lessons, looking for work and has just passed her driving test (she never drove in Ukraine).

Their decision to leave Ukraine may have already saved their lives, as their house in Zolochiv was hit by a Russian bomb and badly damaged. Occupying the house at the time were several refugees from the east. All were injured, some seriously. Andrii stayed in Poland, where he was able to secure employment as a transport worker, while Oksana and the children returned to repair the house.

Victor was there to help with the house restoration. He remains in Zolochiv with wife Maria and daughter. Their son Yuri, like almost all the young men, is somewhere fighting Russians.

At eighty-six, Aunty Anna remains in Pidlyptsi with her family. Her grandsons Bohdan and Igor are in the army

History repeats but is not forgotten.

We live in hope.

Glory to Ukraine. Glory to the Heroes.

Notes

1 Growing up in Germany – Maria, 1920s

1. Thirty-one years earlier, Adolf Hitler, the seventh of eight children, was born. Only he and his younger sister, Paula, survived infancy.
2. It was a love that she later passed on to her children and grandchildren. If ever we came across a sick bird or animal, we took it to Nana – she would always know what to do.
3. She would fly, some sixty years later.

2 Growing up in Ukraine – Leon, 1927–33

4. In Ukraine, the woman's name always ended in an 'a'. Leon said 'Maria' when referring to his mother. However, her baptised name was Marika.

4 Story Time – Leon, c. 1934

5. The 'tickled to death' joke was not new. People have passed the story down for generations. I came across it in Anna Reid's book *Borderland*.

5 First Memories of Hitler – Maria, 1933

6. They would have used the word 'throne' because, formerly, German leaders had always been kings.
7. Literally, the Leader, but the title is more akin to referring to a supreme, unrestrained commander.
8. The producers of the literature may have anonymously hired innocent children to hand it out.
9. Maria may not have known but the authors of the leaflet may well have been paraphrasing Hitler when they referred to 'heads will roll'. He used those words in the Supreme Court when intimating what he would do once in power. Peter Ross Range, *The Unfathomable Ascent: How Hitler Came to Power*, The History Press, p. 202.

7 Did You Join the Hitler Youth? – Maria, c. 1935

10. Short for *Appelplatz*, which means 'roll call'. Maria must have been marked 'Absent'.

9 Die Jude Eisfeld – Maria, 1936
11. Timo Bullemer, *Dates from the Jewish History of Cham*.
12. The Klosterkirche Maria Hilf Catholic Church is still located in the centre of town.
13. It is interesting that the Eisfelds were known according to their religion first, and then by their last names.
14. Sounded like Rambach.
15. The gentleman's name sounded like Ugarn.

10. Milestones – Leon, 1937
16. Stephanie Sneesby, interview and major work.
17. Leon spelt it 'Shimmel' in English.

11 Brückls, Stepfather, Referendum – Maria, 1937–1938
18. Concentration camp specifically for political prisoners.
19. William L. Shirer, *The Rise and Fall of the Third Reich*, Simon & Schuster, p. 350.
20. The voting age was twenty and Maria was eighteen. Voting was not compulsory.

12 Julik – Leon, 1938–1939
21. Steffany Sneesby, interview.

13 What Happened with the Czechs? – Maria, 1938
22. Maria's grandson was three at the time.
23. They are still there and popular today.
24. Before 1919, the Sudetenland was part of a larger region known as Bohemia. Maria and many Bavarians still saw it that way.

14 First Came the Russians – Leon, September 1939
25. An interesting observation, given that the Russian and Ukrainian language, whilst similar at times, can be quite different. Many Western Russians were able to speak Ukrainian as most Eastern Ukrainians today speak Russian.
26. Ironically, they did only stay a few years but only because the Germans forced them to leave. Independence would have to wait for quite a while.
27. Poland would have been a huge disappointment. The Nazis would not have welcomed wealthy, learned or aristocratic Ukrainians into their fold. They were systematically murdered.
28. Anywhere other than Germany would be better. Some managed to get to places like Canada and the US.

15 War Begins – Maria, 1 September 1939
29. Georg Brückl's son.

16 Germany Invades Russia – Leon, June 1941
30. Most likely, it was a Junkers or a Stuka. While they were

dive-bombers, they also carried machine guns.
31. From Aunty Anna's account.
32. At the height of its power before the First World War, the Austro-Hungarian empire occupied nearly all of Eastern Europe, including most of Ukraine. Hence, Leon's grandmother spoke German, the language of the empire.
33. Galicia broadly speaking refers to the area that existed as an independent kingdom in the middle ages and then became eastern Poland after the First World War. Its population was about as diverse as you could get and included Poles, Ukrainians, Galatians, Magyars, Jews, Russians and Lithuanians.
34. Henri-Philippe Pétain, the disgraced ex-French general who became leader of Vichy France, the Nazi puppet state, during the Second World War.
35. Literally 'commando' units, ostensibly to restore order and deal with resistance and political dissidents. In reality, they were mass murderers.

17 Why Did We Attack Russia? – Maria, 1941
36. The country's love of Hitler at that point, in terms of fanaticism and adoration, resembled the Beatlemania crowds in the 1960s. One difference was that the Beatlemania fans were mainly female and the Hitlermania fans were young and old of both genders. Of course, the biggest difference being that the Beatles were all about love whereas the Nazis were all about hate, at least when it came to pretty much anyone who was not German.

18 The SS (Schutzstaffel) Arrive – Leon, 1941
37. Steffany Sneesby, interview with Leon.
38. Ibid.
39. Steffany recalled 'Pop' became very emotional during her interview with him, when he described the deaths of the Hershki family. When I interviewed Dad in 1998, he murmured, 'I don't know, shot.'

19 Two Heinrichs – Maria, 1941
40. Harold Nicolson's *Diary, 1907–1964*, Phoenix, 2008, p. 227.
41. http://www.bbc.co.uk/history/worldwars/wwtwo/hitler_russia_invasion_01.shtml
42. Arguably the second most powerful figure in Nazi Germany. As Reichsführer SS, he was in command of the Schutzstaffel, SS Protection Squad. His portfolio included the Einsatzgruppen, Gestapo and secret police. Ironically, he

showed few of the Aryan attributes he professed were essential for Nazis in the Thousand Year Reich.

20 Holocaust – Leo, June/July 1943

43. The powder would have been lime. Lime increases the rate of decomposition of corpses. The helpers were either Ukrainians or the last Jews to die.

44. Some of them were still alive. Leon was reluctant to go into detail, but, to make that assumption, he almost certainly saw them writing in agony in the pit before the soldiers leaned in and sprayed them with more bullets.

45. Leon may have witnessed such murders on more than one occasion.

46. Ironically, the Ukrainian National Committee was fighting a lost cause. Eventually, they were to be enslaved. Shimon Briman, *Ukrainian Jewish Encounter*, 13 July 2016. https://ukrainianjewishencounter.org/en/lviv-Western-ukraine-view-israel/

47. Shimon Briman, *Ukrainian Jewish Encounter*, 13 July 2016.

48. Ibid.

49. Ibid.

50. Anna Reid, *Borderland*, p. 148. By the end of the war, Nazis had murdered an estimated 2.2 million Ukrainian Jews.

22 The Pilot – Leon, 20 April 1942

51. The name given by the Germans to the invasion of the Soviet Union.

24 The Bomb – Leon, April 1942

52. Stephanie Sneesby, interview and major works.

53. The Tryzub is Ukraine's national symbol.

26 One From Each Family Must Go/The Journey – Leon, Mid-1942

54. Leon said the message arrived on a 'stick'. Initially I thought it might be a scroll: the type that is unravelled from both ends to reveal a message. However, a flat sliver of timber makes sense. It would be easy to carry, and more durable than paper or a scroll.

55. We react to smell to warn us that something is foul or fresh. Known scientifically as 'olfactory adaptation,' after a while, the body adapts so that it can divert its attention to other, potentially more important things. Hence, the best jobs in the concentration camps were tending to the latrines. The Nazis would not go there and the cleaners had lost their sense of smell.

56. The general name Germans gave to those who came from Eastern lands to work in Germany.

57. Her son, Paul, is the Ukrainian Catholic priest in Newcastle.

58. It was to be over seventy-five years later that Zofia's daughter, Halina Wlodarczyk, and Milla Sneesby made contact through Ancestry DNA, to discover our second cousin relationship. Zofia and Leon lived literally just down the road from each other in the tiny village of Pidlyptsi. It is not known if they travelled in the same carriage. Leon did say that there were four or five girls. It is likely that one of them was Zophia.

59. Ukrainian for brother. Leon explained, 'In Ukraine, it's a brother, not cousin. All brothers and sisters, you see. That's how it was over there, and still is now. When I write a letter to my cousin, I write sister or brother – that's tradition in Eastern Europe.'

27 The Tide Is Turning – Maria, 1943
60. Attributed to Admiral Yamamoto, from his diary.

28 Verflucter Ausländer, Arbeit – Leon, 1942/43
61. Leon described the distance in relation to our local shopping centre in Newcastle.

29 Meeting Leon/The Doctor – Maria 1942/43
62. Rachel Hand interview.

30 Georg Brückl – Leon, mid-1943
63. Leon used to joke to his children that to save time, Leis would belt him before he did anything wrong.

31 For Whom the Bell Tolls – Maria, Winter 1944
64. Albert survived another eight months. He died in March 1945, as the war drew to a close.
65. Maria called it '*Rolle für victory* – Roll for victory'.

32 Soviets Regain Ukraine – Leon, 1944
66. 'I will be Home in a Year', a song by the author, available on YouTube.

33 To Help a Friend – Maria, 1944
67. United States Holocaust Memorial Museum, https://collections.ushmm.org/search/catalog/irn5880
68. She never did learn to drive.
69. Maria said 'five kilometres'. She may have meant one stop or even fifty kilometres, or perhaps she was right. That would have meant that you could only travel within the district and even then most trips would exceed five kilometres. If she was correct, then that would effectively rule out civilian rail travel from late 1944. Regardless, she carried a ticket that was well in excess of

the maximum distance civilians were allowed to travel.

34 Work and Leisure – Leon, late 1944

70. Sepp Brückl, during the Pilgrimage, took us to the Keil house, and recalled to me the location of the ice rink and his memories of skating there as a child.
71. I remember as a child going to Ukrainian Mass with Leon/Dad. He always stood in the front row.

35 To Altötting, Maria, Late 1944

72. It was not created with Nazis in mind, but the Devil and his demons. However, it was a good fit; the Nazis were the 'demons'.

37 In Hiding – Maria, Winter 1944

73. Maria's love of scripture never faltered. She always welcomed anyone of religious persuasion into her home.

38 The War Is Nearly Over – Leon, 1944–45

74. Rosa possibly heard the most infamous of the launchers, Stalin Organs, named after the eerie sound they made as they simultaneously fired multiple missiles.

39 Stephan Mykulyshyn – c. Late 1944–Early 1945

75. From Olga Mykulyshyn's account, translated from Ukrainian.
76. Anthony Beevor, *Berlin: The Downfall*, Viking Press, 2002.
77. Posted on 7 August 2015 by World Peace Foundation, https://sites.tufts.edu/atrocityendings/2015/08/07/german-pows-deaths-under-allied-control/

40 Death March – Maria, April 1945

78. Daniel Blatman, *The Death Marches*, pp. 153–154, Belknap Press, 2011.
79. Ibid.
80. https://giconcentrationcampberga.weebly.com/death-march.htm
81. https://en.wikipedia.org/wiki/Cham,_Germany
82. The fifty kilometres was correct. Maria may have been mistaken about their origin. Those buried in Cham were said to have come from Flossenbürg. They had already endured a fifty-kilometre walk to reach the outskirts of Cham.
83. Daniel Blatman, *The Death Marches*, p. 99.
84. Wikipedia, Flossenbürg concentration camp.
85. Inaudible on the recording. Maria named places that sounded like Radebe and Anaheim.
86. https://encyclopedia.ushmm.org/content/en/article/death-marches-1

87. https://www.holocaustcenter.org/visit/library-archive/oral-history-department/oral-histories-ns/raimi-rejngewirtz-saul-bezalel/

41 The Last Battle – Leon, 1945
88. Literally, 'People's storm'. Similar to the 'Home Guard,' where civilians were tasked to carry on the war effort.
89. Brückl's son recounted the story to me as we looked out over Haschaberg from the newly constructed lookout on the Bleschenberg.

42 Trapped in a Battle – Maria, April 1945
90. It was a big call after all that she had been through.
91. Snakes were her biggest fear.
92. Even though it was a very serious, life-threatening moment, Maria could laugh when she told the story. She laughed at her own brazen but honest response.

44 The Ceasefire – Maria, 1945
93. Maria then told me to go and ask him for myself. Fortunately, I did.

46 Aftermath – Maria, Autumn 1945
94. Anthony Beevor, *Berlin: The Downfall*, Viking Press, 2002.
95. The Japanese fought on until 14 August. It wasn't until 2 September, after the surrender was formally accepted, that the war officially ended.
96. Mengele died a free man and never received justice for his heinous crimes. Barbie died in jail; he had remained on the run until 1987, when the French government managed to have him extradited from Bolivia to face trial. Eichmann, captured in 1960 in Argentina by Israeli operatives on a daringly successful kidnap mission, met with the executioner in 1961 in Israel.

47 Revenge – Leon, Autumn 1945
97. Also called Pontoon or Black Jack. Dad passed his love of cards on to his children and there was never a family get together without a game of cards. The favourite games were Nominations and Sheba (Hearts). He also taught us how to play a game called Thousand, that involved a good deal of mathematical and statistical speculation. While most people took a minute or so to determine their hand, Leon was ridiculously fast at predicting the exact value of his hand.

48 Engaged and Married – Maria, 1946
98. We knew her as Maria. In Germany she was known as 'der Maryl'. After learning that on our trip to Germany, that was my name for her thereafter.

49 Stolen – Leon, 1946
99. Yugoslavia was controlled by President Tito, a revolutionary communist with close ties to the Soviet Union.

50 I Am Nothing – Maria, 1946
100. Eleanor Roosevelt was in Germany from 15 to 18 February 1946. She visited the ruined cities of Frankfurt and Berlin and several refugee camps. Her writings do not mention a visit to Windischbergerdorf, although theire is no entry for 17 February. I assumed that if they had met, it must have been at the camp, but it could have been elsewhere. Eleanor Roosevelt, 'My Day, February 15–18, 1946', *The Eleanor Roosevelt Papers Digital Edition* (2017), accessed 18/10/22, https://www2.gwu.edu/~erpapers/myday/displaydoc.cfm?_y=1946&_f=md000263
101. Maria had no idea at the time that by marrying Leon she had given up her nationality. Her son Victor recently investigated whether he could obtain German nationality but was unsuccessful. Despite the fact that he was born in Germany, he was ineligible because his mother inadvertently renounced her citizenship when she married Leon in 1946.

52 Poverty, Faith – Maria, 1948–1953
102. Hebrews 13:2.
103. Maryl recalled the story to me one day after I complained about my Christmas present.

53 Post-war – Leon, 1948–58
104. Victor's recollection of the first time he saw his father.
105. Wasyl was seconded into the German army. He fled to Austria in the last days of the war, desiring to start a new life. He went on to marry another Maria (a very common name), and together they had six children. He never returned home.
106. There were two grandchildren at the time.

54 Leaving Germany – Maria, 1954–1969
107. Translated from German from a cassette found amongst Maria's possessions.
108. The account comes from Victor, who was seven at the time.
109. Victor did return to Germany but never settled. He was pleased to return to England.
110. Rachel Hand, née Grist, recorded her grandmother's memories some fifty-six years later on the eve of her ninetieth birthday.

56 Why Did We Go To Australia? – Maria, 1968–69
111. Cape York in north

Queensland is the northernmost point in Australia and the Great Australian Bight is the distinguishing feature along the southern coast.

112. From Rachael Hand's interview with Maria (her nanna), in 2010

Epilogue

113. From Rachael Hand's interview with Maria (her nanna), in 2010.
114. The author lived the furthest away in Muswellbrook, a hundred and fifty kilometres north-west of Newcastle.
115. Like many others, they added a 'j' to the end of their name.

Acknowledgements

To Maria Winder (Maryl), our beloved sister. She and I travelled to Germany together for a week in 1985, where we met our cousins especially, Ziglinde, Great Uncle Alois and Uncle Adolf.

To Milla, for her planning and organising the Pilgrimage. For sharing her deep interest in and knowledge of our family history.

To Josephina, for the Pilgrimage journey, her wisdom, and much more.

To Elizabeth for her recollections, support, advice, and her passing on of valuable letters and documents. For being there on the Pilgrimage.

To Victor. He and Maryl were born in the Poorhouse in Döfering. His knowledge of family history, recollections and understanding of postwar days in Germany and England is unprecedented. His memories stretch back further than any of us.

To Leon, who joined the Pilgrims during our stay in Lviv. He was the first in the family to travel to the Ukraine. For his friendship, knowledge and generosity.

To my niece and nephews on the Pilgrimage: James, Steffany, Chris, and Michael. We had so much fun. Your support was endless. To Steffany for her organisation, editing and research.

To Rachel Hand, for her interviews with Nanna.

To our family in Zolochiv and Pidlyptsi, especially, Andrii, Viktor, Olga (who sadly passed away in 2021), Oksana, Maria and Aunty Anna. So many beautiful memories and valuable contributions to this account.

To our family in Haschaberg, especially Sepp, Marili, Oliver and Claudia. You were of great help. We had an unforgettable time. To Oliver for the photos and correspondence throughout.

To Henryk Gierlik. Local legend and historian shared his wisdom and gave us the best seats in the house.

To Ira Iruna, Aunty Anna's granddaughter (therefore my niece), for her invaluable correspondence, especially in pointing out the location of key landmarks in Pidlyptsi.

To Helena Wlodarczyk, Zofia's daughter, for sharing her mother's story.

To Julia Sokulsky for the artwork on the maps.

To Kay and Matthew Sokulsky for their advice and support.

To Timo Bullemer at Cham archives for his invaluable knowledge and assistance.

To the following for their invaluable contributions: Betty May, Narelle Austin, Louise Stokes Chapman, Eric (Enrico) Villari and Brittany Spooner

To all those in the Ukrainian community in Newcastle for sharing their wisdom and their stories; especially Father Paul Berezniuk, Ihor and Nika Jaremus, Maria Brylynsky and Ivan Semciw.

To Olia Mykulyshyn for help in translations and information about all things Ukrainian.

To Stephen Matthews OAM. I cannot thank you enough for your patience and work, and for believing in this book.

To Mum. She was the heart and soul of our family. She was happiest outdoors, feeding the birds, or by her grotto. She loved cooking for otherst, praying, singing with her beautiful voice, and being with family.

To Dad. He worked hard to make a home for us in Australia. He was always proud of his family and their accomplishments. He was most content content working, relaxing, building, planting, fixing things, and being with his family. His favourite saying, tongue in cheek, was 'Nice to see you come, nice to see you go.'

How fast the years have gone.

www.ingramcontent.com/pod-product-compliance
Lightning Source LLC
Chambersburg PA
CBHW070504120526
44590CB00013B/749